The Dog Did
What?

D1041763

*Chicken Soup for the Soul: The Dog Did **What?***
101 Amazing Stories of Magical Moments, Miracles and… Mayhem
Amy Newmark. Foreword by Miranda Lambert
Published by Chicken Soup for the Soul Publishing, LLC www.chickensoup.com

Front cover photo courtesy of iStockPhoto.com/GlobalP (© GlobalP).
Interior photo courtesy of iStockPhoto.com/graphicphoto (© graphicphoto).
Back cover headshot of Miranda Lambert courtesy of Randee St. Nicholas.
Childhood photo provided by Miranda Lambert.

Cover and Interior Design & Layout by Brian Taylor, Pneuma Books, LLC

Distributed to the booktrade by Simon & Schuster. SAN: 200-2442

Publisher's Cataloging-in-Publication Data
(Prepared by The Donohue Group)

Chicken soup for the soul : the dog did what? : 101 amazing stories of
 magical moments, miracles and… mayhem / [compiled by] Amy Newmark ;
 foreword by Miranda Lambert.

 pages ; cm

 ISBN: 978-1-61159-937-4

 1. Dogs--Behavior--Literary collections. 2. Dogs--Behavior--Anecdotes. 3. Dog
owners--Literary collections. 4. Dog owners--Anecdotes. 5. Human-animal relation-
ships--Literary collections. 6. Human-animal relationships--Anecdotes. 7. Anecdotes.
I. Newmark, Amy. II. Lambert, Miranda, 1983- III. Title: Dog did what? : 101 amazing stories of magical moments, miracles and… mayhem

SF433 .C45 2014
636.7/02   2014940366

PRINTED IN THE UNITED STATES OF AMERICA
on acid∞free paper

24 23 22 21 20 19 18 17 16 15 14   01 02 03 04 05 06 07 08 09 10 11

The Dog Did What?

101 Amazing Stories of Magical Moments, Miracles and... Mayhem

Amy Newmark
Foreword by Miranda Lambert

Chicken Soup for the Soul Publishing, LLC
Cos Cob, CT

Contents

❶
~Who Me?~

❷
~Learning to Love the Dog~

❸
~Who Rescued Who?~

❹
~That Little Rascal~

❺
~Four-Legged Therapists~

❻
~What I Learned from the Dog~

❼
~Who's in Charge Here?~

❽

~Meant to Be~

❾

~There's No Place Like Home~

❿

~Bad Dog!~

Foreword

Sometimes people ask questions like "Do you remember that song, 'Fishin' In the Dark'?" You might say, "Oh yeah, I remember where I was the first time I heard that song," or "I remember singing that into a hairbrush in front of the mirror with my best friend." Other times someone will start singing an old TV theme song like "Now this is a story all about how..." And you chime in, "my life got flipped, turned upside down." Who can forget Fresh Prince, right? It causes you to walk down memory lane to the place where you instantly relive the experience.

Other things are such a fundamental part of your life that you can't remember a time without them. It's that way for me with the Chicken Soup for the Soul book series. It's also that way for me with dogs. I can't remember back far enough to know life without either of them. So it was a natural fit when I was asked to be a part of *Chicken Soup for the Soul: The Dog Did* **What?** I started thinking about funny things my dogs have done and memories that I have with each of them. Then I looked a little further back, at the bigger picture. It was then that I learned where my lifelong love for dogs started and where my passion for them was rooted. I learned a little bit about myself that I hadn't realized until now.

My first pet was around before I was born. He was a yellow Lab named Cooter Brown. My parents were a little worried about how he was going to accept a new baby in the house. Until my birth in 1983, he was their "baby." That proved to be an unnecessary concern. The story goes that when I first arrived home he walked up to me, kissed my face and became my constant companion and guardian. He moved himself from my parents' bed and took up lodging under my crib, and then later moved into my bed. In my parents' house is one of my favorite pictures of all time… a photo of me, around two years old. I'm outside in overalls, and I'm singing and dancing with Coot. It says everything about how I grew up and who I would become… a singing country girl hanging out with a dog. Cooter was my best friend.

I've had many, many pets since Cooter passed away when I was six, but I can't write a foreword for *Chicken Soup for the Soul: The Dog Did What?* without thinking about what Cooter Brown did. He alone created the lifelong love that I have for pets and animals in general. He taught me trust and acceptance. He taught me how to care for others and be cared for by others. During our tea parties, while sitting patiently at the little table with a bonnet on his head, he taught me about meaningful conversations and about listening without judging. Our relationship was the textbook definition of unconditional love. He taught me that I never have to be alone because as long as you have a dog, you have a friend. He taught me what it means to depend on something and be depended on. I have carried the things I learned in those first six years, lessons about love, trust, acceptance, and friendship, throughout my life. That's what the dog did. As a grown woman, I still practice those lessons.

A few years ago I recorded a song called "The House That Built Me." The first time I heard it I was coming home from the Dallas airport with my husband, Blake. He popped in a CD with some "pitch" songs sent to him by his producer. The third song was "The House That Built Me." By the end of the first chorus I was in tears. Actually it was more like crying profusely. Before the song was over Blake looked at me and said, "I know this song is a huge hit but I'm not going to record it. This song belongs to you." Sometimes in life, even when you aren't looking, something that belongs to you finds you for some reason. "The House That Built Me" turned out to be a signature song for me because it's a song I relate to and I think we all can relate to. The song hit #1 on the Billboard chart and stayed there for four weeks. It won Song of the Year and proved to be the biggest crowd-pleaser on tour. The song is about losing yourself in the world, getting away from your roots and going back home to find out who you are again. In that song, at the end of the first chorus there is a line that says, "Up those stairs in that little back bedroom is where I did my homework and I learned to play guitar and I bet you didn't know under that live oak my favorite dog is buried in the yard." At my childhood home, the "House That Built Me," there really is an oak tree where my favorite dog is buried, and that dog is Cooter Brown. That house is my "Chicken Soup for the Soul." And that song is a reflection of what my dog did for me.

My hope for you is that you rediscover something about yourself in the pages of this book. I hope you read something that reminds you of your favorite dog and suddenly realize that the relationship with him or her helped to create the thread of the person you became. I hope that you laugh and that you cry while reading it. Most of all I hope that you remember your "chicken soup for the soul" place and moments and that you discover what the dog did for you.

Don't forget… love a shelter pet.

~Miranda Lambert
May 15, 2014

Introduction

We are so pleased to bring you our latest collection of stories about dogs, and this time with a special guest, Miranda Lambert, writing the foreword. In addition to being one of the most popular and well-liked entertainers on the planet, Miranda has been an incredibly dedicated and effective spokesperson for animal welfare and for the benefits of working with and adopting rescue animals. She is a big supporter of the American Humane Association and we are happy that the royalties from this book will go to the Association to further its good work.

Chicken Soup for the Soul makes every effort to support the work of shelters and to promote adoption of dogs and cats. We use rescue dogs and cats as models on the packaging for our pet food, and we have been contributing to shelters for years. With this book, through the generous participation of Miranda Lambert, we undertake our biggest effort yet to financially support the welfare of animals.

You will read many stories in this book about the love and devotion between dogs and their human families. You'll read about dogs that save lives, dogs that demonstrate surprising intuition about the needs of their humans, and dogs that teach people important life lessons. You'll read about the wonderful volunteers and professionals who have found new meaning and joy in their lives by adopting, fostering, and working with pet rescue organizations and shelters. You'll also read dozens of really funny stories about the mischievous things that our little rascals do. It seems like every dog owner can't help but smile, even when relating his or her dog's most dastardly deeds!

Most importantly, the stories in the book make the point over and over again—shelter dogs and abandoned dogs are fabulous! They add so much value to your lives, and you have saved them from a grim future. So enjoy these stories from your fellow dog people, make some new stories of your own with your dogs, and remember to adopt those abandoned dogs... and don't forget the older ones. Senior dogs really need you too.

~Amy Newmark

Chapter
1

The Dog Did What?

Who Me?

The Rescue

A dog will teach you unconditional love. If you can have that in your life,
things won't be too bad.
~Robert Wagner

When I turned eight, we adopted a sweet, timid, Blue Heeler puppy. Skeeter was the runt of her litter, but she made up for her size with grand obedience and abundant intelligence.

My mother soon adopted a canary as well. It filled the house with trilling and chirping—a new song invented after every molt. The bird was a strange, tiny creature, indeed, next to our wholesome, standard-sized brown dog, but Skeeter would sleep beneath its cage, accepting the new family member.

And even while constantly flanked by my faithful dog, I also wanted a different type of animal companion, like my friends had. My parents obliged me by adopting a little hamster who I named Quincy. He lived in a sawdust-filled cage, complete with the requisite wheel, in my room.

I loved Quincy, though our relationship wasn't very close. I rarely took him out of his cage, except to clean it or, most often, put him in his hamster ball. At first I kept Skeeter away from Quincy when he was out, worried that she, following instinct, would chase and hurt him. After all, she took great pleasure in pouncing on the shrews that lived in the bushes outside. But Skeeter only watched with one small black eyebrow cocked as Quincy rolled his way through the living room, experiencing his captive freedom.

One day, somehow, Quincy went missing from his cage. We were visiting family for the day and when we all returned, with Skeeter in tow, we found the canary happily singing, but the hamster cage bleakly empty.

I'm surprised now by how upset we all were. I cried and we debated where he could have gone, as Skeeter wound her way between our legs, sensing worry. For three days we tiptoed through the house expecting to find Quincy, lifeless or injured, but he was simply gone.

The fourth night, we all, including Skeeter, curled up in front of a movie. I sat on the floor with my back against the couch and, consumed with the screen, didn't notice that Skeeter had left my side. When I looked up, I saw her approaching with something in her mouth. At first I thought it was one of her prized and well-chewed fuzzy tennis balls, but as she got closer I saw it was of a different shape and color altogether. She held it carefully between her tiny front teeth, gingerly tipped her head and dropped a still living, unharmed Quincy into my lap. He was alive! It was a miracle! He had somehow managed to survive, undetected, in the house for half a week until a very clever canine nose sniffed him out.

But when I looked up at Skeeter, still standing there, watching Quincy and me expectantly, I thought she was the real miracle. This furry member of our family had sensed the value we placed on Quincy. She knew that he was not a rodent to be caught and killed like the poor wild shrews. Skeeter knew we were worried when he was gone and she knew that, as a member of the family, she should help bring him back.

When I set Quincy back in his cage, he sniffed around a bit and then hopped right back on his wheel, as if the past few days were little more than a vacation. Skeeter sat patiently at my feet, happily waiting for the next affection I could offer her. And petting her soft, sweet forehead, I thanked her for showing me the meaning of family. And love.

~Kelsey Kate Bankert

2

Matters of the Doggy Heart

Love makes your soul crawl out from its hiding place.
~Zora Neale Hurston

have never heard a canine love story quite like the story of J.J. and Bailey. For J.J., a large, black Lab mix, it was love at the first sight of Bailey, a Cairn Terrier.

Bailey was a year and a half old when she came to live with me in January 2000. Her experience with other dogs was limited to a canine companion in her previous home with whom she did not get along. I worried about how Bailey would interact with the many dogs in my neighborhood, and it turned out I was right to worry. It took Bailey years to make friends with only a handful of very sweet dogs. I resigned myself to the idea that she would never get over her fear of larger dogs.

J.J., who originally hailed from Florida, came to live with my neighbor Dianne when Dianne's daughter, Avery, went to work overseas. J.J. was one of the most obedient and well-behaved dogs I have ever had the pleasure of knowing. He would sit and listen to human conversations with an expression of intent interest on his face. With no proof to the contrary, I am convinced that he did in fact understand everything he heard — including the reason Bailey didn't like him — because she was afraid after having been attacked by a supposedly "friendly" black dog.

It seemed that no matter how J.J. acted toward her, Bailey wasn't interested in being his friend. Things changed, however, one night when J.J. came up with an idea. J.J. saw Bailey and me walking past his house, and began to cry for Dianne to let him out. Before she could open the screen door, J.J. turned and ran to the kitchen, then rushed back to the door. Neither of us realized at the time that he ran to get one of his dog treats, which Dianne kept by his dog dish. J.J. ran straight over to Bailey and deposited one of his treats at her feet. Never one to pass up food, Bailey immediately snatched it up while J.J. stood by, smiling and wagging his tail. Dianne and I laughed—commenting that he was taking his courtship of Bailey seriously! We had no idea that first night that J.J. intended to provide Bailey with treats for the rest of her life.

From that night on, every evening before their walk, J.J. would deliver a treat to Bailey. If the treat bowl was empty, J.J. would cry and carry on until Dianne gave him something he considered a suitable present for his best girl. Not that Bailey minded, because this occasionally resulted in the gift of a rawhide or, best of all, a human cookie. Regardless of how delectable the treat, J.J. carried it straight to Bailey and deposited it at her feet. As he did the first time and every time thereafter until Bailey's death in 2007, J.J. stood smiling and wagging his tail as he watched her enjoy his gift.

And to those who think J.J. must have shared his treats with others, rest assured he did not. Never before he met Bailey, and never after she died. Ever faithful until his death a few years later, J.J. never brought treats to another dog, remaining steadfast in his love and devotion to Bailey, his one true love.

~Katharina Cirko

Ubu Saves the Day

The better I get to know men, the more I find myself loving dogs.
~Charles de Gaulle

The year my daughter was born, I was struggling with many issues. My husband chose to leave our marriage to seek a more carefree lifestyle. I owned a home that was a money pit, and my funds were limited as I was working on a freelance basis so that I could parent my daughter. And, as all new parents are, I was horribly sleep-deprived and felt overwhelmed.

The one constant in my life was my dear dog, Ubu, who was quiet when the baby slept, gentle when she would crawl onto his back, and always near me making me feel loved.

Each day, I would take my baby for a stroll around the neighborhood with Ubu in tow. Ubu had been trained to walk with me without a leash and was very responsive to my commands, so I never worried about his behavior on our walks.

One day on our walk, my daughter started getting fussy, so I sped up and headed for home. While I told Ubu to come, he stood next to a house around the corner from me and just looked at me. Since my daughter was warming up to a full-blown crying fit, I told Ubu I was going home and that I couldn't wait for him.

I got home and found the source of my child's distress, took care of the problem, and sat on the front porch to await Ubu's arrival. Fifteen minutes passed and he was still not home, so I loaded up the stroller and we set off to find him. The first place I looked was successful. Ubu was lying next to the front stairs of the house where we had left him.

As I approached Ubu, and inquired as to what was so important, I heard the noises of several crying kittens. I'm allergic to cats and did not want to get involved in whatever was going on under the stairs, but Ubu would not budge.

I knocked on the front door and the older woman explained that a stray cat had come onto her property and she suspected the cat had given birth. I asked her if she would like our help in retrieving the cats, but she was not a cat lover and told us that we could just leave them there.

Ubu did not agree, so I asked the woman if it was okay for my dog to go under her porch and try to retrieve the kittens. She scoffed and said, "Don't come crying to me when that cat claws your dog."

I told Ubu to stay put and that I would be right back. I went home and called Animal Control to ask them what we could do. The man said that he would send someone over, and I gave him the address. Then I changed into sweatpants in case I had to crawl under the porch, donned working gloves, and grabbed a laundry basket that I covered with sheets. I loaded everything into the stroller, and we headed back to the house.

When I arrived, Ubu was not there. I felt a bit of panic, thinking that the cat might have attacked him. But as I moved closer to the stairs, I saw he had crawled under the porch and was guarding the opening.

When the man from Animal Control showed up, he was surprised that Ubu was standing guard. He chuckled and said, "Is he waiting for a free meal?" I found no humor in that and suggested that we get on with saving the kittens. He said that he was not going to crawl under the porch to retrieve the kittens, so I pushed the stroller closer to the hole and kept up a lighthearted conversation with my daughter. The opening was only about twelve inches tall. I looked at the opening and attempted to fight off my claustrophobia and the idea that there could be spiders, rotting leaves, and who knew what else under the porch. But even as I tried to overcome my fears, there was no way I would be able to crawl through such a narrow opening.

I looked to the Animal Control man for guidance, but he just sneered and said, "Send the dog to get them."

I sat down next to Ubu and explained what had to happen. He needed to crawl under the porch and bring the kittens out. He needed to be very careful and gentle. While I was talking to Ubu, the Animal Control man started laughing and said, "Now, I've heard everything."

My frustration with the situation and this man's attitude grew. I said, "You have been of little help and absolutely no encouragement, so I'm going to make you a wager. If my dog retrieves the kittens, you are going to buy him a large bag of dog food, the premium kind."

The man's smirk turned to a grin. "You're on."

So I went back and sat down next to Ubu and explained again what I needed him to do. He belly-crawled to the back of the porch and one long minute later came out with a tiny kitten nestled gently in his mouth. When I asked him to give me the kitten, he hesitated. I found that perplexing so I told him again to give me the kitten; he did not. I don't know what made me think of it, but I turned, put on my work gloves, and brought the laundry basket over to Ubu. He not only gently placed the kitten in the basket but nudged the sheets over it as well.

Ubu "delivered" twelve kittens in the same manner. The shock on the Animal Control man's face was reward enough for me. I handed him the basket of kittens and headed for home.

Later that afternoon, he returned with a fifty-pound bag of dog food. "You told me that you were allergic to cats, and while your dog was rescuing those kittens, what really amazed me is that he wouldn't let you touch them. It was almost as if he knew you were allergic."

I smirked at him. "He did."

~Judith Fitzsimmons

Marmadufus

Things that upset a terrier may pass virtually unnoticed by a Great Dane.
~Smiley Blanton

As I pulled into my driveway, I noticed the stray dog sitting by the gate as if waiting for me to come home. The big, clumsy puppy bounced happy circles around my feet, tripping me several times before I got to the front door of my house. He also jumped up to bite at my hands with his sharp puppy teeth. What a nuisance, I thought as I struggled to get inside my home without being mauled. Where did this puppy come from? He looked happy and healthy, but definitely was not well mannered!

We phoned our neighbors to ask if they were missing a puppy. After making sure no one was looking for him, I decided to foster the new arrival until he could be adopted. I often foster homeless pets, and with a little guidance and fine-tuning, I thought this one would make a nice dog for someone. Because of his large size and color, I decided to call him Marmaduke after the lovable cartoon Great Dane.

The new puppy made himself right at home, meeting me with joyful abandon each time I stepped out of the house in the morning. Leaping and pawing at my clothes, he'd pull on my sleeves with his teeth while I stumbled over him. It wasn't long before I realized that, in spite of his resemblance to a Great Dane, the name Marmaduke didn't fit this big fellow at all. He was proving very hard to train. A scolding meant nothing to him. As happy and cute as he was, I had to admit that he wasn't the smartest puppy I'd trained. After one exasperating session, I frowned at him but then caught myself laughing. With his thumping tail, head tilt and lolling tongue, how could anybody resist such a silly pup? From that day on, I called him Marmadufus.

As Marmadufus continued to grow, his enthusiastic games became rougher. Several times he caused me to fall, and my hands and ankles bore the marks of his playful nips. But the problem that worried me the most was his aggression toward, of all things, his own tail.

I first noticed the obsession with his tail when Marmadufus was resting. He would curl around, grab the end of his tail in his mouth, and chew on it. At times he bit it so hard he yelped. He kept it damp and the skin became irritated. Most alarming, though, was his reaction when we fed him. He would begin to eat, then stop and stiffen. His lip would curl and he'd give a throaty growl. Then he would suddenly spin and snap at his tail. His snarling and growling became so fierce that, even though he was the only dog in the yard, it sounded as if a terrific dogfight was occurring right outside the front door! Peering out the window, all we saw was Marmadufus spinning in circles and snapping.

I read all I could find on dogs who spin circles and chase their tails. I tried several suggestions, even giving him a veterinarian-prescribed antidepressant, without success. I began to suspect that the chances of this foster puppy finding a home were becoming slim indeed. Few families would be interested in a large breed, food-aggressive, tail-chasing Dane!

To our horror, we returned from church one summer morning to find Marmadufus had actually caught his tail while we were away. He greeted us as usual, wagging a tail that was now about four inches shorter and freely dripping blood.

"This is not how I want to spend a Sunday afternoon," grumbled my husband as he and our son loaded the happy pup into the pickup for an emergency trip to the veterinary clinic. As Marmadufus underwent surgery, I stayed behind to scrub the front porch and glass door and remove all traces of what had apparently been a very traumatic morning for the young dog. As I cleaned, I had to wonder what kind of a silly dog bites off his own tail?

The next morning, ol' Marm was quite a sight when he came home from the veterinary clinic. He had a bandage on his short tail and a big Elizabethan collar on his neck. For ten days he clumsily bumped and crashed into things, but the collar did the job and allowed the tail to heal without further injury.

Marmadufus is now two years old. His manners have improved, but he still does his crazy spinning and growling when he's fed. In spite of his quirks, he's a handsome dog and truly devoted to our family. I never found anyone interested in adopting a huge, silly, bob-tailed Great Dane.

On second thought, I guess I did find someone. Marmadufus is very much loved, and here to stay!

~Pamela Jenkins

Oops

All knowledge, the totality of all questions and all answers,
is contained in the dog.
~Franz Kafka

"O ops," I said while tapping my foot against the rug, where I'd dropped a breadcrumb. Kafka the English Bulldog bolted off the couch and stuck his snout right into the rug to slurp up the miniscule piece of food. That wasn't enough though, so he continued to sniff around the rug to make sure he got every last crumb I might have dropped. When that wasn't enough, he stared at me, willing me to drop the bread and butter in my hand.

That was Kafka's relationship to food: beg—and stare—until he got more food, or until it was gone and there was none to be had. From the moment we got him, one of the first "commands" he understood was "oops."

My husband Tyler and I should have been more careful about our use of the word, something we learned quickly on another evening.

It started innocently enough. Kafka was actually behaving by playing with his tennis ball on his own—rather than shoving it at my legs and refusing to drop it. Tyler was in the kitchen pouring himself a drink, and I was heading his way for a snack.

But then the glass slipped out of my husband's hand. Water went everywhere, and Tyler uttered the one word Kafka without fail responded to: "Oops."

Kafka bolted across the living room, through the hallway, and right into the puddle, sliding through the spilled water. His paws scrambled as he tried to get some traction on the wood.

But he couldn't stop, and he crashed right into the trashcan as if he were a fifty-pound bowling ball and the trashcan a single pin.

Tyler and I laughed so hard tears came to our eyes.

"Kafka, are you okay?" we both tried to ask through our laughter. Kafka strolled over to us and lapped up some water. When our laughter still hadn't ceased, he looked up at us and cocked his head to the side as if to say, "What's so funny?"

Oh, Kafka, if only you realized how much you entertain us!

~Elizabeth SanFilippo Hall

The Dastardly Duo

Sometimes when you get in a fight with a skunk, you can't tell who started it.
~Lloyd Doggett

My husband realized it too late. That black tail did not belong to our cat.

On pleasant evenings, Bob enjoyed strolling along a circular path that wandered from our yard, across a field, through an abandoned apple orchard, and back to our home. Our young inexperienced Weimaraner hunting dog accompanied Bob, the pup nosing at every interesting (sometimes cow-pie "ripe") smell along the way. Our black cat, tail always high, trotted behind them.

One evening at dusk, as this trio strode among the apple trees, Bob thought the dark shape twenty feet ahead was the cat. But, too late, he noticed a white stripe along the creature's back.

Bob instantly swerved backward. The cat crouched low beyond Bob's feet and hissed. But the dog bounded ahead, yelping with excitement. Game to flush!

Bob tried to run and tripped over the cat. The dog howled in surprise as he caught the skunk's spray full force. Breeze-blown smells settled on Bob. Somehow the cat escaped.

My husband arrived home and rang the doorbell. I answered and shouted, "Retreat! Retreat! Down the driveway. Strip off everything out there." Then I slammed the door.

Skunk odor as one passes along a breezy country road smells bad, but bearable. Skunk odor close enough to wage full attack on both nostrils encourages upchucking.

Fortunately, darkness had descended, so Bob, near the end of our ninety-foot-long driveway, removed his stinking clothes without fear of the neighbors gawking at him. Nude, he raced up the front steps and into the bathroom, slamming the door.

With one hand I held my nostrils closed. With the other I passed Bob two quarts of my freshly canned tomato juice. He bathed—and bathed—and bathed—and soaped and rinsed—until the hot water heater ran cold. Finally he invited me in for a smell-test. I declared him fit to leave the bathroom.

Again holding my nose, I lowered Bob's clothes into a black trash bag, tied it tightly and dumped it at the end of the drive for garbage pick-up. However, this black plastic apparently was not designed to contain smells.

On the driveway next to the garage, I filled a galvanized tub, immersed the dog in soapy water and slathered his silver-gray hairs completely with more tomato juice. I worked the juice deep, into all of his skin. After half a dozen washings, I wrapped the shivering pup in an old cotton blanket and carried him, odor-free, into the garage. His ears drooping, eyes downcast as if ashamed, he curled up and whimpered nonstop.

The next morning, the garbage collector phoned me from the far end of our block. "If I load that bag into my trash carrier, imagine what will happen when I scramble and compact my load. Half the folks on my route would phone my boss asking why I hadn't washed out my truck." He pleaded with me. "Please don't make me take that smelly bag. Don't you have a burning barrel? On county property, you can dispose of that stuff yourself."

Skunk-odor-filled clothing burning in a steel barrel does not resemble breeze-filled sniffs when out on a drive. In self-defense, I gathered the dog and cat into my little Honda and drove the fifteen miles to town, hoping for a couple of pleasant hours while the kerosene-doused burning barrelful smoldered and dissipated.

I'd warned the neighbors about leaving the barrel without fully extinguishing the fire. One friend, half a block away, promised to call the fire department if the barrel's fire blazed out of control. She thanked me for destroying the skunk-perfumed clothing at a time when no wind blew toward her house.

I had reached city limits when Bob phoned me. "Please pick me up from work right away. I'm taking a sudden vacation day. I'll be waiting outside the building."

When Bob shut the car door, the dog howled from the back seat and clawed at the window. The cat hissed and flattened herself under the passenger seat. Bob immediately untied his shoes and ordered, "Stop!" I slammed on the brakes.

He jumped out and dumped his smelly leather footwear into the nearest trashcan along the street, banging the lid down tightly. The dog cried a moment longer, but calmed down with the offending leather shoes gone.

After Bob climbed back into the car, he explained. "I was at a meeting with my boss when he sniffed and said, 'I smell skunk.' My partner, Howie (who knew the truth) said, 'Hmm, I don't smell anything.'"

Bob chuckled at his friend's loyalty. "However, I hightailed it out of there."

My husband explained, "We need to buy me new wingtips right now." Why hadn't he noticed the horrible smell at home when dressing? Was his nose still suffering last evening's assault? We don't know.

We glanced around to be sure no one had seen us dump the shoes in the trash, then raced away, headed for the nearest shoe store.

From then on, whenever Bob called the pup for an evening's trek through the orchard, the dog slunk on his tummy toward his master, whining pitifully. Only weeks later did the animal agree to accompany Bob on evening jaunts. But the pup always trotted close to my husband's side, never ahead. And only if the black cat stayed home.

~Geni J. White

An Angel on Earth

Angels have no philosophy but love.
~Adeline Cullen Ray

It began as a normal weekend jaunt to the local flea market. I pulled my old, red VW into a parking space. My husband got out and started walking over to a pickup truck parked a few spaces down. As I approached the truck bed, I saw a litter of six Rottweiler/black Lab puppies. My husband already had one in his arms, but I told him there was no way that we could get another dog.

I was rational: "We just lost our last dog two months ago. We live in a tiny apartment. We can't afford a big dog."

He reluctantly put the puppy back into the truck. We strolled around the flea market. Everywhere we turned, there was a little kid holding one of the puppies, trying to sell it to the other browsers. It really began to bother me. They were cute.

My husband pleaded his case as we got closer to our car to leave: "Please? I promise I'll take care of it!"

He was pitiful. I was looking at a grown man who had suddenly morphed into a five-year-old. But, I did miss having a little fur-face around the house. I told him to ask the guy if he'd sell us a puppy for twenty-five dollars, thinking he would turn it down. I went back to the car to sit and wait. Five minutes later, my husband got into the car, along with a puppy.

He was jet black with a Rottie body and cropped tail. Although he was itty-bitty, he had huge paws. I looked down at those big brown, soulful eyes. What had we gotten ourselves into? We named him Jack.

I was teaching at the time, and on spring break, so it was convenient for me to house-train Jack. He was completely housebroken in two days. He was very intelligent. I had always thought my previous dogs were smart, but they were nothing compared to Jack.

I taught him some basic tricks. He learned so easily that many nights my husband would come home from work only to discover that I'd taught Jack yet another trick. He was the best of both breeds, and we marveled at him.

Jack loved squeaky toys and had a big wicker laundry basket filled with them. Every evening, he'd do what we called The Toy Parade—one by one, he'd grab a toy and squeak it non-stop while parading in front of us and wagging his little bunny tail. Although he had over fifty different toys, if we told him to get a particular one, he'd run to the basket and dig around until he found the right one.

Three years later, I was pregnant with our first child. In my fifth week, I began to bleed and was put on total bed rest, which meant I lay on the couch. I was beyond stressed out, but I followed doctor's orders and would not leave the couch except to go to the bathroom. Not only was I worried about the baby, I had just lost my mother a few months before and it weighed heavily on my mind.

As soon as my husband left for work, Jack would take his place on the floor beside me. He'd entertain me once in a while by bringing me a toy to throw for him. Mostly, he kept vigil.

One day, I was overly melancholy. I lay on the couch praying to God to protect the baby, yet I felt so alone. I missed my mom terribly and wished she were there with me. I ended up in tears and fell asleep from exhaustion.

I had no idea how long I slept, but I heard a familiar harumph-sigh. I turned my head to see Jack sitting just inches from my face, his whole body wiggling as he sat on his big Rottie butt, wagging his little tail. He rose to his feet, gave me a big slurpy lick across my face and then barked. I opened my eyes and could not believe what I saw. My whole body and the couch were covered with all of his toys.

From my chest all the way down to my toes, this dog covered me tenderly with his most prized possessions. He swaddled me with a "toy blankie." I grabbed him and held onto him, laughing and crying at the same time.

I ended up having a miscarriage, but Jack was there to see me through it all. He was with us for eight beautiful years. I believe God sent him to us for a reason.

~Jodi Sykes

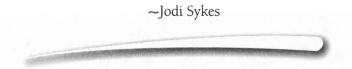

Chi Chi and the Hungry Hawk

Let sleeping dogs lie.
~American Proverb

My husband and our dog Chi Chi, an eight-pound Pekingese, were on our deck. When the weather is nice we often sit outside in the afternoon and watch the local wildlife. Our deck overlooks a large creek that is home to mallards, wood ducks, Canada geese and blue heron, not to mention an irascible resident muskrat and the occasional beaver. Our back yard is overrun with squirrels, chipmunks, and birds, lots and lots of birds.

Among the feathered freeloaders that hang around our place are a couple of red-tailed hawks that perch in the trees on the opposite side of the creek. They watch the goings-on in my yard with keen interest. They'd love to swoop down and devour one of our feathered or furry inhabitants, but they don't dare. There is something scary standing in their way… me!

My husband and I have always enjoyed the nature show, but not so our dog. Chi Chi is oblivious. She couldn't care less. We'd nicknamed her "Road Kill," because of her unnerving habit of sleeping with her head down and front and back legs splayed out as though she'd just been run over by a truck. Most times she looks like a furry splat.

One day I was working at my computer when I heard my husband speak in a strained whisper. He sounded excited.

"Come outside. Quick! Hurry! You've got to see this!"

I went to the door and was surprised to see a large female red-tailed hawk perched on the deck railing, not ten feet from my husband.

"Get the camera!" my husband whispered, trying not to scare the hawk away. "We've got to get a picture of this."

The hawk was behaving strangely. She had her back to my husband and was staring over the yard and creek. Every minute or so, she would sneak a look over her shoulder. At first I couldn't figure out what she was doing. Then it hit me. The focus of her attention wasn't my husband. It was the dog.

Chi Chi took no notice of the hawk. Her eyes were barely open. She was settling in for her late afternoon snooze, as opposed to her midafternoon siesta, or early afternoon nap. The dog was nearly narcoleptic!

The hawk kept turning its head in Chi Chi's direction. With every glance, it inched closer to the semi-comatose canine.

It didn't take a genius to see what was happening. It was mealtime and the hawk was hungry. Our little mutt was about to become the main course. To the hawk's way of thinking, I couldn't possibly object since the dog was practically dead already! She was doing me a favor disposing of the remains.

The hawk was ready to pounce when I charged out the door, yelling at the top of my lungs and waving my arms like a lunatic.

The startled hawk took off like a shot. She'd have to seek her dinner elsewhere.

My husband was furious with me until I explained what the hawk had been up to.

The commotion woke Chi Chi. Sleeping beauty opened one eye and glared at me, as if to say, "How rude!" Couldn't I see she was trying to sleep? She closed her eye again, and a second later she was sound asleep.

That afternoon Chi Chi got a new nickname. We didn't call her "Road Kill" anymore. From that day forward she was known as "Hawk Bait"!

~Mary Vigliante Szydlowski

Peace and Quiet

I just want to live in peace and quiet.
~Agnetha Fältskog

When we moved to the mountains of West Virginia, we brought all our animals with us including our dog, Honus. While Honus didn't seem to enjoy the humidity, he did seem excited to be in the forest where he barked at squirrels, chipmunks, and birds. His constant barking was a little annoying, but there wasn't much we could do about it. So much for living in the peace and quiet of the forest!

Honus was sixteen years young and this was an adventure for him, but I worried about what might happen if he came in close contact with one of these creatures. Would his animal instincts kick in? Would something a little bigger be able to hurt Honus?

"Worrying about it isn't going to change anything," my husband said. "Honus has never been around other animals, but hopefully if he does get into a scuffle, it will be with something small and he won't get hurt. You know he really is a gentle soul; I don't think he'd hurt a flea!"

My husband was right. Still, I hoped there wouldn't be any trouble and that the forest creatures would stay away from Honus. After all, he was a dog.

Honus was pretty quiet in the morning, but each afternoon the barking and whining started up. On one beautiful fall afternoon, I'd just finished dusting the bedroom when I noticed how quiet it was. I suddenly felt sick as I realized something must be wrong with Honus—it was the time of day he usually barked and whined at his forest friends.

"Please let him be okay," I said out loud as I ran to the window that looked out to the yard. There I saw Honus, lying on his stomach with his head extended in front of him, a few inches away from his food bowl. His eyes were wide open and he was lying perfectly still while a feral cat and her five kittens ate the leftover food from his bowl.

Running into the other room, I hollered for my husband to come and see. "I told you he wouldn't hurt a flea," said my husband as he put his arm around me. "I don't think you need to worry about him anymore!"

We spent the next couple of months watching the mother and her babies feed from Honus's bowl each afternoon. Arriving at the same time each day, Honus would wag his tail when he'd see them coming, then lie down in his usual position and watch them eat. It was a beautiful sight and it came with an extra special bonus: For the first time since moving to the mountains, we finally enjoyed the peace and quiet—the way we'd imagined it would be!

~Jill Burns

When Natty Rescued Nami

Nothing but heaven itself is better than a friend who is really a friend.
~Plautus

Tsunami, our two-year-old Akita that we called Nami for short, did not take readily to our new country home. When my husband Ken and I lived near Washington, D.C., we took her to the dog park for a romp at least twice a week. She played beach ball soccer with the other dogs and permitted curious toddlers to unfurl her trademark, curled tail.

We praised her for how patiently she permitted admirers to ooh and ahh over her white foreleg markings, so symmetrical that one lady actually called across the field to ask where I had purchased her cute snow boots.

When I retired, though, we moved to a country home in Northeast Washington State, far from such civilized canine playgrounds. Because our pastures were fenced with barbed wire, easy for even a large dog to crawl under, Nami could only play outside attached to her nylon lead. We hooked two together to give her a forty-foot range, and provided her with an array of Kongs, balls and rope toys. But when we put her out to romp, Nami would give her Kong a listless nudge or the ball a disconsolate sideways kick, and then plop down and yawn.

Our veterinarian neighbor's trio of retired racehorses roamed on the other side of the fence. Whenever they emitted a snort, nicker or whinny, Nami would glance disdainfully in their direction, making it clear to us that she knew they were some other strange species, not tall dogs, and certainly not worthy of much interest.

We soon learned that people frequently left litters at The Flour Mill, a local feed store, in hopes that the unwanted kittens, pups or bunnies would be adopted. I brought home three little kittens, but Ken warned me that Nami probably would regard them as potential snacks rather than playmates. Other than emitting an occasional halfhearted growl of annoyance, Nami simply appeared bored with the kittens' antics.

"We have to get her a pet," Ken soon announced. He headed for the Mill that afternoon and returned toting a seven-week-old livewire, a shaggy black mongrel with a dapper white chest.

"A notice on the litter box said that the dad was a Great Pyrenees and the mom a Heinz 57 combo," he said, handing me the wiggling ball of fur.

The pup didn't weigh much more than the kittens. "He looks so natty," I said. "I'm calling him Natty."

"I'm calling him Nat then," Ken rejoined. "No diminutives for my buddy here."

We took Nat out to the yard, where Nami was dozing in the sun. He bounded over, climbed up her flank and nibbled on her ear. For the first time since we moved, Nami perked up. All day she lay contented while the puppy gnawed her ankle, swatted her nose with his tiny paw, and nestled under her chin to sleep.

Nat trotted after Nami as she roamed the yard. He began to join her in batting balls, playing tug-of-war with fringed ropes, and chasing the kittens if they strayed into their territory. He soon learned that he could play keep-away tag with Nami, running just outside the circumference of her lead. As Nat grew, they began to wrestle, and Nami sometimes rolled over and appeared to let him win. Apparently she knew how to keep her playmate motivated to continue the contests.

Then one winter afternoon while the dogs gamboled in the yard, I ducked into the house for a moment. When I returned they were gone. Nami's hooked-together nylon leads had somehow unsnapped.

Ken and I drove up and down the nearby roads, stopping now

and then to call their names. Alas, they had vanished, most likely into the surrounding hills. "Don't worry," Ken reassured me. "When they get tired of roaming, they'll come home." But I did worry. Nami was trailing that nylon lead behind her, and I kept imagining it getting tangled in shrubbery, trapping her in the woods.

A little after sundown, while Ken drove off again to search, I went outside to call their names. After a few minutes I thought I heard sounds from the back pasture. Sure enough, here came Natty, panting, damp, out of breath. He flopped down at my feet, tongue hanging out, and eyes wild. I bent and patted him. "Where's Nami... where's your Nami?" I pleaded.

Nat kept staring back across the pasture from whence he came. I began to shiver in the icy moonless night. "Natty, where's Nami?" I asked once more. Nat, still panting, lurched to his feet, and trotted back across the dark field. I thought I heard some distant growls and grunts. Soon I could make out the white patch on his small dark form as he slowly trudged back towards me. Then I saw the much larger Nami limping behind. As they drew closer I saw that Nat had the end of Nami's nylon lead in his mouth. After every step or two the pair paused. Then Natty would step forward and tug and Nami would inch forward, more and more haltingly.

I rushed out to help, but Nami weighed nearly as much as me so I couldn't carry her. She barely made it up the step to the side door, then heaved herself inside and collapsed on the carpet. I could tell she was in a lot of pain.

"They came home, but she's hurt," I told Ken when he returned. "There's something wrong with her legs, but Natty brought her out of the pasture with her lead in his mouth." Ken gave me a skeptical glance. "Are you sure? That sounds highly improbable."

"I saw it, Ken. Natty brought her home from the field."

The next morning we took Nami to the vet. She had ruptured her anterior cruciate ligaments and would require surgery. Apparently on their excursion she had jumped over fences. Large dogs such as Akitas are prone to such injuries, the vet explained. Nami underwent two operations, one leg at a time. Natty remained by her side during the weeks of her recovery. In the meantime we had the back yard securely chain-linked-fenced so that the pair could play outdoors freely.

Nami's nearing eleven now, and Natty's nine. Nami's still much larger, but the lifelong companions on occasion still wrestle and play tug of war as equals. Nami, of course, even though arthritic, remains the alpha dog, a regal queen reigning over her backyard realm. Natty, her devoted servant, more loyal than royal, despite partial blindness from cataracts, follows her around faithfully.

He may never merit a crown, but brave Natty certainly deserves a medal. We got him one. His dog tag reads: "Natty H." The H stands for Hero.

~Terri Elders

The Dog Did What?

Learning to Love the Dog

Mosby No

*We could have bought a small yacht with what we spent on our dog and all
the things he destroyed. Then again, how many yachts wait by the door all
day for your return?*
~John Grogan

knew I wanted a Pug. Our older Pug had passed away six months earlier, and I told my husband John that our other dog Riley needed a friend. But really I was getting the dog to fill our empty nest. Prior experience had proved that Pugs had everything we wanted in a dog; they were quiet, calm, and intimidated by cats.

"What do you think of this cutie pie?" I asked John after weeks of searching a pet adoption website. A year old, his name was Tyson and he was described as "the best little Pug ever."

"Go for it," he said. Words I would repeat later when he claimed to have told me we didn't need another pet.

Tyson was housed at an organization called Smashface Rescue about an hour away. During the drive there I pictured a back yard filled with Pugs lounging in the sun. What I found instead were several active Pit Bulls, a Mastiff, and a few other large breed dogs. Tyson sat placidly amongst them. I'm sure now he had been drugged. With his little squished face and plump curled cinnamon-bun tail, not only was he incredibly cute, he seemed quiet, calm...

"How's he around cats?" I asked Jeff, the man in charge.

"Loves them," he said. As if to prove his point he carried Tyson out front and sat him in front of a sleeping feline. Both remained unruffled.

"I'd like to fill out an application form," I said, assuming there would be a lengthy adoption process including a call to my vet and a home inspection.

"Oh, there's no application. You can take him today," Jeff said, "after you pay the fee." This should have been my first clue.

I had no crate or leash with me but they weren't needed. In the car, Tyson slept sweetly and soundly. At home, he quickly woke up. The first thing he did was tug on Riley's scruff, and then he lifted his leg and peed on the sofa. Next he scrambled up my husband's easy chair and jumped like a mountain goat from the back of the chair to our table and barked at my Siamese cat who, terrified, leapt to the top of our kitchen cupboard. I stared in disbelief.

"I don't know if that dog's a good fit for us," my husband said with alarm, and I had to agree. We hadn't gotten a puppy because we didn't want to deal with housebreaking, but this dog had issues beyond potty accidents. I immediately renamed him. Tyson was too reminiscent of the boxer who had bit off an opponent's ear. Our favorite sitcom at that time had a loveable character named Ted Mosby, so we christened our new pug Mosby. The name quickly became Mosby No.

"Mosby, no!" John yelled when he dropped his favorite guitar pick and Mosby swooped in like a shark and crunched it in his crooked little teeth. His words were repeated when Mosby gnawed on the kitchen chair legs instead of on his chew toys, when Mosby grabbed the end of the toilet paper and ran until the roll unwound, and again when John opened the dishwasher and Mosby leaned in to lick the crud off the plates.

"Mosby, no!" I screamed when he caught sight of our other cat in the hall and chased her up the stairs. I did not witness the battle that ensued, but Mosby returned with one eye closed. It cost me $500 for several vet visits and medications to heal the cat scratch on his cornea.

I dug out the old plastic gate from the garage that we had used years ago to confine our toddlers in one room. Mosby leapt over it like a horse. I spent $100 on a new, taller gate that would keep him in our family room/kitchen area, away from our cats and carpet. I spent another $75 on vaccinations, and $100 on obedience school registration. Our best-little-Pug-ever was costing a fortune.

I had high hopes that I could train him, but the only thing Mosby got out of the parks and recreation class was kennel cough that he passed on to Riley—another vet bill. I skipped the final "exam" so that I wouldn't embarrass myself when Mosby stopped to pee on a fence post or bark at a skateboarder.

"Are you keeping that dog?" my husband asked as Mosby's behavior got worse. Whenever we went to the other side of the gate, Mosby desperately yelped and bit our heels. On walks he pulled so hard that he nearly dislocated my shoulder. If I passed another dog walker, he quietly sniffed and circled the other canine until the duo continued on their way. Then he barked frantically and pulled even harder. At home he marked his territory every time I left him alone: sofa cushions, exercise machine, doorframes, and once my shoe, which I didn't discover until I put it on.

Frustrated by what a poor choice I had made in getting Mosby, I contacted several rescue groups. But after describing his issues, I was told they were "at capacity." I felt guilty that I didn't want him, but who would?

Then one day I read a newspaper article about a couple who adopted a toddler from an overseas orphanage. Their first few years of adjustment were difficult at best. The child had frequent tantrums, and timeouts weren't working. At a baseball game, when the mother went to get a beverage and the child had a melt down because "mommy might not come back," the couple realized that the root of the child's every problem was fear of them leaving her—separation anxiety.

Bingo. This is what Mosby had too.

"Beverly Hills," is what Jeff had said when I had asked where Mosby had come from. He explained that the original owner was cited for having twelve dogs and had to give up some of them. Next, he went to a pregnant lady who realized she couldn't handle him and an infant. So she surrendered him to Jeff at a Starbucks. I don't know how long

Mosby lived with Jeff and the Pit Bulls; he wouldn't understand the term "forever home" if he heard it. But he knew what it felt like to have loved ones leave you.

So did I. My two children had left for college. My dad had died. Close friends had moved away. By bringing Mosby home, hadn't I made a commitment to be there for him? Always?

"Mosby, you're a real pain in the ass," is what John says now when our dog barks excitedly as we arrive home from an outing or when we discover he has removed his bellyband diaper and peed somewhere.

We've had Mosby a few years, and he's only slightly calmer and quieter. I'm not going to lie and say he's become "the best little Pug" we've ever had, but every time he curls up in my lap with his pink tongue sticking out, snoring and randomly passing gas, for better or worse, I've accepted he's mine.

~Linda Delmont

The Barking Dog Contest

A dog's bark may be worse than his bite, but everyone prefers his bark.
~Author Unknown

O ne morning, after I got my kids off to school, I turned on the radio. I tuned in halfway through a contest. This particular day, WYSZ-FM was offering a barking dog contest. The radio station wanted to see whose dog barked the most in one minute.

One by one, listeners phoned in and coaxed their dogs to yip it up for the radio audience. Stopwatch in hand, the DJ counted the number of times each dog barked. The station buzzed with calls.

It was a lighthearted hour, filled with fun and laughter, as each dog tried to bark its way to local stardom. Percy, Max, and Noodle Poodle barked in various octaves. Duke howled. Babe entertained us with her whining. One old dog only barked twice and I think his owner must have pinched him or he wouldn't have barked at all.

The phone lines were flooded with calls from eager participants. German Shepherds, Cocker Spaniels, Schnauzers, and mixed breeds entertained the live radio audience. Some folks kept pressing the redial on their telephones because the lines were so busy. If they were patient and didn't give up, many were pleasantly surprised to eventually get through.

Periodically the DJ would announce the prizes. "Call in folks!

We have some great prizes and only one dog will win. This is what we will give to this grand prize winner: two concert tickets valued at fifty dollars, and no, you can't take your dog to this concert. Sorrrr-ry! We'll also give the winner a $10 gift certificate for dry cleaning, a fifty-pound bag of dog food, music CDs, and gift certificates to a fast food restaurant. These are great prizes, folks! Make your call now and tell Fido to bark."

Hmmm. Those were great prizes. If only I had a dog. Then a brilliant idea occurred to me. Every time I stepped into my back yard, my neighbor's new dog would go ballistic. This little white fluff-ball would spring into the air along our fence, yipping frantically whenever she saw me. This bundle of energy was named Belle. Although Belle was only a foot tall, there were days I was sure she could clear the top of our four-foot fence. It seemed as though she was on an invisible trampoline. And bark she did!

As the contest hour neared its end, I felt I needed to help Belle feel welcome in our neighborhood and make her a star. Maybe, if the truth were told, I was just greedy for prizes. I hadn't won anything since eighth grade and decades had passed. Maybe Belle was my ticket to contest success.

I quickly called the station and registered "my dog." I took my cordless phone to the back yard while I was on hold. Much to my chagrin, Belle wasn't in the back yard. I started to panic.

Right at that moment, the DJ got on the line. I told him about my dilemma—how I didn't own a dog but wanted to enter the contest. He laughed hysterically. He thought I wanted to bark to win those prizes. When he calmed down, I explained I wanted to enter the neighbor's dog. That was fine with him.

I covered my receiver as I yelled to my neighbors through their screen door. "Bring Belle out here quickly—I need her—HURRY!" The little neighbor girl peered quizzically at me through their side window. Her older sister jumped into action when she heard the urgency in my voice. She flung open the door and out pounced Belle. Just like I had expected, Belle charged toward our fence and barked so ferociously that you could hear her all the way down the street. Her entrance was like perfect clockwork.

With stopwatch in hand, the DJ couldn't believe what was happening. Belle yipped with such passion that she made me proud. Yip, yip, yip, yip, inhale, yip, yip, yip. The DJ almost couldn't keep up with the count because she barked so fast. Belle was on a yipping marathon and SHE WON! Belle set a record several times over the nearest competitor.

The DJ had a hard time composing himself. He was still in stitches from our previous conversation. The adrenaline rush from being on the air coupled with hearing the DJ's reaction and delight caught me off guard. I dissolved in laughter, with tears running down my cheeks. Maybe they were tears of joy from finally winning a contest.

The little neighbor girl, head tipped slightly to one side, stared at me with a wrinkled brow and puzzled expression. I'm sure that she and her little sister thought I was strange. No doubt, they wondered what was going on. After I pulled myself together, I was able to explain how Belle had become an instant celebrity.

I was pleasantly surprised when I had the opportunity to meet the DJ a year later, during a beach outing. When I reminded him of his barking dog contest, he broke into a wide grin. He explained that when I called in to enter the contest — and didn't own a dog — it just about pushed him over the edge. It struck him funny that someone would do that, and then win. He mentioned that of all the contests he had presented during his morning radio programs, this was his favorite. And it was my favorite too!

What a happy day it was when I claimed my prizes. The two concert tickets, a $10 gift certificate for dry cleaning, a fifty-pound bag of dog food, music CDs, and gift certificates to a fast food restaurant were now mine. But I did split the prize with Belle. She got the dog food. She also won my affection. Although I still don't own a dog, it's not unusual to see me buying dog biscuits for my winner next door.

~Judy Gyde

Leonidis, MD

You cannot share your life with a dog, as I had done in Bournemouth, or a cat, and not know perfectly well that animals have personalities and minds and feelings.

~Jane Goodall

When my son, Justin, first suggested bringing home a Pit Bull, the thought terrified me. "Absolutely not!" was my initial response. Pit Bulls were evil and mean, weren't they? Justin and many other dog lovers explained that the media hypes up the "vicious Pit Bull" image because it sells stories!

I gave in, but told my son that the first time the dog proved to be aggressive he would have to find a new home. He assured me this tiny puppy would show me how wrong I was about the breed.

When I was growing up, our family had Beagles, Labradors and even a German Shepherd—but my son's puppy, who we named Leonidis, was hands down the friendliest of them all! And I was in for even more surprises.

It was early February and I fell sick... very sick, very fast! I had pneumonia and went to the emergency room just in time. The doctors said if I had waited one more day they would have had to admit me. I stayed in the emergency room for a few hours; I needed IV fluids because I was dehydrated.

The days that followed were filled with drinking lots of ginger ale, trying to rest, and remembering to take my medicine on time. I had to take my medication three times a day. I initially tried to take each dose the same time each day, but the times I took the first two doses fluctuated because I would sleep at different hours. I tried to take my last dose at 10 p.m. so I could sleep through the night after that.

After several days, I was able to move from the bed to the living room. On my second day in the living room, Leonidis ran to my side at 10 p.m. and started barking. He didn't stop until I acknowledged him. He swatted at me to get my attention. I thought he wanted to play and told him, "Go see Justin!" A few moments later he started barking again. "What do you want, Leonidis?" He reached out and knocked over my bottle of medicine on the table.

How could he possibly know that I needed to take my medicine at that time? He was only an eight-month-old puppy. I called it a coincidence and dismissed it. The next day I purposely did not take my medicine at 10:00 to see if he would repeat the "trick" from the night before. Sure enough, at 10:04 he was by my side trying to get my attention by barking and swatting at me. I looked at him and asked, "What's wrong?" He stared at my prescription bottle and started barking. Amazing! I had no idea that he was so smart, let alone so observant.

Almost two weeks after I started my prescription, I was getting better, but at a snail's pace. Except for my breathing; I was having just as much trouble breathing as I did from the beginning. This was mostly my fault. The doctor gave me an inhaler to use every four hours, but I was also taking cough syrup and two different pills. That just seemed like an awful lot of medicine, and I was scared of the potential side effects. However, the doctor knew what he was talking about and I should have used the inhaler as much as he said instead of hardly at all.

It was around nine in the morning and I was fast asleep after a restless night. Throughout the night I'd had a lot of trouble breathing, and my fever came and went. Then I was awakened by Leonidis. His face was right in front of mine and he was barking. When I opened my eyes he started licking my face. I pushed him away and went to tell him to get off the bed when I realized I couldn't speak! My lungs had closed completely. I looked down on the bed and there was my inhaler. And Leonidis was still on my bed barking and swatting at me, looking at me and then looking down at the inhaler.

I quickly grabbed it and took two puffs. My lungs started to open.

How did Leonidis know that I stopped breathing? And how in the world did he know to bring me my inhaler? What an amazing and intelligent dog! I could only imagine how that morning could have ended had he not been there.

For the remaining two weeks that I was sick in bed, Leonidis would spend hours lying next to me with his head resting on my stomach, watching over me until I was better.

~Charlotte Hopkins

Snowstorms

In order to really enjoy a dog, one doesn't merely try to train him to be semi-human. The point of it is to open oneself to the possibility of becoming partly a dog.

~Edward Hoagland

"Leon! What am I going to do with you? Look at this mess!" A snowstorm of fluffy white comforter batting completely covered the utility room floor. I started gathering up the mess our one-year old Dachshund had made once again. "You're determined to be a bad boy!" I scolded.

He gazed at me from his bed with clear, unblinking eyes as I stuffed the thick layer of fresh, white fiberfill into a trash bag. He was trying his best to be invisible but the puffy white goatee dangling from his chin told me he was guilty of the crime. He was adorable.

We had met Leon one evening when he and his sister, Noel, were out for a walk with their family. My husband, Ed, asked their owners if Doxies were good family pets.

"Oh, they're great house pets. They're affectionate and loving. We wouldn't have anything but a Dachshund," the man said. "This younger one, Leon, is for sale if you're interested," he added.

With his nose to the ground, the short-legged wonder zigzagged along our driveway following the scents from past visitors. He was sturdy and agile with an auburn coat that glistened in the sunlight. His eyes were warm and filled with curiosity. It was love at first sight.

Leon was terrified after leaving the only home and family he'd ever known. He peered at us from under the patio table with questioning expressions: Who are you? Why am I here? What's going to happen to me?

Within a few weeks, however, he was running through the house as though he'd lived with us since puppyhood. He stuck close by and only vanished for short periods to take snoozes behind the king-size pillows on our bed. He had captured our hearts with his engaging, people-pleasing antics.

Leon was a charmer and a perfect fit for our family, but his behavior was not exemplary. He had his own room, which was a converted utility area with a doggy door. His room adjoined a large bedroom and full bath so there was plenty of space for him to wander. The problem arose when we put him in his room and closed the door to leave and run errands. As soon as the door closed, he became a dog on a mission to destroy anything that was soft, stuffed or fuzzy.

In just a few months, Leon had destroyed countless pillows, comforters, sleeping bags and throw rugs. He shredded one king-size comforter into thousands of tiny puffs of simulated snow. Throw rugs were nibbled into a frayed mass, and then he'd drag them outdoors onto the grass. It was clear Leon wanted to make a statement, but what was he trying to say?

"I'm at my wits' end with this dog! He's loveable and smart and it seems he wants to please us, but I've about had it with his destructiveness. Something seems to snap in him when we leave him home alone. It just doesn't add up!" I complained.

One day after work, Ed burst through the front door. "I think I've figured out what's going on with Leon," he exclaimed.

"Talk to me! He chewed the corners off another pillow today so I'm open to any reasonable suggestions," I said with a sigh.

"I think he's angry and hurt. He gave his other family his loyalty and devotion, and then in return they gave him away! It has to be the ultimate betrayal for a dog." Ed was convinced he'd solved the problem.

"Okay, I'll give you that he might have abandonment issues, but what can we do to stop his destructiveness?" I asked.

"We're going to leave the door to his room open when we leave. I totally believe that when we put him in his room and close the door, he's terrified about who will be on the other side of the door each time it's opened."

"I'm not sure about all this," I said, shaking my head.

"He'll be able to see us come and go, day in and day out, which will alleviate his fear of being carted away by strangers. He needs to feel safe when we're away and secure that only you and I are coming home to him," he insisted.

"You might be right about him needing to feel safe," I conceded. "But I'm still hesitant about leaving him alone with our best overstuffed couches, chairs and pillows."

"Think about it," Ed said. "He's only destroyed his stuff, nothing of ours. We need to leave his door open when we go out so he can roam about the house just as if we're home. Let him look out the windows and explore the house as he pleases. He'll soon feel safe and secure and the destruction will cease. Trust me, this is going to work!"

I started by leaving Leon loose in the house for a few minutes while I ran to the post office—no problems. Over time I tested him for a couple of hours in the afternoon—nothing was touched. Then we left him when we went out for the evening—everything was in its place upon our return. Within a few months, we trusted him for a couple of days with only a pet sitter looking after him.

Ed had realized Leon's problem. Feeling safe and secure in his new surroundings was the key to calming his frustration and easing his fears. He became a changed dog, never destroying anything again. His fear of abandonment has stayed with him throughout the years but now he cuddles when he's fearful instead of destroying things. Leon is now enjoying his golden years curled up on a cozy, warm comforter where snowstorms only exist in his past.

~Cynthia Briggs

15

Learning to Love Lucy

Trouble is part of your life, and if you don't share it, you don't give the person who loves you enough chance to love you enough.
~Dinah Shore

I found Lucy in a small black cage outside a pet store one hot July morning. A black Lab mix puppy with a white belly and perky ears that stood at attention, Lucy had been abandoned at a nearby house. The homeowner had kindly taken her to a vet, paid for medical treatment and transferred her to a shelter. The shelter volunteers brought her to their weekly adoption event at the pet store.

What drew me to Lucy was her serenity. All the other adoptable dogs were panting and barking and yelping and scratching. But not Lucy. She just sat in her cage, watching people go in and out of the store, with a Zen-like calmness. I crouched in front of her cage and looked into her dark eyes.

"Hi there," I said.

She blinked back at me and cocked her cute little head.

"She's so calm," I said to the friend who was with me.

I envisioned long days of writing with Lucy as my companion stretched out at my feet. I drove home and brought back the entire family to test her out. My three- and five-year-old boys played with her and walked her. My husband examined her teeth and paws and personality. She received unanimous approval.

It took three days to process the paperwork and for the shelter staff to research our suitability as dog owners. When the call came that we were approved, I drove back to the pet store to retrieve her for good. In that three-day time period, however, she had morphed into a different dog—a strong, hyperactive one I could barely control. I wondered if they had given her a sedative for that adoption event. She practically jumped out the window on the way home. I chalked it up to her being excited to have a new family.

On our first visit to the veterinarian the next day, I brought my boys so they could be a part of the entire dog-caring process. The two vet technicians giving her shots discussed her breed possibilities while they held her steady on the table.

"Hmmm. Lab and… Pit Bull?" one said.

"Yeah, definitely some type of terrier in her," the other said. She examined her snout more closely. "Yeah. Pit."

"I have a PIT BULL?" I said.

"Mix," they said together. "Pit Bull mix." As if that made everything okay.

Suddenly, I was afraid of my cute puppy. From all the horror stories I'd read in the newspapers, I assumed that all Pit Bulls were evil, dangerous, child-eating machines. I had two children. And a Pit Bull mix.

I held Lucy's leash all the way home in the car to make sure she didn't snack on the boys while they were strapped in their car seats. But she just curled up on the passenger seat and went to sleep. When we got home, I called my husband at work and told him the terrible news.

"Maybe you're overreacting," he said. "After all, she's part Lab too."

I tried to focus on the Lab part of the mix and concentrate on training and loving Lucy, even as a tiny voice was telling me, "Give her back, give her back." But another voice was saying, "Give the poor unwanted creature a chance. Don't judge. She's only a puppy, after all." So I gave her a chance.

Whenever we walked her in the neighborhood and someone asked what kind of puppy she was, both my boys would gleefully announce, "She's a Pit Bull!" I would quickly step in. "No, no, she's not. She's a Lab

mix. We don't know what else she's mixed with. Could be anything."
The people usually eyed me suspiciously and hurried away. I made
the boys practice the line: Lab mix. Lab mix. Lab mix.

And then it happened. About a month after we adopted Lucy, I
was at the stove cooking dinner and she was in a down-stay at my feet.
A man walking two big, fluffy white dogs down the street appeared
out the bay window and Lucy decided they needed to be annihilated.
Immediately. She sprang from her spot, sprinted to the window and
smashed through it. Glass shattered. I screamed. The poor man walking
the dogs clutched his chest. I envisioned the canine bloodbath that
was about to ensue and hollered at Lucy in a scary voice I didn't even
know I possessed to GET BACK HERE NOW!

To my utter surprise, she stopped and slowly backed through the
shards of broken glass until she was all the way back in the dining room.
She then sat perfectly still and silent while I gaped at the large hole in
the bay window and the shards of glass strewn all over the carpet.

"I'm so sorry!" I called out the hole.

The man and his frightened dogs stumbled away, leaving me
alone with the destructive and unpredictable beast that I knew now
we couldn't keep. Lucy lay down and put her head on top of crossed
paws. She knew she had crossed the line.

"Too late!" I told her. "Bad dog!"

Our pet adoption contract was still on the counter. My heart
hammered in my chest as I scanned the list of things I had agreed to.
Number seven was highlighted and starred: If for any reason I could
not keep my pet, I agreed to return it to the Humane Society or to
the foster parent.

I called the phone number listed and left a pleading message on
the answering machine: Please call me back as soon as you get this. I
cannot, I repeat CANNOT keep Lucy. I need to return her ASAP.

"No, Mommy! No!" the boys protested.

No one from the shelter called back that night or the next day.
I left two more urgent messages. It wasn't until almost a month later
that someone called me back. "I'm so sorry it took so long. When can
I come and get Lucy?"

In the span of that month: 1) the window was fixed, 2) my older son repeatedly fell asleep curled up with Lucy in her crate, 3) Lucy went to sleep-away training and came back much more civilized and 4) I taught her to sit, give a high-five, roll over, play dead, "speak" and dance.

When the person from the shelter finally called I was cooking dinner and Lucy was playing hide-and-seek with the kids.

"You found me!" I heard my older son say. "Good girl!"

"My turn," my younger son said. "Down, Lucy." Lucy dutifully obeyed.

"Actually," I told the woman, "thanks, but don't bother. We've fallen in love with her."

Lucy just turned twelve. It's hard to believe we almost gave her back.

~Julie Richie

16

Comrade in Arms

*For me a house or an apartment becomes a home when you add
one set of four legs, a happy tail, and that indescribable measure
of love that we call a dog.*

~Roger Caras

When my fiancé Shawn and I purchased a townhouse, I decided it was time to realize my dream of dog ownership. Growing up, we had cats for pets, but instinctively, I knew I was a dog person. Unfortunately, my fiancé was not so sure.

"Puppies pee everywhere," Shawn warned. "A dog would wreck the carpeting." Undeterred, I researched until I found a breeder of a Poodle-Schnauzer hybrid willing to bring his puppies over for a home-visit.

"We don't have to decide now. I'll just look at them," I told my leery fiancé.

Shawn was not convinced, especially after he discovered the visit would be when he was at work. I told him not to worry and promised to take pictures.

The day of the visit arrived. Amidst a soundtrack of high-pitched yips, the breeder left the Schnauzer mother in his station wagon and carried out the two remaining puppies. One pup was completely jet black. The other was shades of gray. The black puppy refused to move, but the gray pup confidently wobbled to my outstretched hand. I admired his complex coloring: the black fur on his back faded to smoky gray on his sides and silvery white on his paws. He sniffed me with a wet, black nose. I smiled, flattered by his attention. Then his thin black lips parted, and he licked my fingers. His tail was docked and the remaining nub twitched back and forth frantically.

"Which one do you like?" asked the breeder.

"The gray one," I said.

I picked up the puppy and brought him inside. I held him against my chest; he felt as warm as a swaddled newborn. His fur of soft curls with black wiry ends tickled my skin, making me smile. All else seemed to fall away when I felt the quick pulsing of his little heart as he snuggled my neck and licked my chin. The breeder talked about kennels, leashes, and puppy food. I nodded, only half listening. I lifted the gray puppy so our eyes could meet. My gaze locked with the dark chocolate eyes hooded by bushy white eyebrows. In those shiny brown eyes, I saw trust, loyalty, and love.

Hours later, Shawn returned from work to discover his fiancée sitting in the living room, cuddling a sleepy gray puppy.

"I knew it!" he said. "You bought it, didn't you?"

I smiled guiltily. "I'm naming him Sammy. Isn't he adorable?"

Shawn reached out to pet Sammy, but the pup barked, frightened. "He doesn't even like me!" Shawn complained. He was clearly not impressed.

The next few weeks were rough. With every accident we had to clean up and every night's sleep cut short by whines for attention, Shawn grew more frustrated.

"I told you we weren't ready to have a dog," he grumbled as he aggressively sprayed the carpet with pet odor neutralizer.

It appeared my venture into dog ownership was not working out. Then, I received life-changing news from my National Guard unit. We had received deployment orders. In just three months, I would be off to six months of training at Fort Hood, Texas, followed by a year of refueling helicopters in Iraq.

In the next chaotic weeks, my fiancé and I organized our wedding, prepared for my deployment, and somehow managed to housetrain Sammy. On a clear brisk day in January, Shawn and I married in my hometown church, surrounded by family and friends. Just four weeks later, the dreaded day I had to fly to Fort Hood came. That morning, I kissed Sammy's furry head as I placed him in the kennel.

"Take care of Daddy," I whispered.

I knew if I said anything more, I would burst into tears. Shawn drove me to the airport in the pre-dawn darkness. We didn't talk much, but we held hands with a fierce tightness.

"Call me as soon as you can," Shawn kept repeating. I nodded, eyes filling with tears. Would we get through this? Would Shawn be okay without me?

"I love you, so much," was all I could say.

"I love you, too, baby. Call me as soon as you can, okay?"

I came home for mid-tour leave the next year at the end of January, the week of our first wedding anniversary. After a tearful reunion with family at the airport, Shawn and I drove home. We couldn't stop smiling as we held hands in the car.

"Just wait until Sammy sees you," Shawn said. "He's going to flip out."

I was excited to see Sammy, too. When Shawn brought Sammy downstairs, I didn't recognize the adult dog who jumped on me, smothering me with wet kisses.

"He's huge!" I groaned from under his weight.

Sammy was fifteen pounds heavier than the puppy I remembered. His coat was lighter too. The black that once highlighted most of his furry curls was reduced to a thin strip along his back. Sammy was so excited to see me he had a little accident on the kitchen floor. When I noticed the puddle, I glanced nervously at my husband. I braced myself for an annoyed reaction. Instead, Shawn continued smiling as he grabbed the cleaning spray and paper towels.

"Man," Shawn laughed, "he really is excited to see you!" His calm reaction was the first clue something had changed between Sammy and my husband. I noticed Sammy followed my husband everywhere, shiny eyes fixed loyally on my husband's face. It became clear our dog was no longer a momma's boy. I commented on this change to Shawn.

He scratched Sammy behind the ears and confessed, "I couldn't have made it through these past months without him."

He explained that Sammy was the one who was always there for him during my absence. He helped my anxious husband sleep by filling my empty spot on the bed. It was Sammy who raised Shawn's spirits with his infectious playfulness and constant ploys for attention. Thanks to him, Shawn didn't have to come home from work to an empty, lonely house. Instead, Sammy was always there to greet him by running around in circles of frenzied excitement and jumping on Shawn's legs until he knelt to receive a series of doggy kisses. Sammy would even lick Shawn's tears when he cried.

"Come on Mr. Floppy Ears, let's go upstairs with Mommy!" my husband cooed in baby talk to Sammy as we carried my Army duffle bags upstairs.

I smiled. Observing the loving bond between Sammy and my husband comforted me. The previous fall I had impulsively bought a friendly gray puppy because I knew I was a dog person. Now, it was very clear my husband was a dog person too. When the time came to return to Iraq for the second half of my deployment, the drive to the airport was once again tearful. However, this time, my anxiety over my husband's welfare was absent. I knew my husband would be okay; he had Sammy.

~Joan Oen

Monster

If your dog doesn't like someone you probably shouldn't either.
~Author Unknown

Twenty years ago, Mia's little friend Holly stood at our front door and yelled, "Happy Birthday, Mia!" Then, Holly pushed a hairy, squirming puppy into Mia's hands. "We got him at the Humane Society. He's six weeks old. Isn't he cute?"

I swallowed hard.

Of course, Mia squealed with delight.

Legs running, pushing air, squirming, with his tongue slurping at anything in reach, he was too rambunctious to hold. Mia dropped him to the floor, where he squatted and peed.

Screams erupted again. The girls turned and ran for paper towels.

I couldn't hide my horror.

Holly's mother saw my face. She flinched. "You said it was okay to get a dog."

"Yes, but...." I exhaled. I wanted a dog that would be sweet and gentle with us. That would let us put pink bows in its hair and paint its toenails when we painted ours. I needed a dog that would fit into our new all-female post-divorce world.

I didn't need this giant Mastiff in the making.

A cough, a gag, the hairy beast heaved twice and upchucked onto the floor. And, with a sad look, he flopped down in it.

"He's sick." Relief flooded through me. We could take him back.

"Kennel cough. They were going to put him to sleep." Holly's voice caught as she swiped at the goo with a paper towel. "We had to take him. We saved his life."

Undeterred, Mia swooped the puppy into her arms.

"Mom, we have to keep him. He needs us."

There it was.

Mia named him Coco. I called him Monster.

Monster grew, and grew… into a wild looking dog: part Chow, part giant, and a lot of whatever got over the fence. I guessed wolf. His head hung low between his well-muscled shoulder blades as if he had no neck. This caused his fur to stand up, creating the look of a lion's mane. His walk made strangers believe he was rabid. He swaggered sideways, unable to walk a straight line. Monster's head remained cocked stiffly to one side, like his muscles had atrophied and locked there. Worse, when he growled, and he growled a lot, the coarse hair running down his spine bristled straight up. He was the image of power and insanity all wrapped up in one dog.

Strangers never messed with Monster. They called Animal Control. Some even called the police.

He was one ugly dog. This turned out to be a good thing. Since nobody messed with Monster, nobody messed with Mia. He stayed by her side wherever she went. Watching. Brooding. Growling. Loving Mia.

Monster won my admiration.

Like most divorced mothers, I worked, which left my kids alone after school. They had to fend for themselves. Not by choice. But with sporadic child support, and nobody volunteering to help, I didn't have a choice. Staying home was not an option. Even then, sometimes, I couldn't make it. I called my dad twice for help.

I lived scared, knowing that every day we were one paycheck away from homeless.

Monster gave me the ability to go to work. He became the protector of our home. Monster kept us safe. He provided comfort. He loved us when it seemed no one else did.

One day, Mia came running down from the hill behind our house. Terrified, she gulped out, "Snake."

"Were you bitten?" I grabbed her and searched her arms and legs.

"No, but Coco... he jumped in front of me." She sobbed.

I pulled her close, kissed her, then took off yelling for Monster. Mia wiped her tears and followed.

Within seconds Monster loped around the corner and crashed into my arms. Frantic, I clawed through his thick fur.

"Did you see it strike?"

"Yes."

Monster flipped over, presenting his belly. Frantic, we both searched every inch of him and didn't find any teeth marks. I assume his thick fur protected him.

Later, we went up the hill to where Mia saw the snake. There it was. A rattler. Torn to shreds. Monster sniffed it, hit it with a paw and then stood proudly back, as if to say, "Don't worry... it's dead."

After that, Monster slept in Mia's bed with his head on her pillow. I guess he figured she needed extra protection. I probably should have objected, but with constant money problems... I didn't fight the Monster-craze. There was no point. I was as sold on Monster as Mia was.

He comforted me too. Sometimes I'd wake up hearing the house creak and creep out of bed, only to be met by Monster, smiling his scary-looking grin. I'd know we were fine because the hairs on his back weren't standing straight up.

You see, Monster didn't like solicitors or, as Mia grew older, any of the pimply-faced boys who showed up on our doorstep. But he never bit anyone. He didn't have to. He'd just smile, baring his teeth.

Monster grinned all the time.

It was unnerving.

Time passed. Things improved in our little female enclave. I got promoted. Our money problems eased. We collected all our back child support. We had options, like college for Mia.

Both Monster and I were sad when Mia moved away. Monster

crawled into her empty bed and moped. I tried to coax him into mine. After all, I was lonely too. I offered dog treats and hamburger balls, all to no avail. He stayed true to his girl even when she wasn't home.

Mia acted like most college kids, dashing in and out in between semesters and summer breaks, delighting Monster and me. Then one day, Mia brought home a lanky young man. Monster sniffed him, high and low, and walked away. Then, he flopped on the floor, at Mia's feet. No growl. No snarl. No nothing.

I almost fainted when that same young man reached down and patted Monster's head. His tail wagged. A blessing formerly reserved solely for Mia.

Mia married that young man and they had a child.

I fell in love, married and moved into my new husband's house. I gave our home to Mia. Monster stayed in the house with Mia and her new family. By then, he was an old dog and settled in his ways. But he was happy. He spent his retirement lying around, somewhere close to his girl.

One day, Monster died. Devastated, Mia and I cried and cried.

We buried Monster in the back yard, under his favorite tree.

Mia has another dog now. But, I am sure Monster hasn't given up his post. He still watches, protecting Mia, as he always did.

~Karen Ekstrom

Crazy for Daisy

Properly trained, a man can be a dog's best friend.
~Corey Ford

'd lost three Basset Hounds in the span of only ten months to various maladies. I was suddenly dogless and lonelier than I ever could have imagined. I lasted three months before beginning the quest for another.

I had raised puppies before. The prospect of sleepless nights, shredded shoes and swabbing puddles of piddle off the floor had lost its appeal. Daily, I searched the local pounds and shelters for adult Bassets, but found none. Then an ad appeared in the newspaper: Basset Hound, female, 1 year old, $150. Patience and Dolly, two of my former Bassets, were both a year old when I adopted them. Both were wonderful dogs. I called and drove out to see the dog in the ad.

When I walked up to the front door and rang the bell, I heard the baritone bark of a Basset, music to my ears. Ah, a good watchdog! Score a point in favor of this candidate. Our former Basset Hound, Patience, could never have been mistaken for a watchdog. A doorstop, perhaps. The people introductions were brief. We got straight to the matter at hand—that is to say, paw.

"This is Daisy." The lady held the glossy, tricolor Hound firmly in check with a choke collar. The dog was clearly healthy. Score another point. Daisy strained at her collar as though she were in training for the Iditarod. Perhaps this dog was too healthy.

"You can release her now," I commanded. The next instant she was all over me like lint on a lollipop. I retreated to the couch and sat. Good human! Daisy catapulted from the floor to my lap, planting her forepaws squarely on my chest. A sixty-pound Basset is no lap dog, but Daisy wasn't aware of this or any other rules of acceptable canine conduct.

When she upturned to have her belly scratched, gazing at me with Hershey's Kiss eyes, I melted. The scales tipped further in her favor when I was assured that I could have her for free; the $150 was only to deter any Cruella de Vil trolling the classified ads for dog #102. Daisy even came with her own leash, bed and sky kennel. I'd found Barbie's Basset Hound!

"She'll try to dominate you," they told me. The warning fell on deaf ears. The sight of their battle-torn family room should have served as clear enough portent of my fate, but budding puppy love is blind.

I should have bolted for the door. Instead, I asked, "Do you mind if I take her for a walk?"

"Sure, go ahead." She had never been on a leash in her life, but by the time she dragged me halfway down the street, I was heeling perfectly.

I didn't take her with me that afternoon. I drove home and thought it over for a whole hour. Then I called and asked Daisy's soon-to-be-ex-mom to drop her off on the way to work the next morning for a one-day trial. After three months I still had her, even though Miss Daisy was driving me crazy.

She woke me hourly every night until 6 a.m. for the morning feeding. I began to imagine I could hear her whining at my bedroom door, even when she wasn't. She was as snappish as a crocodile in a sushi bar. The first time I came too near her food bowl, I was nearly a double amputee. I should have sent her back to her former owners before I grew too attached, but it wasn't long until we'd bonded like peanut butter and jelly. I was the jelly.

After many years of receiving love and attention from me that she never got from her first owners, Daisy became a good dog—sort of. Several weeks after I adopted Daisy, I drove to the SPCA to donate the last of Patience's senior diet kibble and her battered wicker bed.

Daisy rode beside me in the same seat Patience had. If I squinted hard enough, I could see my sweet old girl sitting there next to me. I'd been through a lot with Daisy the Doggy Disaster. She was nothing like our calm, gentle Patience. For two cents, which is more than Crazy Daisy cost me, I would have left her there at the shelter. Anyone in her right mind, or less determined to make this canine/human relationship work, probably would have.

I felt a moist nose nudge my hand. I stroked Daisy's silky fur as she sat beside me in Patience's old co-pilot's seat. Then those chocolate eyes met mine. In them I clearly saw the unflagging trust and devotion I've read only in the eyes of my dogs. In that instant it was understood that she would still be sitting beside me when we returned home that day. I knew that in the years to come I'd be driving Miss Daisy, and she'd still be driving me crazy.

~Sue Owens Wright

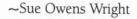

My Chilly Chis

Dogs have a way of finding the people who need them,
Filling an emptiness we don't even know we have.
~Thom Jones

Dog owners tend to be drawn to a particular breed or breed type, and our choice was the Border Collie. We'd had various breeds and mixes but our Border named Bongo stood out for his astounding loyalty, obedience, intelligence and ability to practically read our minds. He was so smart that my husband suggested that, instead of the kids, we should send the dog to college.

When you get a puppy and raise it along with your children, it becomes a part of their childhood and a part of your family history. When my older son went to college and my younger went to heaven, Bongo dutifully stayed to ease our grief for as long as he could. When it was time to put him down, we knew we were losing the last vestige of our children's childhood. If you've ever had to say goodbye to a loved one, you know that you give a piece of your heart to hold onto until you meet again in heaven. We didn't think we could give our hearts to another dog after Bongo passed.

"It would be unfair to any dog that should come into our home," I said. "We could never love it like we love Bongo." Everyone agreed. Anyone who knew Bongo lauded his special personality.

Months passed, then years. We shared Bongo stories and how we could sometimes "feel" him jump on the bed or catch a glimpse of him out of the corner of our eyes. Bongo could never be replaced, just as our own little boy could never be replaced.

My adult daughter and I often walked up and down the rows of cages at the city animal shelter, wondering if we were ready to volunteer. We agreed no dog would come home with us.

One day, as we passed by the cages, one small brown dog reached her tiny paw through the bars as though to stop us. It was a Chihuahua mix. Despite her obvious trepidation about the shelter cacophony and blur of passing strangers, she wagged her tail and licked our fingers, coaxing us to stay with her.

"A Chihuahua?" We looked at each other. No, not the neurotic yippy-yappers. But then, we remembered Bella the Chi we once dog-sat for a friend. That Chi wasn't an anxiety-ridden noisy small breed. Neither was the sweet therapy Chihuahua, Nellie, who visited my daughter during her long infusions at the hospital. Maybe with an open mind both my daughter and this rescued one could have a new life of purpose becoming a therapy team, too. This Chi mix had a perfect, easygoing temperament and was obviously social and gentle.

When she came home, she slipped into her new home life quickly and easily. It's not good to treat a dog like a child, I know, but her size just begged to be babied. Soon, I found myself warming a blanket in the dryer, bundling her up and cradling her in my arms. Just the sight of a blanket makes her eager for the next cuddle session. She always seemed so chilly that I bought her a sweater. My husband warned me not to spoil her, but I ignored him.

Sweet little Suki slept in our bed under our blankets with us, and she ate kibble, canned food and treats from our table. Love and adoration beamed from her large, brown eyes. Over the next year, Suki gained weight. Bony when we got her, she ballooned unhealthily. We showed our love with hugs and kisses and big dog portions of food from the drive-thru. Whenever we passed by a fast food place, she licked her lips. This was not good. Our love had to be kept non-edible. No more fast food. And more exercise.

The perfect solution? A new friend. It was such a happy time for us to return to the animal shelter, this time on a mission to find a new family member. It didn't take long.

If we thought Suki looked terribly thin and forlorn when we first saw her, this little Chihuahua mix looked like a shivering waif straight out of *Oliver Twist*. An oversize, threadbare T-shirt made him look even more pitiful. His legs were thinner than chicken bones. Yet, he had the bounce and energy of a tightly wound spring. Gizmo was the perfect, annoying little brother for Suki. He got her running and losing the weight she'd put on during the previous year.

You'd think our little pack was happy and complete, but I was hit by the most curious urge to adopt just one more Chi. A third. My husband thought I was crazy and it took some time to convince him that I was not becoming an animal hoarder. We'd never had more than two dogs at a time before but this feeling was hard to resist. Two Chis were terrific. Three would be thrilling!

"No more Chihuahuas!" my husband said. "If we ever get another dog, it will have to be a Border." It only seemed fair. But the thought of having three Chis was overwhelming, so I went to the animal shelter website to see what Chis were available. As I clicked on the pages, one particular little dog caught my eye. It was described as a Chi mix but it looked like a Border Collie. Closer inspection revealed that it was a rare Border Collie-Chihuahua mix. I couldn't believe it. I rushed to the shelter, knowing that my husband would have his Border and I would have my Chi.

Bongo was named after the bongo drum, which my husband played, so it seemed only natural to name his new Bochi (Border-Chi) Quinto, the name of the companion drum. My husband was over the moon when he saw Quinto's soft, playful face. And now our three little Chis have filled our home with a lot of joyful antics. We can't lie on the sofa without being covered by happy Chihuahuas, bubbling over with glee.

I never considered myself a Chihuahua person. Dogs, to me, aren't fashion accessories. But they still do look irresistibly cute wearing a T-shirt or sweater. As for Quinto, while he is the size of a Chi, he has plenty of black and white fur and the look of a Border—so we decided to keep his couture limited to a tiny red bandana, which seems to suit him quite well.

So, in the name of good dogs everywhere and especially our precious, irreplaceable Bongo, we have rescued three homeless dogs from the shelter and become members of the ASPCA. Alas, none of our Chis turned out to be therapy dogs, except for the therapy they provide us at home. The amount of love they bring into our lives still amazes us.

We wonder if Bongo looks down upon our pack and approves. If he were here, he would have loved to play with these three chilly Chis. I imagine that someday he'll be herding us all into heaven, where he'll look at us as if to say, "And you didn't think you were Chihuahua people!"

~Lori Phillips

Chapter 3

The Dog Did What?

Who Rescued Who?

Early Warning System

A dog is man's best friend, and vice versa.
~Author Unknown

I gave myself a month to grieve when my very first dog passed away. Then I adopted a two-year-old blond Cairn Terrier from Pet Rescue who had been abused and abandoned by his previous owner.

Naming him Toby, I showered him with love and kindness, yet it took months before he understood he would not be abandoned again. The change in his behavior once he realized that was like a reborn animal—happy, playful, eager to go with me wherever I went. We became inseparable.

He'd follow me into every room of the house, then settle at my feet. I couldn't take a bath or shower without him demanding to be in the room with me.

I never realized how deep Toby's love for me was until the early morning hours a few days before Easter Sunday. It was a hot, muggy day that continued into the night. Rain was forecasted, but by midnight I was too tired to care and went to sleep in my second-floor corner apartment, sharing that bed with Toby. I left the window open beside my bed, hoping for some cool wind to reduce the heat and humidity.

I was awakened rudely from a deep sleep by a short bark and hard nudge in my back from Toby to face the sounds of heavy rain, thunder, and the sight of lightning outside my window. Wow. The clock on my night table read 12:50 a.m. I had been asleep less than an hour. I rose and kneeled by the window to admire the lightning display and enjoy the cool wind blowing through the screen.

Toby leaped off the bed and barked again. I turned to see his blond body, reflected from the outside parking lights, standing in the doorway of my room. The look in his eyes seemed to say, "You idiot, I'm outta here." He barked again, expecting me to follow.

Seconds later the power went out. Darkness enveloped the entire neighborhood. The lightning, thunder, and heavy rain swiftly cut off. There was a dark, ominous silence. You could hear a pin drop.

I peered into the darkness at the tall forest of trees beside my building, listening to their soft sighs as they began to bend. Strange, I thought, the trees aren't swaying back upright. Then, abruptly, I heard snapping. The sound grew louder the closer it came toward my building. At the same moment Toby barked again, urgency in his tone.

I raced into the hallway, screaming for him, unaware he was right at my heels until I reached the hall closet.

The loud roar drowned out my voice. The entire two-story apartment building vibrated as I grabbed Toby with one arm and leaped into the hall closet. I knelt down and struggled to close the door while I watched the far wall of my bedroom and the roof above it rip off, the tornado fighting desperately to tear the door handle out of my hand and suck me and Toby into its vortex.

In what seemed like minutes, yet was no more than seconds, the roaring sounds and vibrations ended. The tornado had passed.

It was quiet and still. I waited, afraid to move, still clasping Toby under my arm. He had not made a sound throughout the tornado's passing. I prayed it was over.

Suddenly I heard another roaring sound and the building shook. A second tornado struck, following the same pattern as the first. Through the closet door, I heard things crashing and splintering inside my apartment. Items on the closet shelf jumped and fell, hitting me as I held Toby tight to my chest with one hand, the other clinging for dear life to the doorknob.

I felt a loud boom from the other side of the closet, shaking the entire building, spilling even more debris off the shelf and onto my head.

My eyes tightly closed, my body filled with terror for what seemed an eternity, and then the second tornado passed. It was silent again. But soon, I heard shouts and yells from my neighbors.

I let another minute pass before daring to open the closet door and step out into the dark hallway. I stared into my bedroom, the debris so thick I couldn't enter. I could see the sky, the large hole in the wall where my tall dresser had stood. A huge tree now lay across my bed and protruded into my second bedroom as well, barely ten feet from the closet where Toby and I had hidden. The bed the two of us slept in moments earlier was gone, smothered under the debris and thick tree. The tree had slammed down so hard it had put a hole through the concrete floor and into my neighbor's bedroom below.

With Toby at my side I left the apartment, climbing over tree branches on the stairs. All my neighbors in our four-unit apartment section were safe, yet as frightened as I over what had happened so quickly and violently.

We gathered at my neighbor's apartment across from me on the lower floor, Toby trying to climb up my leg, not wanting to be separated. As I settled on my neighbor's sofa, sharing it with Toby, I petted him and calmed his shaking body, gazing into soft, dark brown eyes as they gazed into mine. I easily saw his love and trust for me, aware my own reflected the same. My adopted little hero had saved my life.

~charly s.

Choosing Ophelia

Acquiring a dog may be the only time a person gets to choose a relative.
~Author Unknown

Ophelia is the dog we almost didn't want. My son's living arrangement wasn't working out and, unable to find a place that allowed pets, he debated whether he could keep his new German Shepherd puppy. Adding to his stress were complications with his job and the ending of a long-term relationship.

I will never forget Barrett sitting on our kitchen floor with three-month-old Ophelia in his arms as we discussed the possibility of returning her to the breeder. "She's such a wonderful dog," he kept saying, while she looked up at him trustingly. There was an edge of grief in his voice.

After several discussions, my husband and I suggested Barrett move back home until he found a place to live. "But you don't want a dog," Barrett said.

He was right, we didn't. "We'll make it work," I promised.

Ophelia arrived with her crate, toys, dishes, and puppy food. A timid little soul, she soaked up hugs and praise, and couldn't seem to get enough of us. I braced myself for dog hair drifting across the floor, "toilet training" gone awry, chewed furniture, and a house that smelled doggy.

Accidents did happen; in fact, one morning I almost stepped in a large, fragrant one in the kitchen. She chewed through the phone cord and tore off a chunk of wallpaper with a ripping sound that brought me running. The vacuum cleaner remained permanently plugged in. Sometimes the house smelled like a dog.

But something else happened, too. A miraculous creature with a passion for stealing socks and an astounding capacity to give and receive love bounded into my heart. In my mind's eye life is now divided into Before Ophelia and After Ophelia.

Before Ophelia, I was annoyed by a cupboard door left ajar. Before Ophelia, a speck on the couch was vacuumed immediately. And no one could wear shoes in the house Before Ophelia. After Ophelia, not even a dog hair floating in my coffee, or muddy paw prints on the sliding door fazed me.

Now a year old, Ophelia follows us from room to room, reluctant to be separated for even a few minutes. Her greeting when we come home is equally joyous, whether we've been gone half an hour or all day.

Her beautiful tail almost reaches the floor. Her huge ears stand up perfectly and her coat is glossy and soft except for a bit of unruly business on her back that swirls crazily like a cowlick and makes me laugh.

One day Ophelia and I were interviewed by Vicky, Recreation Manager and Volunteer Coordinator of Chateau Gardens, a long-term care residence. Ophelia's enthusiastic interest in people and sweet spirit made her a good candidate for pet therapy.

"Where's your leash?" I asked.

She looked at me, head cocked, expectation shining in her dark eyes.

"Get your leash, Ophelia," I said. "Let's go."

She smiled (German Shepherds can mimic an owner's smile), bounced out of the room and came back, carrying her leash in her mouth, tail wagging excitedly; at fifty-nine centimetres that tail has sent cups on the coffee table crashing to the floor.

She took up the entire back seat of my Echo, ears brushing the roof, and watched as I fastened my seatbelt and turned the key.

Vicky met us outside and we sat on a bench where Ophelia promptly decided to leap on me. Vicky laughed, which seemed to egg on Ophelia. She rolled on her back, legs in the air and began chewing on her leash.

"Ophelia!" I said sternly. This wasn't going the way I envisioned.

As we chatted, Ophelia jumped on Vicky, tried to chase a bird, and ripped open her bag of treats. By now my reassurances that she was well behaved sounded feeble and contrived.

But Vicky was encouraging and gave Ophelia a pat on the head before sending us on our way with paperwork to fill out. We were scheduled for our first visit in a few weeks; Torin, a resident with multiple sclerosis, couldn't wait to see us.

To my surprise, Torin appeared to be in his forties and beamed at us despite a debilitating battle with his disease. Before coming to live at Chateau Gardens, he owned a German Shepherd named Whitney. Giving her up broke his heart; and when he heard she'd been put down, the wound was ripped open again.

Ophelia eagerly entered Torin's room, ears up and tail wagging. She snuffled his hand, into which I'd placed a doggy treat, put her paws on his pillow to get closer and then, to everyone's astonishment, made a gigantic leap into his hospital bed and lay down beside him.

I stood there, wondering in a sort of panic if such a thing was allowed and what the staff would do, but they crowded into the room and began clapping. Although Torin's body had betrayed and trapped him, it couldn't quite contain his laughter. He grinned and shook with almost soundless delight and tried to pet Ophelia with a pale, uncooperative hand. Ophelia put her head on her paws and snuggled closer.

I wouldn't have expected Ophelia to be such a natural for pet therapy. She is, after all, just a year old and brimming with energy, yet she's endlessly curious and gentle with the residents. She hops on their beds, pokes her head into purses, licks frail, trembling hands, does tricks for treats (her high-five is everyone's favourite), and gladly accepts petting and fondling. When I brought in cupcakes to celebrate Ophelia's first birthday, an elderly woman in a wheelchair couldn't stop giggling as Ophelia carefully licked all the icing off her fingers and then drank the water out of a Styrofoam cup she was holding.

Next month Ophelia and I are scheduled to begin orientation with the St. John Ambulance Therapy Dog Program. The program has grown to become a recognized leader in animal-assisted therapy and is a wonderful opportunity for the two of us to work even more closely together, providing comfort and companionship.

To me, Ophelia is much more than a dog. She's a reminder each day that challenges are meant to be met as a family; the overwhelming and impossible become the strong, true lines and spacious rooms of a sanctuary we build together. Some of its finest features are designed by the most difficult circumstances.

Barrett's career as a pilot could take him almost anywhere, but I've told him that Ophelia stays. And I think he's okay with that. She is part of our family and she is loved. Her life has become entwined with the lonely and vulnerable, and the joy of it fills us both every time we enter Chateau Gardens. It's there when she looks up at me and nudges my hand with her nose as we walk down the hall, and in the way she expectantly enters a resident's room.

One of the nurses said it well, "You don't choose an animal; it chooses you."

~Rachel Wallace-Oberle

Saving Grace

I do not at all understand the mystery of grace—only that it meets us where we are but does not leave us where it found us.
~Anne Lamott

t was October of 2012 when I got the call that shattered my heart. The love of my life, my nine-year-old Yorkshire Terrier Louis, had been stung by a bee and was in cardiac arrest. I was an hour away. I had a sick feeling this wasn't going to end well.

Just six months earlier, I was fired from my job of almost nineteen years—a job I loved. It was another call that wiped away what I thought was my identity and collapsed my world entirely. I felt like all I had left were my two beloved Yorkies, Lily and Louis, who had been with me through it all.

When I first got Louis, he weighed under a pound. I was worried that raising a furry little boy would be too much with my crazy work schedule, but I was desperate for a companion. Louis was a tiny little guy, the runt of the litter. He looked more like a mouse than a dog... he didn't have a lot of fur or a lot of energy but for some reason I fell for him. I think it was his intense, dark brown eyes. When he looked at me, I melted. I could tell he needed me and I needed him.

So when I got the call that Louis had a heart attack and might not make it, I wasn't sure that I would make it. I was in anguish as I rushed to the hospital. When the vet told me Louis was going to be okay, I felt so relieved. My dog walkers were there with Lily and handed her to me. I asked to see Louis, and the staff told me it would be just a minute. So I went to my car to get my credit card. Moments later the vet rushed out to me. "I'm sorry," he said. "He arrested. Louis is gone. We couldn't save him."

I turned around in shock. "What? I thought you said he was okay?"

"He was. We don't know what happened. He's gone. I'm so sorry."

I went in to hold Louis one final time. At first, Lily jumped on him. She was excited to see him. Then she realized he was gone and hid her head in my lap. She started to cry and didn't stop for days.

Lily and I went home. It was the hardest day of our lives. Friends flew in from around the country, literally. Everyone knew this loss was devastating for us. And after losing my job, they weren't sure I could take anymore. Lily and I didn't sleep for days. Lily stopped eating. She stopped playing. She kept her eyes down. She was heartbroken. I was heartbroken.

Many months later, my vet told me Lily needed a friend. I wasn't sure.

I called Sonya Fitzpatrick, a well-known pet psychic and medium, to see what she thought. She told me that Louis thought yes, it was time to get another dog. In fact, he thought I should get a small white dog and name that white dog Grace. Sonya went on to say that Lily agreed. She wanted someone to play with because she was lonely.

"Hmm, okay," I said.

After our call, I searched the web for puppies who needed homes. I found one dog, a Biewer Yorkie who was soft and furry but not totally white. He was black and brown with a little bit of white fur. I put Lily in the car and drove an hour to meet this dog. When I arrived and introduced the puppy to Lily, she would not look at him. I mean WOULD NOT LOOK. She did everything in her power to avoid eye contact; she buried her head into my lap and turned away. She whined and cried until I finally gave up and left. This was really odd behavior for her, as she usually loves other dogs. I thought maybe she wasn't ready. But I came to find out that particular puppy just wasn't "the one."

A couple of weeks later, I was at a local kill shelter in L.A. when

I saw a tiny white puppy in a cage. This puppy looked more like a bird than a dog. She was emaciated, dirty and sickly, but there was something special about her eyes.

She had dark brown intense little eyes—a lot like Louis.

I picked her up. She laid her head against my chest and looked straight at me.

I swear I could hear her say those famous words from the movie *Babe*: "Will you be my mom?" She was the most imperfect dog, but I didn't care. She needed a mom and I was up for the task.

Lily needed a playmate and she seemed like the perfect fit.

The vet told me the dog had been found on the street and was very sick, and probably wouldn't make it. The vet didn't think I should risk bringing a sick dog into my house, so I put her back in the cage and left.

The next day I couldn't stop thinking about the little white dog at the shelter, so I called to see if she was still there. They told me she was gone—they wouldn't reveal if she had passed or if she had been adopted. I was devastated.

A week later, I got a call from the shelter vet. There had been a mistake. The puppy's paperwork had been switched and she was still there! The puppy was alive and getting stronger. If I was still interested, the vet thought she was healthy enough for me to bring Lily in to meet her.

At this point, Lily had refused all other dogs I'd considered. So I worried this puppy would also garner a bad reaction, but was going to give it a try.

I picked up Lily and brought her to the shelter.

I set Lily down in front of the puppy and waited.

Lily slowly walked up to the puppy and sniffed her.

The puppy sniffed her back.

Then she licked Lily's nose.

Lily pawed the puppy's face.

Then they chased each other around the room.

It was the first time I had seen Lily play since Louis died.

She was happy again.

It had been eight painful months and finally Lily had found her saving grace.

And I had found mine.

~Lisa Erspamer

Easter Surprise

The art of love... is largely the art of persistence.
~Albert Ellis

It was the Friday before Easter and I was working in my flower-beds when I saw a black dog in a field across the street. We live in a rural area with only a few neighbors, and I knew I had never seen this particular dog in our neighborhood before. I wondered where she had come from.

She certainly looked well fed. Maybe she came from one of the houses further down in the valley. She looked over in my direction and then slunk off to the vacant lot next door, and disappeared into the woods.

Later that evening, as I watered my plants on our back deck, I heard faint yelping coming from somewhere in the woods. We have all kinds of wildlife in our area, and I assumed it was just some animal making noise.

That Sunday, my mother-in-law and I sat on my front porch waiting to go out for Easter dinner. I saw the black dog again coming out of the woods, only this time she looked a lot thinner and was moving much more slowly.

Oh, no! She'd had a litter of puppies! I remembered the sounds I had heard on Friday night. That was probably when she was giving birth.

I told my mother-in-law what I thought had happened. Without hesitation, she said, "We need to find those puppies."

I had seen the dog go into the woods at the far end of the lot, but I knew those yelping noises had come from somewhere closer to our house. We entered the woods from that side, and it was like walking into a sauna. The humidity was high and the foliage was so thick that hardly any light could get through. Within minutes, we were both sweating through our clothes and our make-up. I lost an earring, and my mother-in-law had to retrieve her shoe from a rabbit hole as we stumbled along aimlessly, listening and looking for any sign of the mother or her pups.

Then we heard a low growl from somewhere on our left.

"We must be close," I said.

We went in that direction, pushing heavy pine boughs out of the way, when we saw a blur of black fur run past us.

"She's trying to divert us away from her den," I said.

We went a little further and found a huge oak tree that had blown over in a storm. Beneath the root ball and cloaked in a thick mass of honeysuckle vines were seven healthy, beautiful puppies all rolled together in a tangle of ears and tails and fur.

Their eyes weren't open yet, and I knew not to touch them until we had won their mother's trust. So we backed out, forgot about Easter dinner and went to the store to buy two huge bags of dog food. With nursing seven babies, she would need the extra calories and vitamins to build her strength back up and keep her milk flowing.

That afternoon, my husband and I took two bowls of food and water to the edge of the woods. We heard growling. We left the bowls, and Jerry and I watched from our bedroom window as "Mommy Dog" emerged a few minutes later. She hesitated at first, but she went over to the bowls. She devoured the food and water as fast as she could, then ran back to her den.

This continued three times a day for the next several days. Each time, we would move the bowls a little bit closer to our house. We hoped to lure her to our back deck, which sits about eighteen feet off the ground and would provide a good shelter for her and her pups.

We were watching again from our bedroom window when she came all the way to our side yard. It was the first time we had gotten a good look at her. She was pitiful. Her ribs showed and her fur was filthy and matted. I kept looking at her right eye as she wolfed down her food.

"What's that thing on her eyelid?" I asked my husband.

He leaned closer to the glass and said, "I think it's a huge tick."

My heart broke. Apparently so did my husband's, because early the next morning, I awoke to the sound of loud hammering coming from below our back deck. I threw on my robe and went outside to ask him what in the world he was doing. He said he was building a shelter for the dog and her puppies so we could take them out of that sweltering, tick-infested hole that they were living in.

The plywood structure had a roof, and square hole on one side for the dog and puppies to go in and out. We spread fresh straw along the ground and put bowls of food and water right inside the entrance. We managed to lure Mommy Dog over, but she wouldn't bring her puppies.

A few days later, I coaxed her over to our front porch. She lay down on the cool stone floor, and with a pair of tweezers I took dozens of ticks off her. I stopped counting at fifty. She never once flinched. Then we used the garden hose to give her a bath. We had to lather her up three times to get her clean. To our amazement, we discovered she was a German Shepherd-black Labrador mix. She had been so filthy the only thing you could see on her was the black. We could also see she was gaining back weight and muscle tone.

After her bath, she fell asleep in a patch of sunlight. Jerry went over to her den with a large laundry basket and brought the puppies over to the shelter. Mommy Dog came around the corner of the house just as we were placing the first puppy into their new home. She stopped in her tracks. We didn't move, fearing she might attack us. But she came over and stuck her head inside the basket and sniffed her puppies and then looked up at us as if to say, "Okay." It was like she knew we wouldn't hurt her babies.

The puppies stayed in the shelter until they were weaned and ready for adoption. We found homes for all of them, and when the last one left the nest, my husband asked what we were going to do with the mom. I looked over at her sleeping on her straw bed and I thought about all that she had gone through.

"Well," I replied, "we can't very well keep calling her Mommy Dog. She looks like a Sadie to me."

My husband shook his head. "No more dogs," he replied. "We agreed when we had Peabody put down that we wouldn't have any more dogs. We'll put out food and water and she can sleep outside until we find her a home."

It's been a little over a year since then, and Sadie is now queen of her castle. And I'm not talking about a doghouse. She's healthy, happy and has the sweetest disposition of any dog we've ever had. Sometimes she puts her head on my lap and looks up at me with those soulful dark eyes — it's almost like she's trying to tell me she knows what we did for her and her babies.

Oh, and by the way, Sadie sleeps on her own special blanket at the end of our bed with her head on my husband's feet.

~Cheryll Lynn Snow

From Foster to Agility Champ

Until one has loved an animal, a part of one's soul remains unawakened.
~Anatole France

first met Keta at an adoption clinic being held by an animal rescue organization in my old neighbourhood. I went to say hello to all my friends from the dog park—people that I used to see a couple of times a day before I moved. My friends were all there—and so were Keta and her puppies.

Keta had been a breeding dog for a "backyard breeder"—really just a small-scale puppy mill. The rescue group picked up her and her puppies, cleaned them and vetted them, then put them up for adoption. Her puppies were the star attraction at the adoption clinic and were quickly adopted. When she saw her last puppy walk out the door, poor Keta went to pieces—howling, crying, and shaking.

Keta was only about a year and a half old at the time, in good health, and a good-looking German Shepherd-Lab mix. But no potential adopters came for Keta that day—no wonder, since she was such an emotional wreck at the time. At the end of the clinic, all of us still there were in tears. "She can't go back to the shelter!" the rescue volunteers said. And then, looking at me, said, "Why don't you take her home to foster?"

I already had a large German Shepherd mix at home. I didn't

really need another large dog. But I took Keta home with me that day, and she has been there ever since.

The next year, I decided to try agility with my dogs. Agility is a team sport for handler and dog. The handler directs the dog around a timed obstacle course that includes jumps, tunnels, an A-frame, weave poles, and a seesaw. If the dog takes the obstacles in the correct order, without knocking down any jump bars, and is under course time, it is called a qualifying run, or Q. Earning a Q entitles you to a ribbon or rosette. The goal is to collect Qs in order to earn titles at higher levels. With each title comes another rosette, usually a large one at that!

All that summer and the next, Keta and I practiced. We enjoyed it, but I never thought we would enter competitions—those were for professionals! But in our third summer of lessons, when Keta was five years old, I decided to enter an upcoming competition. Keta was amazing! We Q'd almost every event we entered. I was hooked. Once you start earning those rosettes, it's hard to stop!

Over the next few years, we entered more and more competitions. Keta really loved running in the agility ring. People would often comment, saying, "I just love watching you two run. Keta looks like she is enjoying herself so much!" Personally, I think Keta always had her eye on the cookies she would get after the run. She always picked up speed on the last three or four obstacles!

Keta was never that fast—but she was fast enough to be under course time. And she was consistent, rarely going off course or dropping a jump bar. Keta qualified for the Agility Association of Canada National Championships in four consecutive regional competitions, and even placed second in her division in 2010—our first and only time on the podium!

From her rather inauspicious start, the doubts about her speed, her problems with hip dysplasia and arthritis—Keta overcame all of her own obstacles and earned a Lifetime Award of Excellence at the age of nine and a half. Earlier in Keta's agility career I had met a couple of people who had reached the Lifetime level. At that time, I never dreamed that we would complete the 225 runs required for the award!

My journey into agility with Keta has truly been a wonderful experience. I have spent quite a large number of my weekends at agility trials, in beautiful and not so beautiful weather. I have learned a lot more about dog training. I have bought dog crates, dog warm-up coats, supplements, and agility practice equipment. I have met a whole group of wonderful people at the trials, people who truly care about their dogs, and about the sport—and who cheer you on through your difficult periods and celebrate with you when you succeed. And, by spending so much time practicing, travelling, and competing together, Keta and I became a true team, attuned to each other's moods and energy, and enjoying every minute of our journey together.

I am so proud of my little girl. I knew when I brought her home I was changing her life, but I had no idea she would change mine! We achieved goals I never even thought possible. More importantly, running in the ring with Keta has shown me that it's not whether you win or lose, it's running joyfully that counts. And maybe making sure there are plenty of treats thrown in along the way!

~Beverley Stevens

25

Saving Each Other

Where there is great love there are always miracles.
~Willa Cather

Her teeth gripped the metal cage bars. Saliva ran down the sides of her mouth as she lunged forward in anger. The chunky brown and white Chihuahua had every reason to be angry. After seven wonderful years together, her human guardian had abandoned her in the local kill shelter.

Pure panic clutched the Chihuahua as the shelter staff reached into her cage with a catch pole — a long metal pole with a rubber loop on the end — and pulled it tight around her neck, allowing her to dangle in the air at head height. I couldn't take a breath until her little feet landed safely on the ground. The moment her paws hit the floor and a leash slipped over her head, her tail began to wag.

Margo wagged her coiled tail and her eyes seemed to gain a spark. We knew we had to save her. What other choice did we have? We didn't know anything about her, other than the fact she would die if we didn't pay the safety fee and walk out the door with her by our side.

Margo sat on my lap with a sense of contentment as she looked out the front window of the Jeep. Never again would she know the pain of being locked away in a shelter. Never again would she be next on a list to have her life ended. Never again. From this point forward, as we promise every pet we rescue, Margo would only know love and compassion. From this point forward, Margo would be safe.

The bond between us grew instantly. Margo stuck by my side and

I stood by hers. She followed me around as a puppy would. She slept snuggled up next to me at night. She wasn't fond of anyone else, only me. After a period of time this began to concern me. I loved the bond that we had, but knew if Margo were ever going to have the chance of being adopted into a forever home, she would need to learn to accept others.

I began to take her on short drives, on regular walks and she was always present when regular company arrived. She would always throw her small fifteen-pound body in front of my legs when another human approached to say hello. She would snarl and bark; she was protecting me. Having endured a terrifying case of sexual assault and stalking in my personal life, I became concerned that Margo was sensing my fear of the world. Was Margo protecting me because she knew I was terrified of being harmed again? Was she simply protecting me the way I had protected her?

It is well documented that animals have a keen sense of intuition. If Margo was picking up on my internal struggle to reconnect with the world, I had to change. Although it had been several years since the incident occurred, I had never sought therapy, feeling that I was too strong to need assistance. Margo made me take another look at myself. When doctors diagnosed me with generalized anxiety disorder, which included frequent panic attacks, I knew it was time to take action. Margo had shown me that in order to take care of her and train her properly, I had to first take care of myself.

I began to talk to a therapist and I discovered yoga. When I would pull out my yoga mat at home, Margo would rush to my side. As I stretched, Margo would lie on her back, all four paws up in the air, staring at the ceiling. As I began to re-embrace loved ones in my own life, Margo began accepting others into hers. Margo's progress encouraged me to continue working on myself. We were going through a journey of discovery together. I was happy to have a partner on my side and I think Margo was too.

Margo demonstrated a newfound sense of freedom in her life. She began to play with toys; she ran freely in the yard with other dogs; she greeted guests at the door. She was healing.

The day came when we received an amazing adoption application, nearly six months after her rescue. I admit, my heart sank, but it also fluttered. I had been fostering pets for nearly a decade and yet there was something about Margo that won my heart. We had been through an emotional journey together; we had an unbreakable bond. Was I ready for this? Was Margo?

Laura was everything her application had indicated. She was kind, calm and most of all she was patient. On adoption day, we brought Margo to her new home. Margo hid by my legs, but when Laura bent down with a small piece of chicken, Margo looked at me as if to ask if it was okay. I nodded as she took a step forward towards Laura's hand. That was the start of their friendship and of my goodbye. Margo trotted after me as I approached the front door to leave that evening. I nearly broke down in tears, but I knew my emotions were being carefully read by Margo. So I bent down, gave her a big kiss and told her that she was going to have the happiest of lives here with Laura and that she would forever be in my heart.

I didn't sleep for three nights after Margo's adoption. It was bittersweet—it always is. You become so attached to your foster pets, yet you want to see them find a forever home surrounded by love. If you didn't reach that goal, it wouldn't be possible to save additional pets in need. Every pet, regardless of age, size or breed, deserves a safe, loving and forever home.

Nearly a week after her adoption, Laura contacted me with an update. Margo was not only sitting on Laura's lap and following her around the house wagging her tail; she was sleeping with her in bed and loving life. Margo had found exactly what she needed, and along the way, she helped me begin my own journey of rehabilitation.

Margo's strong spirit remains with me always. We're all on life's journey and life is best lived when we help each other out along the way. Whether or not you remember those who lifted you up when you most needed it, what's important is that you have learned who you are and that you have surrounded yourself with love. Really, is there anything better than that?

There is a wonderful quote, author unknown, that sums it up for me: "It's so much better to look back on life and say, 'I can't believe I did that' than to look back and say 'I wish I did that.'"

~Stacey Ritz

26

The Eyes Have It

An animal's eyes have the power to speak a great language.
~Martin Buber

A soft rain was falling the day we buried Sergeant Murphy. The weather seemed appropriate for a funeral, although it was unusually warm for late February in the Willamette Valley. Gary and I stood in the shelter of an old oak tree and shared memories of how Murphy had impacted our lives.

I thought back to the years he had been my partner, sitting beside me with his alert brown eyes taking in every movement outside our vehicle. Nothing escaped his notice. His casual demeanor, with his elbow on the armrest, belied the speed with which he could leap from our ride when the situation demanded. He even put up with my singing along with the local country music station.

The day we first met it had also been raining. This rain was far more typical of a Northwest spring. Hard, driving rain, with the wind blowing branches from the trees. It was a depressing Sunday afternoon. I had no desire to leave my warm house and go to work, but knew I must. When I parked and ran into the office, my co-workers were standing in a huddle discussing one of our inmates.

Looking through his door, we watched him stretched out on his blanket, calmly looking back at us. Gail unlocked the door and we both went inside. We wanted to treat his wounds one last time. He was a solid mass of infected bite wounds from his muzzle to his tail. Murphy was a Pit Bull, not long from the fight ring. Despite his obvious discomfort as we worked on him, he made no attempt to bite. He would cry and push us away with his paws, but never gave the slightest indication that he was even thinking of biting us.

Gail looked at me and shook her head. "I can't do it." We both looked at the kennel manager, who just shook his head. I looked into Murphy's eyes and I am still not sure exactly what I saw in them, but I knew it was something special. I filled out the adoption papers, clipped the fee to the forms, and buried them deep in the stack from the previous week.

I called my vet, and she agreed to meet me at her clinic. The first thing she did when she saw him was ask why I wanted a Pit Bull. I told her that I hadn't the foggiest, but when all three of us were unable to put him down, there had to be something about him that was worth saving. She sedated him, and we worked together for the next hour and a half cleaning and dressing his wounds. He was still groggy when we got home, and he crawled under a table and went back to sleep.

A few weeks later, we went to an animal control conference in Seattle. One of the officers demonstrated what could be accomplished with the aid of a dog specially trained for animal control work. My co-workers and I discussed the idea on our drive home. We decided to see what Murphy could do.

I enrolled him in the next K-9 program, and he passed with flying colors. We had to teach him to bark, and he would only do it on command, but that was deemed acceptable. Next he got his advanced training, learning how to lure dogs within range of my catchpole. With most strays, he didn't even need my help. I would open the big cage, and Murphy would trot out to the dog and engage it in play. They would circle back toward the truck, and Murphy would jump in, usually followed by the stray. Then Murphy would jump out and I would slam the door.

One night I received a call about a dog running in and out of traffic on a busy street near the park. When I arrived on the scene, I saw a large mixed breed running along the edge of the park. No owner was in sight, so I got out and called the dog. He came right to me, and I put a lead on his neck and started back to my truck. At that moment, the owner jumped from the bushes and ran toward me brandishing a large knife. Murphy leapt from the truck and took the man down, but received a punctured lung in the process.

I rushed him to the emergency clinic where we worked to stabilize him. We transferred him to the regular vet the next day. During the time he spent in the hospital, he refused to eat or drink unless I hand fed him. I spent the next two weeks camped on the floor of the recovery area, hand feeding Murphy bites of steak and chicken while he recovered enough to go home.

About a year later, I accepted a position in Oregon, and Murphy was no longer allowed to work with me due to county insurance regulations. He was, however, allowed to come in when a new officer was being trained in the use of the catchpole. Final score: Murphy 4, trainees 0.

Oregon summers can be brutally hot, with high humidity, and I frequently left windows open while I was at work. One afternoon some deputies were chasing a suspect through the yard. Murphy leapt through the window and joined the pursuit, bringing down the suspect. Without command, he went to heel at the nearest deputy's side, still focused on the suspect. From that day on, the local deputies would ask to borrow Murphy if a county K-9 was not available.

Life went on in this manner for several years. Murphy had pretty much retired except for his training classes with the City and County K-9s on weekends.

As he got older, we dropped out of the classes too. I worked with him at home on tracking, which is not nearly as hard on his body. My neighbor's five-year-old was our usual victim, and Murphy would literally jump with joy when he found her. I had seven acres of heavily wooded field to train in, so the training was quite realistic.

One morning about 2:00, I received call from dispatch asking if Murphy was available to search for a missing child. I explained that he was now fourteen years old and hadn't tracked for several years. When the dispatcher explained that a two-year-old was lost in the mountains in freezing rain, I agreed that we would try. I pulled Murphy's old tracking harness out of the closet, and the moment he saw it I swear that dog lost ten years. His eyes glowed and he danced in place while I buckled it on. We arrived on the scene just as the report came in that the child had been found in a far pasture, and was safe but cold. I put Murphy on the trail to go out and meet the rescuers so he would have the experience of "finding" the child. The little boy got lots of Pit Bull kisses, and Murphy got a hug for his reward. When we got home, he went straight to bed and stayed there until the next afternoon.

We knew the time was approaching when we would have to say goodbye. On a Wednesday afternoon in February, he had a massive stroke and could no longer walk. He would drink a bit of water if I handed it to him, but he refused all food. I had to carry him out to the yard to relieve himself. His vet came on Friday evening and released him from his worn-out body. It was the first time I had seen the vet cry while euthanizing a dog. I sat on the floor holding Murphy while he went to sleep for the last time. For nearly an hour afterwards, we sat around talking about him and the life he had lived.

Murphy was more than just a dog. He was destined for great things, and his expressive brown eyes told all of us that on that rainy Sunday in the kennel.

~Kathryn Hackett Bales

27

Music to My Ears

The one absolutely unselfish friend that man can have in this selfish world,
the one that never deserts him, the one that never proves ungrateful or
treacherous, is his dog.
~George Graham

I never wanted my dogs. My sister foisted them on me with the plea that they would end up in the shelter if I didn't give them a home. Knowing that Beagles are often not adopted, I sighed and agreed to take them. But I didn't choose them.

My dogs are annoying and nearly impossible to train. They steal the covers and lie on my feet until circulation to my toes has all but ceased. If I don't watch my food, they'll steal it in stealth maneuvers so impressive that they could teach the Army Rangers a thing or two. At fifty dollars per dog per infraction, I've had to bail them out of "doggy jail" on several occasions. Once they catch a scent, they'll follow it until a dogcatcher hauls them off. Worst of all, their howls make the windows vibrate and, on occasion, ears bleed.

However, it was that same howling that saved our lives.

It was a bitter cold day in January 2009. It was so cold, in fact, that my husband Matt, a diehard hunting fanatic, decided to stay home. We later learned it was the coldest day of that year.

After returning home from a long day, and an even longer week teaching, I lay down in my bed, deciding to renew myself with a quick nap before a supper of venison stew and biscuits. The house was quite cozy, a fire roaring in the wood stove.

While I slept, Matt played a historical strategy computer game. He was happily taking over Pompeii with his virtual army when he heard our two Beagle pups, barely a year old. The howl was eerie and unlike any he'd heard before. He immediately went into the living room to investigate.

Alice and Twain, named for Alice Walker and Mark Twain respectively, each stood on a different piece of furniture. With hackles raised, both stood stock-still, howling directly at the fireplace.

After considering their strange behavior, Matt realized something must be terribly wrong. Hurrying outside, Matt found thick, black smoke billowing out of the eaves next to the chimney.

I awoke to the sound of him calling my name. At first I thought it was dinnertime, but then I processed that he'd said the house was on fire. I could hear the fire in the second floor, the rush of air that sounded like a distant freight train. The crackles and snaps were discernible through the ceiling above the bed. I leaped up, my heart pounding. Not even stopping to locate my glasses or put on shoes, I grabbed the leashes and led the dogs, who never stopped howling, into the driveway. My husband called the fire department to report that our house was on fire. As we stood in the road, watching the second floor burn, the smoke detectors finally issued their shrill warnings.

I stood on the frozen ground in my wool socks, holding the leashes of the dogs, who had calmed considerably. Usually, they pulled and tugged when put on a leash, always wanting to follow some unseen scent trail. After one extremely challenging walk, we had agreed to quit trying to train them to a leash, for fear the next nightly walk might end up in whiplash.

On this day, though, they seemed to sense my fear and shock as the firefighters ran across the yard, pulling hoses and shouting, trying to save our house. The Beagles, for once, stood quietly beside me, only barking when they saw Matt. Worried that I was cold without a jacket or shoes, my neighbors tried to convince me to go into their house, but I refused to leave the dogs.

After the fire had been put out, the fire marshal told us that an ember from a fire had escaped through a crack in the mortar of the chimney. It smoldered behind the plaster walls, possibly for days, until it reached an air pocket, which caused the house to catch fire in earnest. Since the fire started between the walls, the smoke detectors would not have detected the fire until much later.

As it stood, we lost part of the second floor of the house. I could see the cold January sky through the ruins of my living room ceiling. Whenever people would exclaim how terrible the fire must have been, Matt and I always would shrug and reply, "It's just stuff." Thanks to Alice and Twain, that's all we lost.

When guests come by and wonder how we can stand the canine opera, I just smile and shrug. It's music to my ears.

~Amanda Kemp

28

Finding Spirit's Spirit

Call it a clan, call it a network, call it a tribe, call it a family.
Whatever you call it, whoever you are, you need one.
~Jane Howard

Her name was Spirit, but looking at her you wondered if she had any left. The gold and black German Shepherd-Pug mix lay under the table the SPCA had set up at our small-town festival. A cage filled with kittens stood nearby and got a lot more attention, despite the fact the dog under the table was young and had an intriguing look.

As a family with three small children, I turned the stroller holding the baby toward the kittens, assuming my four-year-old and two-year-old were headed that way. Their father stepped up and began a conversation with the associate manning the table. I looked ahead of me. My daughter was talking to one of the kittens, but my son was absent. I looked to my left and beheld a nerve-wracking yet amazing sight. My son had crawled under the table and looped his arms lovingly around the dog's neck. An astounding transformation ensued. She lifted her head and her warm brown eyes brightened. Her tail lifted and she followed my son out from under the table to stand next to him. The associate was surprised, noting this was the first interest the dog had taken in anyone since the pup had arrived at the SPCA.

My husband, a softie despite a tough truck driver persona, fell in love at that moment. He hid it well, though, talking to the associate a bit more, playing with the kittens with our kids and then turning away to walk through the rest of the festival. His interest in the dog became apparent a bit later, as the kids went through the fun house and rode the carousel.

"What would you think of going down to the SPCA tomorrow to look around?" he asked.

I was surprised. Our house was already inhabited by two dogs, a cat and three ferrets, all but one of the dogs a rescue. My husband was the one who had said no more animals. We had three kids, one of them a newborn.

On Sundays, our SPCA opens at noon. We were there shortly afterward. We walked through, but didn't see Spirit. A volunteer told us she was in an outside pen and asked if we would like to take her for a walk. Yes! During our walk she bounced around us, licking the two older kids and even managing to give the baby a kiss while I had her in the sling. She was gentle despite her high energy level. The volunteers were all very surprised at her change in behavior, as she had never shown this much interest in anything before. We brought her home to foster. In the three days we had her, she got along well with the other dogs and showed curiosity in the cat and ferrets but obeyed commands to leave them alone.

She showed how well behaved she could be and was anxious to please with house-training, despite some accidents due to excitement. She obviously adored all three children, establishing herself as the dog that wanted to run and play with them and receive their hugs. She even checked on them when they were in different rooms, making sure everybody was okay. At a little less than a year old, she was the perfect age to grow with them and seemed happy to do so.

After our trial period, she was so well suited to our family that we knew we couldn't give her back. I called to discuss the adoption fee and was told we needed to bring in Spirit for shots if we were adopting her.

I took her into the SPCA with three young children in tow. The shelter manager asked what dog I had with me. When I answered, "Spirit," the manager did a double take. When Spirit was at the shelter, she was timid and despondent even when shelter workers brought her into the office to work one-on-one with her. She would hide under the desk and not respond to anyone, even when offered treats. The dog before them now was nothing like the pup they knew before. She was so much happier and outgoing after just three days as a part of our family.

Since then, we have found that Spirit loves camping, running excitedly during the day and sleeping calmly at the end of my sleeping bag at night. She obeys commands from the children as quickly as she obeys the adults. She understands her place in the household and enjoys it very much. While I didn't understand exactly why the SPCA chose to take such a withdrawn animal to the local festival that day, it makes a lot more sense to me now.

We found Spirit's spirit. It was hiding at our house, among our family.

~JoEllen Wankel

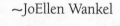

Kibbles to the Rescue

The bond with a true dog is as lasting as the ties of this earth will ever be.
~Konrad Lorenz

"Dad, please, please, please, can we have a dog?" My sisters and I begged. We already had an old tomcat, named Thomas. But he was a dignified, independent spirit and not too keen on letting children cuddle with him. A roly-poly puppy is what we desperately desired!

"We promise to take care of him, to walk him, to feed him, and to brush him." My sisters Julie and Jolyn, little brother Michael and I pleaded with our father. My mother, the practical one, would have said no. For good reason—she knew the burden of taking care of the animal would eventually fall to her, and she already had four children and a daycare to run.

Not too long after this discussion, a white puppy swirled with black and brown markings entered our world. "It's a Collie mix," my father informed us. "It will be a smart dog. Collies are known for being clever."

We loved Kibbles and played with him, but we also had our school lives, friends, and sports activities. The burden of taking care of Kibbles mainly fell to my mother, as expected.

My parents were fond of camping, so several weekends each summer we would pack up our station wagon with our massive tent, sleeping bags, coolers full of food, and all clamor in, including Kibbles. Then we headed to one of the many Minnesota state parks. We would throw around the softball, swim in the local creeks, build campfires, and complain that we would rather spend time with our friends than roast marshmallows with our parents.

On one of our camping trips, my oldest sister Julie wanted some time to herself and went to read a book in the tent several campsites away from where we all lazily sat around the campfire. We didn't know she had taken the gas lamp into the tent so that she could read.

I must have dozed off around the campfire, because I awoke confused at the commotion all around me. I could hear Kibbles' warning bark in the distance. He had pushed his way into the camping tent and was barking frantically over Julie's limp body. She must have gotten cold, or forgotten my father's warning about the gas lamps and the need for air, because she had zipped shut most of the windows in the tent. She had passed out from carbon monoxide poisoning.

My father dragged Julie outside. We were miles away from the closest hospital. But thankfully the fresh air did the trick, and my sister regained consciousness. After what seemed like ages, but was probably just several minutes, she could speak and, though groggy, seemed herself.

To this day I shudder at what would have happened if it weren't for Kibbles. As we all sat around the campfire that evening, my thirteen-year-old sister would have slowly asphyxiated as she read in the tent. It would have shattered our family. Today, she is the proud mother of five children.

~Melissa R. Meyers

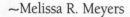

Danger in the Woods

Dogs are not our whole life, but they make our lives whole.
~Roger Caras

My daughter Kira was only eleven, just two weeks into her first year of middle school, when her dad died suddenly. Tom and I had divorced a couple of years earlier and it had not been amicable. Now he was gone and the mending I had hoped might someday occur could not happen. Given what a mess I was, I didn't know how I could help my wonderful daughter recover from losing her dad.

I did know one thing that would help — we were going to take Tom's dog home to live with us. Charlie was a fluffy five-year-old, white and gray Shih Tzu. Kira adored Charlie. Having lost our own beloved dog less than a year earlier, I knew having Charlie with us would be important to help her to heal. When Kira's uncle drove up with Charlie a few days after Tom's death, Kira was overjoyed.

From the moment he entered our home, Charlie brought light and joy. He loved everyone. He loved to play and be outside. He often attempted to play with our cats — one of whom was his size — but to no avail since they were, after all, cats.

We have a big yard and often when I was outdoors working in the garden or puttering about, Charlie would run into the woods to play and bark. The first few times, I went chasing after him, fearing he'd get lost. But after a while, I'd let him roam in the woods and swamp, from which he would come home wet and stinky. He clearly was having a great time and was never gone for long. He'd generally bark and bark, so I knew what part of the woods he was in.

On one of those gorgeous late summer New England September mornings, I decided to sit on our back porch to do my work. Charlie scampered down the stairs and took off into the woods, barking happily.

He was in the woods for a while, barking and barking as he usually did.

Suddenly, the barking changed to a cry. Something was wrong.

I started yelling Charlie's name and went flying off the porch and into the woods. I ran to where I had last heard Charlie's bark, just on the edge of the woods.

A coyote had Charlie in its mouth!

I ran at them, screaming and flailing my arms. Miraculously, the animal dropped the dog. Charlie had a number of wounds but was breathing and alert.

I ran back to the house with Charlie in my arms. We immediately called our vet, who told us to go to the local animal hospital only a few minutes from our house. Kira was home sick from school that day, which turned out to be a blessing because she could hold and comfort Charlie while I drove.

When we arrived at the vet's and explained what had happened, they took us in immediately. Most people couldn't believe a coyote had gotten hold of Charlie, since he was still alive. I didn't want to leave him, but Dr. Pyun said, "He's going into shock. We need to take him now."

The next few hours were awful. I tried to keep a calm front for my daughter. My stomach was in knots, though, and I said many prayers.

We got a call a couple of hours later. Charlie not only had come through surgery fine, but we could take him home later that day. Kira and I drove back to the veterinary hospital late in the afternoon. Dr. Pyun and the team at Chase Veterinary Clinic had saved Charlie's life.

When they brought out Charlie, he was in pretty rough shape. He had white plastic tubes sticking out of him to let the wounds drain, and he looked a bit like an alien.

Charlie was in terrible pain. That first night, when I took him outside to "do his business," he nipped at me when I tried to lift him because he was so sore. He slept in his dog bed right next to me that night. After that, because it was so painful for him to be carried up and down the stairs, I slept with him on the pullout couch in our living room so I didn't have to lift him as much. Kira thought I was a little crazy, but I wanted to keep a close eye on him. I wouldn't completely believe he was healed until he could get around on his own and started eating again.

Charlie didn't eat for almost a week, and that worried me. But finally he started to take his supper again.

I feared that after such a terrifying event, Charlie's personality would change, that he'd be more wary and cautious, and maybe not as loving. This had happened to one of my dogs when I was a kid—he had gotten hurt and become very snippy.

Happily, this has not been the case with Charlie. He still loves everyone and everything… and still tries to run into the woods. He isn't allowed to do that anymore, unless I'm right by his side. I've learned to never let a small dog go out alone now that there are so many coyotes out there.

When people ask me what I was thinking (doing something so idiotic as) running after a wild coyote, I tell them I had only one thought going through my head—there was no way we were going to lose that wonderful dog.

Charlie is our miracle dog, now in more ways than one, and I knew it wasn't time for him to leave us.

~Laurie Doyle

Chapter 4

The Dog Did What?

That Little Rascal

No Peas, Please

The belly rules the mind.
~Spanish Proverb

Lucca is not a finicky eater. My Pomeranian mix has a palate that includes homework pages, stuffed-animal insides, raw carrots, pizza off someone's plate, stolen fried chicken, cat food, lots of grass, hornets, and even dog food now and then. He is clearly driven by food—human food, pet food, burnt food, food from the garbage—he is not too selective. Good thing he gets a lot of exercise.

My husband is not really "finicky"... just "vegetable challenged." He does not like broccoli, green beans, cauliflower, beets, or peas. His mom did not like peas, he does not like peas, two of our three children do not like peas—and his dog does not like peas, apparently.

Now and then I feed the dog some scraps from our plates. Yes, I know that pets are not supposed to eat people food, but what could be bad about a little tuna casserole? I make it with egg noodles, tuna in water, cream of chicken soup, a little sour cream... and frozen peas. I put the peas in only half the casserole, to please all family members.

One tuna-casserole-night, when I was cleaning up the dishes, I scraped some casserole leftovers into the dog's dish, and mixed it with the standard dry food. Well, in his typical style, my furry friend went to town on his dinner. I was cleaning up, listening to some crunching, a little pause here and there, more crunching—then quiet. I looked over. Lucca was sitting next to his dish—it was empty, licked clean.

But on the floor, in a semi-circle around the dish, sat the peas. He had greedily chowed down, only to spit out the peas quite carefully.

Really? Had my husband given the dog a certain look, telling him that peas did not fit into a guy's diet? Perhaps my youngest son had whispered in Lucca's ear, telling him that "real men" did not eat peas? I got out my camera and took a few photos of Lucca looking quite guilty. I sent the photo to all my animal-loving family and friends. Everyone agreed it was about the funniest thing they had ever seen. I, on the other hand, did not think it was that funny. I walked the dog the most, fed the dog the most, cleaned up after the dog the most, played with the dog the most. And yet, like a child, I could not count on him to eat what I told him was good for him.

The next day, the guys all went out for burgers. Lucca got his own—and left not a trace.

~Antonia Everts

Upward Mobility

The difference between try and triumph is a little umph.
~Author Unknown

My husband Lee and I had a mystery on our hands. We discovered it one evening after returning home from dinner and a show. Before we left the house, we'd fed our dogs—Conan, a Dachshund mix, and his partner, Lisa, an Aussie mix—and given them plenty of hugs and treats before leaving them outside in our fenced-in back yard.

Our grassy yard is safe and comfortable, with access to the garage in case of bad weather. But the dogs, especially Conan, hated being locked out. They stared after us mournfully through the sliding glass door, whining like they were being marooned on an island.

But when we returned home from our evening on the town, Conan was in the house, barking and wagging his tail. He was delighted to see us.

Lisa, still in the yard, scratched at the door whimpering to be let in.

And the sliding glass door was still locked.

We exchanged quizzical looks and looked from one dog to the other. "You must have forgotten to put Conan out," Lee said, letting in Lisa.

"No. I remember putting both dogs out, and seeing them in the yard before we left."

"Well, you must have," he said. "How else could he have gotten in?"

Lee checked the doors and windows throughout the house. They were closed, except for our bedroom window, which we'd left open for fresh air. He eyed the window, looked at Conan, and back at me.

"Could he have…?" I began.

"No way," Lee said, shaking his head. "He's a foot high at the shoulder. That ledge is almost five feet off the ground. That would be like me leaping to the edge of the roof and pulling myself up."

"I must have forgotten to put him out," I said, shrugging. "How else could he have gotten in?"

The mystery was solved when we went out to dinner a few days later—after leaving the dogs in the yard and locking the sliding glass door.

"The dogs are in the yard," I announced as we left the house. "Both of them."

We'd driven two miles before I realized I'd forgotten my reading glasses and we returned home to get them. "I'll be back in a minute," I told Lee, and went inside.

My glasses weren't at the computer desk where I keep them or near the chair where I sit when I read. Thinking they'd be on my bedroom nightstand, I headed down the hall, hearing some odd thumps and scrabbling sounds from outside our bedroom.

Suspicious, I entered the room silently—in time to see Conan's face and front paws appear at the window ledge. I watched, awestruck, as that smart little twenty-five-pound dog pulled his upper body onto the window ledge and hauled himself inside. Did he just do that? I gaped as Conan leaped nonchalantly to the floor. He looked up at me, tail wagging, tongue hanging, mouth wide, like he was smiling.

He was overjoyed to see me.

~Lynn Sunday

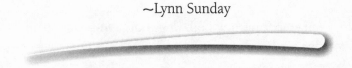

Sunny

If you can look at a dog and not feel vicarious excitement and affection,
you must be a cat.
~Author Unknown

It was nearly Christmas when my first foster dog left for his forever home, and in no time at all, I was a proud foster mom to another. Sunny had been in the care of our rescue before. He had been adopted several years earlier, but when the household's mom passed away, the father had his hands full working and taking care of a young son. The very energetic Sunny proved to be too much and the father decided to bring him back to us.

Sunny was one of the greatest dogs I ever had the misfortune of not keeping for myself. He was just a really cool dog. Easygoing and friendly, he liked everybody and everybody liked him. Everybody, that is, except for one man.

I did not meet this man, but I did meet his wife, his mother and his son. They called several times insisting they wanted this dog. They passed their home inspection, and my director approved the adoption. In retrospect, something niggled at me the day they picked him up. But I had attributed my misgivings to letting Sunny go rather than to the people taking him. A few days later I got a scathing e-mail from this woman stating they did not want the dog and we had to take him back. We would later learn that Sunny was a gift for the man I did not meet, not something our rescue would have approved had the family been honest with us up front. Each e-mail was worse than the one before it. And although she refused to make the trip to return the dog to me, the wife wanted him out of the house.

I was frantic to get Sunny away from these people, no longer sure what they would do with him. It was now three days before Christmas and a dangerous ice storm was predicted. Officials pleaded for people to avoid any unnecessary travel, stating road conditions would be treacherous. I would have to drive three hours north into the storm. In perfect conditions I couldn't arrive before dark. Then I still had to get back home. My car didn't even have front wheel drive. Messages flew back and forth via our group e-mail as we tried to put together a transport, when a message from a brand new volunteer named Mike popped up.

"I don't live far from where the dog is. I'll go get him." He assured us the weather was not too bad yet and he could make it there and back home without a problem. The director approved and I talked to Mike on the phone, telling him Sunny's history and how, to my utter shame and embarrassment, he happened to be in these people's possession.

"So, he's good with people?" Mike asked.

"Yes, absolutely," I assured him. "He was a huge hit with the Girl Scouts who came to my house to make a donation to the rescue. He didn't bother my cats and he was around numerous dogs while he was here. He's a great dog."

"Good," Mike said. "I have to go if I'm going to beat the storm."

"Please," I begged, "be careful and let me know when you get home so I know you are both safe."

"No problem."

"And thank you…." I could barely croak the words out, choked with relief and emotion. But he had already hung up.

I prayed. I prayed to the animal gods, the weather gods, the traffic gods, anybody and everybody's guardian angels and Santa Claus.

Finally, an e-mail arrived.

"We're back. No problem."

I called my director to let her know. "Well, that's one hurdle," she said. "His wife was not on board with this. They're having a dinner party for thirty people tonight." I nearly fainted.

I spent the evening hoping that the theory of mental telepathy with animals was a fact.

"Please behave, Sunny," I begged. "Please!" He was a great dog, but he was also playful and had a sense of humor. The visions I had dancing through my head were not of sugarplums. They were of Sunny snatching the turkey off the buffet table, chasing the cat, even though he had never bothered ours, dumping the tree, ruining evening gowns, destroying carpets, and being kicked out of the house along with his rescuer, shivering in the snow.

"Be a good boy, Sunny, be a good boy," became my mantra as I checked my e-mail every few minutes throughout the evening. It was quite late when I finally went to bed, hoping the adage that no news was good news held true. I was up early, again checking my e-mail every few minutes. Nothing.

I finally heard the little chime announcing the arrival of an e-mail early that afternoon. I opened it and found a picture: Sunny's backside as he was heading under the Christmas tree with no apparent regard for the ornaments or beautifully wrapped gifts. I groaned as I read the caption "I know that cat's under here somewhere."

A second picture: Sunny lying on the sofa next to a woman I would later learn was Mike's wife. She did not look pleased and the caption said: "Ha! She doesn't even let the stupid cat do this." Finally, I got to the message.

"Sunny was a perfect gentleman all night. He sat politely at the front door and shook hands with each and every guest as they entered. He did not beg for food, although I suspect he got plenty. We took a vote when the party started to break up. Keep the dog, 30. Don't keep the dog, 2. One of the two was my wife, the other was her best friend who had to vote no in order to maintain her position as my wife's best friend."

I was so relieved I cried.

"I don't understand why those people didn't want to keep him," the e-mail continued. "This is a great dog!"

Several weeks later the director put her foot down, telling Mike he had to list Sunny for adoption on the website. Mike then admitted he couldn't. Sunny had already found his forever home. That was four years ago, and they are still happily together.

I'm told even the wife loves him, although she doesn't like to admit it.

~Rebecca Muchow

A Hot Dog

Genius is the ability to put into effect what is on your mind.
~F. Scott Fitzgerald

"Dakota, you're freaking me out." It was the kind of hot and muggy night that made your toes sweat. I lay in bed trying to beat the heat and get some sleep, but no air conditioner could keep up with the stifling weather. It didn't help that my 120-pound Akita was sitting in my bedroom doorway, just staring at me.

"Seriously, Dakota go lie down. It's late," I ordered.

That's when the "wooing" started. Akitas, especially my Dakota, communicate by "wooing" instead of barking. Barking is reserved for warning strangers to stay away and chasing squirrels.

"Wooo-wooo," he said.

"Dakota, it's hot and I'm trying to sleep. Please, go lie down," I whined.

He woo'd again, before walking to the side of my bed, laying his big head on the edge, and letting out a sharp huff.

I rolled over, turning my back on my mangy mutt. "Go to bed."

Dakota then put his two large paws on the bed and hoisted himself up, until he was breathing on my head. His hot breath on the back of my neck was not helping.

"Fine." I threw off my sheet. "Do you want to go outside?"

I marched to the back door, yanking it open with more force than needed. "Go!"

Dakota sat down and woo'd at me. Apparently, that was not what he wanted. I slammed the door.

"Are you hungry? Do you need water?" I asked.

I checked his water and food bowls. Both were full, but I emptied his water bowl and refilled it with fresh water. I sat it in front of him.

"Woooo," he replied, not touching the water.

I threw my hands up in frustration. "What do you want?"

Dakota turned and headed back to the hallway. I followed. Getting to the hallway, Dakota started pawing at a large, white, box fan. I turned it on. He then lay down, releasing a big sigh, as if to say, "It's about time."

~Jennifer McMurrain

Bowed In

Sometimes it's best to hide in plain sight.
~David Estes, The Moon Dwellers

A funny thing happens when you are 300 miles from home for several years. You get lonely and homesick, and adopting a puppy seems like a really good way to combat those feelings. I found Boden while attending my last year at Florida State University in Tallahassee. At first I thought the rescue agency named him after the legendary FSU football coach, Bobby Bowden, but it turns out they named him after his own legs. They were extremely bowed in, hence the name Boden. He was a scrawny, floppy little thing with a skinny head who draped himself on my lap and promptly fell asleep for the entire thirty-minute drive home.

One big surprise about Boden is that he loves water. He will jump into just about any body of water that presents itself. He gets so excited he trips over his own legs and practically falls in head first, loving every minute. When he exhausts himself swimming he will find a raft and float. And if no raft is available, he will use the nearest available human.

Boden also loves birds. If he were human he would most definitely be an ornithologist; but since he is canine, we simply call him a bird chaser. He would catch them too, if his legs didn't get so tangled up. That must be why he prefers to swim.

His passion for water and birds came together neatly one cool winter evening while on a casual stroll. My boyfriend and I were walking Boden on his leash through my neighborhood next to a large lake. The manmade lake was large and wound around through several housing developments. It was pretty dark along this particular stretch of sidewalk, but we could see the back porch lights of all the houses across the lake.

As we rounded a curve in the sidewalk that meandered close to the water we came upon a duck. I barely had time to register the duck before Boden slipped his skinny little head out of his collar and took off. My biggest concern was that he would get dirty in the muck and I'd have to bathe him when we got home. That concern became unimportant as we watched him swim across the lake in hot pursuit of the frightened duck, who clearly was the better swimmer. I lost sight of my dog in the dark water after only a few seconds and decided that yelling his name was not going to work. My boyfriend and I split up and ran along the bank frantically searching for him, but there was no sign of him.

We thought that maybe he'd exit on the other side of the lake and we ran around to the neighborhood opposite our walking path. It was late evening so we were hesitant to knock on doors, but we had no other choice because fences blocked access to this side of the lake. I heard dogs barking behind one house so I knocked. A very nice lady answered the door and, after I explained our situation, she invited us to walk through her house to her back yard so we could check the backside of the lake. She explained that they had three dogs of their own and knew how worried I must be. Since the night was cool the owner had all of her back sliding doors open. As we rounded the corner from living room to kitchen the lady looked down at her floor and told us not to slip on the tile. She explained that just before our knock she had noticed several large puddles of water and had been on her way to the laundry room to grab a towel.

The back yard of this house was amazing. As you walked out the sliders you were on the covered patio, which led to a very large swimming pool. Beyond the pool lay a grassy area and then the lake. The only way to access the grass was to walk across a footbridge that spanned a narrow section of the pool. We crossed the bridge, went into the back yard and called for Boden. Silence. No splashing, no barking and no sign of a duck. My panic rose. I couldn't believe I had lost my dog.

We headed back across the footbridge and entered the kitchen. The lady of the house was finishing her puddle cleanup. We thanked her and asked if she'd keep an eye out for a scrawny, leggy, shorthaired reddish-brown dog. I turned to write my phone number on a scrap of paper and, as I did, caught sight of her dogs. To my surprise, or maybe horror, there sat Boden nestled between two of the resident dogs. My dog was just sitting there, tail wagging and dripping pond water, quickly creating yet another puddle. He had apparently been there the whole time, completely unnoticed by the humans. I just know he was laughing at all of us.

~Samantha Eskew

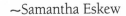

Bamboozled!

The first rule in successful dog training is to be smarter than the dog.
Which is why some breeds are easier to train than others.
~Author Unknown

Not long after moving to the big city on my own, I decided to adopt a puppy. I set out to find an apricot-colored Teacup Poodle and convinced my then neighbor—now my husband—to drive me to the home of the breeder I'd found. This lady had several puppies ready to go.

As I stepped inside her home, a wee bundle of curly fur streaked across the floor, jumped into my arms and licked my face nonstop. She wasn't a puppy; she wasn't the colour I wanted, but neither detail mattered. It was love at first kiss.

For the first few months after I brought Pixie home, she seemed nervous, shy and—I must admit—not too bright. She didn't know how to play or have any fun. She did manage to learn how to pee on the newspaper I'd set on the floor, after weeks of practice. Back and forth she'd go, from one room to the other, until she figured it out. I laughed and conceded that Pixie would never win awards for intelligence, but she was my "special girl" and, in part because of this, I loved her even more.

One day in late spring, not long after Pixie and I moved into Henry's apartment with him and his twenty-four-pound black cat, Chaz, Pixie emerged from the bedroom all aflutter. She scratched the floor and wagged her tail in a blur. I hoped this meant she'd discovered the new placement of her newspaper pee pad on a square of linoleum in the bedroom.

"Did you pee-pee on the paper?" I cooed. She wriggled and squirmed with delight, no doubt in anticipation of the treat she would receive for doing exactly what I wanted her to do. She followed me into the bedroom. I whispered so not to wake Henry, who was napping. "Good girl!" I petted her head, scooped her up and tiptoed to the kitchen cupboard for a chicken treat—Pixie's favourite.

Less than twenty minutes had passed when Henry appeared holding the open treat tin. "She peed again," he said.

It seemed like a lot of pee for such a little dog, but I shrugged and turned back to the book I was reading.

It took our newly formed family about six months to settle into a relatively predictable routine. One chilly day that December I gave Pixie a treat for doing her business and then settled in the living room to get some editing done. As huge snowflakes landed on the railing of our balcony, I heard Pixie at her water dish.

Soon after, Henry called out from the bedroom, "Susan?"

Henry chuckled under his breath. "Come here, would you?"

Really? "Okay, just a sec." I set down my clipboard and pen and meandered toward the bedroom.

Henry whispered, "Come quick!"

He leaned on one elbow and peered over the side of the bed. Chaz sat curled by Henry's knee, the cat's gaze focused on the square of linoleum. And on the floor, next to the newspaper, stood Pixie. As she hunched forward with her nose held high, water dripped from the hair on her chin directly onto the paper in a perfectly round puddle. After the last droplet landed, she peered up at me with a look that could melt the coldest of hearts.

"Has she been going to her water dish all this time? Do you mean that we've...?"

Henry sat up and laughed. "Yup." He lifted her from the floor, cradled her in the palm of his hand against his chest and spoke into the top of her head. "Not so slow after all, are you Pix?" She licked the stubble on his cheek.

"You've got to be kidding!"

Pixie had been duping us both for months, and reaping double treats for the effort.

We'd been conned. Swindled. Bamboozled by a six-pound tiny Toy Poodle!

I vowed, "Never again."

Still cradled securely in the crook of Henry's elbow, my special girl stared over the puddle-marked newspaper at me with a twinkle in her eye and—no kidding—she smirked.

~Susan Blakeney

Losing Boomer

If you have a dog, you will most likely outlive it; to get a dog is to open yourself to profound joy and, prospectively, to equally profound sadness.
~Marjorie Garber

As anyone who has lost a family pet knows, grief can throw you into a tailspin. We recently had our fifteen-year-old Chihuahua put to sleep. Boomer wasn't really my dog. He belonged to my wife, Linda. Still, I found myself pretty choked up the day my daughter Emily and I took him to the vet to be put down.

At times, Boomer was not an easy animal to live with. He barked at strangers, turned up his nose at dog food, and relieved himself on the floor instead of bothering to go outside. A difficult dog, yes, but since his death it's become even more difficult to live without him.

Our family developed a love for Boomer the day Linda brought him home. He was a complex creature, capable of rich and deep emotion. Boomer had a personality with strong and weak points. He also had an incredible patience with children. Our two-year-old son would sometimes grab that little Chihuahua's ears and yank on them until he yelped, but he never snapped.

Boomer may not have been my dog, but he was an excellent running partner. At that time I was a member of Six Rivers Running Club, training for marathons seven days a week. I did most of my running in the mountains behind our home in McKinleyville. Boomer always accompanied me.

I'm not talking a short jog in the forest, here. I mean ten, sometimes twenty miles. How could a small dog run that far? I'm not sure. He must have had a special running gene other Chihuahuas didn't have. My friends called him the Olympic marathoner of small dogs. Together we slogged through mud, wind, heat, and hailstorm. We scampered up mountains so steep they would make a Kenyan distance runner cry uncle. Boomer didn't have an ounce of quit in him.

That dog was treated like a king at our house. Lots of food, a warm bed, and oodles of affection. Linda and I pampered him more than a four-star hotel concierge. When Boomer wasn't sneaking scraps from the table or snatching a cookie from the hand of an unsuspecting child, he was eating steak, ham, and turkey for dinner. Begging for tasty tidbits was his favorite pastime.

When Linda died of cancer Boomer mourned right along with us. He lay in his bed and, shockingly, refused to eat, no matter what kind of tasty morsel was placed in front of him. If there is a God, I suspect He created dogs like Boomer to remind us exactly what unconditional love is all about.

After my daughter headed off to college a few years later, the relationship between man and Chihuahua continued to grow. Though I still refused to call him my dog, Boomer was always there for me, through good times and bad. I took him for walks, gave him treats, cleaned up his pee, and held him in my lap at night.

Then Boomer had a stroke and his health began to fade. Walking became a problem, and his appetite began to diminish. Before long, he completely stopped eating. That's when Emily and I decided to put him down. It was a very difficult thing to do. Boomer had been with us for a long time. He was also our last living link to Linda. It was another heartbreaking hurdle for our family to overcome.

A storm blew in the morning we took Boomer to the vet's office. Rain was coming down in buckets. I was grumpy and out of sorts that day, and I foolishly snapped at the poor receptionist who asked me to fill out a few forms.

"Dad, you sound like a cranky old man," Emily whispered. I apologized and confessed that the thought of watching Boomer die was just too agonizing for me. I'd been through the death of a loved one before. I wasn't sure I could handle the grief again, that period leading up to the last exhale that is so excruciating, so unbearable. Emily understood.

The vet came in to administer the anesthetic. I massaged Boomer's head one last time and stepped out of the room, leaving my daughter to shoulder the burden. I was glad she had the strength to be there with Boomer in those final moments, to ease his passage. I was proud of her.

On the ride home I thought about how much happiness Boomer had brought to our family. I reflected on what a gift he had been. The tears came when I finally understood that Boomer had actually been my dog all along. I'd somehow just failed to realize it.

~Timothy Martin

Gladstone the Escapologist

*All my dogs have been scamps and thieves and troublemakers
and I've adored them all.*
~Helen Hayes

A week before Christmas a few years ago, I went to let the dogs out for a run in the yard as usual. However, as I approached Gladstone's kennel, I realized he wasn't there.

"Peter, Gladstone's gone," I called out to my husband as I rushed back into the house. "How could he have escaped?"

We live on the island of Crete, Greece, a place inundated with stray dogs and cats. We've taken in many animals, and at that time we had nine dogs and eight cats. Set amongst the olive trees on our land, Peter had built a set of enclosures for the dogs.

My husband came out and looked around in disbelief. Gladstone was a cunning escapologist, but there was no obvious way he could have gotten out. It had been years since he had attempted to escape from the yard and I thought we had secured him. How wrong could I have been?

Gladstone was the third dog to come to our home and he had lived with us for over eight years. I remembered the day he had arrived.

"There's a dog tied around one of our olive trees," I had said to Peter one hot August morning, looking through the window.

Peter and I went outside. We didn't have a wall around our yard at that time, so anyone could walk on our land. We approached the dog quietly, not wanting to frighten him, but we were pleased to see that he was friendly. He started to wag his tail immediately. He was cute, with a long body and short legs, and was black and white.

Earlier, we had noticed men in the olive grove next door, so we wondered if the dog belonged to them. However, by evening they were gone. Had they forgotten the dog, or had they deliberately abandoned him? We had two dogs and didn't really want another, but as it was hot, I gave him water and later, food. The island didn't have many animal shelters, certainly not enough to take in all the strays, so what were we to do with him? We decided to sleep on it.

The following morning, the dog was gone. I hoped his owners had come to get him, but later, while I was taking another dog for a walk, he came marching down the road, dragging his chain. His owners hadn't returned; he had escaped. I took him home and tied him back around the tree.

A couple of hours later, the farmer who owned the land next door walked by and started shouting. I was shocked to hear him say that the dog had killed some of his chickens. I tried to explain that the dog wasn't mine, but he said that as I had given him food, the dog was my responsibility.

Nobody seemed to want the dog, so we kept him. He couldn't be an indoor dog as he hated cats. On the other hand, I didn't want him to be tied up, but he had to be kept secure. So Peter built a large enclosure for him. He got to work straight away, and although it only took a few days to build, I worried the dog would escape. I was sure there would be no reprieve if he were caught killing chickens again.

I named him Gladstone and he settled in quickly. He loved his daily walks and cuddling. However, he was wary of men, and it took him time to trust Peter. I wondered what had happened to him in his previous life.

A month later, I came outside and found Gladstone missing. His enclosure had a high fence around it, but there was an olive tree in it. He must have climbed up the tree and then jumped over the fence. Peter and I searched for him with no luck. After a few hours, Gladstone turned up, looking completely innocent. I spent the day worrying the farmer would arrive and accuse him of killing chickens again. I breathed a sigh of relief when he didn't, but I knew it was essential to find a way to keep Gladstone secure.

"I know," Peter said. "We'll put a roof over the enclosure. It's the only way to keep him in."

The years went by and we rescued more dogs. Eventually, we had a wall built around our land. The dogs, although they had their enclosures, could also have time playing together in the yard.

We had no more problems with Gladstone until that fateful December day. I couldn't believe that after so long, he'd managed to escape again. Although he was getting old, he was still lively, and I was anxious that he might still be interested in chickens. I went out to the street and called him, but no luck. Going back into the yard, I heard a rustle in the bougainvillea tree and looked up. There he was! One of our cats, Disraeli, liked to sleep there, so Gladstone must have followed him. It took us all morning to get him down, and we were never sure how he had got out of his enclosure. There was a gap between the gate and the roof, but it seemed too small for him to get through.

Five days later, on Christmas Day, I went outside to find Gladstone gone again. He wasn't in the bougainvillea, so I went out of the yard and found him sitting in an olive tree with Disraeli perched further up! We couldn't think how he'd got out of the yard. Because some of the bigger dogs had managed to scale the wall, we had heightened it with a wire fence. It was about ten feet high, and the wire had just one tiny gap for the cats to use. It seemed unlikely, but there was no other way of escape.

~Irena Nieslony

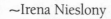

39

Take the First Step

The soul is the same in all living creatures,
although the body of each is different.
~Hippocrates

Thirty years ago, we lived in Edwardsville, Illinois, a small town that charmed us with friendly neighbors, a library that closed promptly at six, and Sunday concerts at the bandstand during the summer. It was a little bit of country, and we liked it.

Our best friends were Annie and Ted Zulmer, a young couple who had four rambunctious kids, all under the age of eight. They lived a few towns over, deeper in the country, so a visit usually meant packing sleeping bags and staying overnight.

Our baby, Lacey, usually clung to me or defended her playpen by throwing toys at any wannabe intruders. Her large, brown eyes viewed our friends' chaotic world suspiciously, especially their dog Max.

Max was a mutt, but once upon a time he'd earned respect as a hunting dog. He was retired now and acted like a grumpy old guy, sleeping in the sun and avoiding the kids. He didn't have the patience for squealing voices or small hands stroking his fur. He didn't bite or snap, just wiggled away if they got too close.

One April Saturday, when the crocuses finally popped out and summer seemed right around the corner, we were enjoying a lazy morning. The kids were watching cartoons in the playroom and the men were outside chopping wood. Annie and I were laughing at my efforts to knit. Nine-month-old Lacey sprawled on a blanket at my feet, playing with building blocks and her dolls.

As my stitches hopelessly tangled, Annie whispered, "Karla, don't panic, but look."

I looked. Lacey had crawled across the room, pushing toys out of her way. She grabbed a handful of Max's fur, struggling to stand up. I edged over quietly, not wanting him to wake up and maybe knock over my baby girl.

His eyes opened. I dropped to my knees, ready to grab her, a silent prayer in my heart. Max wasn't a mean dog and even now, his relaxed body was reassuring.

Somehow, it was okay.

The dog and baby stared at each other for what seemed to be an endless moment. Then, he nudged her, gently, as he would a young pup.

Lacey wavered to her knees, then her legs. Her balance was shaky and she broke into a babble of baby talk.

He stood up slowly and took a step.

She plopped back on her bottom. Her lips quivered. The springy carpet had cushioned her fall, so her wail was pure frustration.

He lay back down and nudged her again.

"I don't even believe this." Annie knelt by my side. "He's helping her. Kids, look."

We all stood transfixed as Max coaxed Lacey to stand. It took several tries, but finally she was successful.

He stepped forward, then swung his head around to peer into her face. Neither the animal or the baby could understand each other, but communication passed between them. His paternal instincts, long dormant, had kicked in. She sensed that he was an ally, able to calm her fears.

Though the old dog could no longer hunt, he could teach. He wanted Lacey to take that first step.

We all did.

Max stepped forward, slow and easy.

Lacey followed him, clutching his coat.

He took another.

Bouncing slightly on her feet and smiling, Lacey took another step.

They managed three steps before she fell into my arms. I hugged her, laughing as she described her wonderful experience in adorable baby talk. I joined the circle petting the old dog, his head lifted as proudly as any father.

"Good boy."

That weekend, we marveled as they repeated the performance. By the time my family left, Lacey was standing and taking a few steps alone.

All it had taken was an old hunting dog, past his prime, but full of heart.

Max never taught another baby to walk, but I told him that one day I'd tell his story as a special thank you.

So, I did.

~Karla Brown

40

Masked Bandits

I think the next best thing to solving a problem is finding some humor in it.
~Frank A. Clark

My dad prided himself on the large, bountiful gardens that he oversaw every summer. He beamed over the juicy tomatoes, crisp radishes, and refreshing watermelons that he produced; however, he was most pleased with his sweet corn.

Yet there was one minor problem with Dad's garden: it was located right next to a wooded ravine with a stream — prime raccoon country. And any gardener worth his salt knows how much raccoons love sweet corn.

And so it went that summer. Upon inspecting his beloved garden every morning, Dad would find telltale raccoon tracks in the soft, tilled dirt. Then he would discover bent-over corn stalks containing empty shanks where ears of sweet corn used to be.

At first, my dad tried a friend's recommendation. Dad ran an extension cord from his workshop down to the garden, and plugged it into my portable radio. Figuring that the all-night musical onslaught would scare the ring-tailed bandits away, Dad smugly went to bed that night.

However, the next morning's inspection revealed that the raccoons had ravaged his sweet corn again. Dad joked to his friend that not only did the masked marauders still get his sweet corn, but they even changed the radio station!

Thus, Dad must've figured that the next best thing to protect his sweet corn would be a live, human guard—namely, me—and my faithful canine companion, Queeny. A mixed-breed mutt that we had rescued from the local dog pound, Queeny was my best friend. We did everything together, so this would just be another adventure. Besides, her eyes, ears, and nose would be indispensable in detecting any raccoons.

So in my youthful ignorance, I allowed my dad to talk me into sleeping out by the garden with Queeny.

There I was—ever vigilant—atop a small hill that overlooked the garden. I was lying on the ground in a cheap sleeping bag meant more for a Friday night sleepover than a hot, mosquito-infested night in July. Next to me lay my trusty ol' Daisy BB gun. At the end of my sleeping bag lay my faithful Queeny. Refusing to sleep, she was poised to pounce on anything. I also had a couple of pieces of cold pizza that Mom had wrapped in aluminum foil next to my sleeping bag.

Under a full moon and a starry sky, this impromptu guard station began its watch. Queeny and I waited… and waited… and waited.

Eventually, I dozed off.

Suddenly, Queeny barked.

In my sleeping bag, I sat upright.

Queeny bolted for the garden.

I unzipped my sleeping bag and leapt up.

Queeny disappeared into the corn stalks.

I grabbed my BB gun, cocked it, and ran after her.

Queeny chased something into the wooded ravine.

I lost sight of her.

"Queeny! Come here, girl!" I shouted.

Within seconds, she was back by my side, running excited circles around my shins. "Nice job, girl!" Queeny and I turned about, and traipsed back through the corn stalks.

"By God, Queeny," I boasted, "no raccoon is going to get any sweet corn on our watch."

Queeny and I departed the garden and marched back up the little hill. At the top, I sat down upon my sleeping bag. There, I lay down my BB gun, and scratched Queeny behind the ears. Then I looked about.

My pizza was gone.

~John M. Scanlan

Chapter
5

The Dog Did What?

Four-Legged Therapists

Seeing with the Heart

Instinct is untaught ability.
~Alexander Bain

We walked onto the school stage, Sage following the sound of my footsteps. I held her leash loosely, for though blind, my Springer Spaniel needed little guidance — she tracked the noise of my boots as I walked the laminate flooring. I stopped and Sage paused; she raised her long muzzle into the air, sniffing the new smells that wafted her way.

A group of fifteen fifth graders sat nearby. I gave Sage a few moments to orient herself. Whenever we made school and classroom visits, I always gave Sage time to acquaint herself, through sound and smell, with our audience and location before embarking upon my presentation. As Sage sat beside me, I began talking with the students about disabilities in pets and how some of the same afflictions that affect people also happen to our pets — such as blindness. As I shared Sage's story about her disability and the disease that robbed her vision, I noted that my blind dog was inching her way toward the audience. Sage's affection for people was strong — she enjoyed hearing voices and receiving pats on the head. And children enjoyed obliging her.

Sage sat in the front row for a few moments as I completed my story about how she and I adjusted to her blindness. I noticed a boy sitting farther behind the group of students, drawing circles on the floor with his finger. He did not appear engaged with my presentation, but I chalked it up to the fact some students are more interested in what presenters have to say than others. I sat on a chair and began reading from the book I'd written about Sage: *Sage's Big Adventure: Living with Blindness*. I read from the chapter in which Sage becomes lost in the woods, distracted from her human's campsite by a scurrying squirrel. A few student gasps and other murmurings made me look up and smile as I noted, "But, as you can see, Sage came out of that experience well—she's still here with us, and she's doing just fine."

That's when I noticed Sage had meandered to the back row and was sitting next to the distracted boy. He was gently and cautiously stroking her leg with his finger.

"Sage had a large gash on her leg from stumbling over fallen timber while she was lost," I added, taking in the moment. The boy looked up at me briefly.

"When things happen to us, it often takes courage to face those problems—just like Sage," I said. "I've learned that great lesson from sharing life with her. She's a very brave dog, I think. Don't you?"

A collective chorus exclaimed a resounding "YES!"

I began taking questions from the audience and in doing so, I glanced back at the boy and my dog. Sage sat statue-still as the boy's cautious finger brushings became full-hand, and he tenderly caressed her shoulder, head, and back. He then hugged my dog with one arm across both of her shoulders. Sage leaned into him and remained stationed in his embrace while I finished answering questions. Prior to leaving, the boy raised his hand. When I nodded his way, he simply said, "I really like your dog."

I gave him a large smile. "And she really likes you. Thank you for taking care of her for me while I spoke. Sage likes making new friends."

As the teacher walked me toward the school entrance, I noticed tears glistening in her eyes.

"That student's parents are going through a divorce—it's been really hard on him. I think your dog was just what he needed today. That was amazing what she did, staying there beside him, like she was singling him out."

I patted the top of Sage's head. "Sage is pretty intuitive," I responded. "She sees with her heart."

I loaded my materials into the car and took Sage for a short walk around the school grounds, once again amazed at my blind dog. I recalled a similar conversation last year with an elementary teacher whose third grade student Sage had also singled out. Just like today, Sage sat next to the youngster as the girl's timid hand first patted my dog's head, then stroked her front legs and eventually down her back. The girl remained quiet during the entire forty minutes I was in the room until the end when I asked for questions. She raised her hand timidly, and simply stated, "I like your dog." I learned afterward from the teacher that the girl's grandfather had died the week before. Somehow, instinctively, Sage knew this child needed comfort and sought her out among the rows of twenty other students.

I also recollected the note I had received from another third grade teacher earlier in the school year after a visit to her class. One of her students was visually impaired, and the teacher told me in her note how much Sage's visit to their classroom affected that particular student. The student told his aide that he didn't know dogs could also have vision problems, and that he and Sage had many things in common. If Sage could be persistent and brave about not having sight, then he could too. I also remembered the countless times Sage lay beside me in my sick bed, providing comfort and companionship. How she learned exactly where to jump to land on the bed or on a chair in the living room was beyond me! Sage was never officially trained as a therapy dog, yet her gentle demeanor and her instinctive abilities led her to offer such services to me and to others.

After getting Sage into the back seat of the car, I placed my hands alongside her cheeks and looked deeply into her sightless eyes. At nine years of age, Sage had been completely blind for most of her life, due to a genetic disease, progressive retinal atrophy. Though she could not see from her eyes, I knew the most important part of her could see.

"You really do see with your heart, don't you, precious girl?"

A swish of her tail and a lick of my cheek told me what her eyes could not.

~Gayle M. Irwin

Who Saved Who?

It is astonishing how little one feels alone when one loves.
~John Bulwer

All my life I had wanted a dog. I had two cats that I adored like children, but I still wanted the companionship of a dog. My cats were spoiled, loved, and very protected. But then I lost them....

Not to some tragic death, but to a bitter, ugly breakup. I had left a twenty-four-year relationship. I didn't take my cats the day I left, and my ex refused to let me have them when I went back for them. He said when I abandoned him, I abandoned them too. I felt I had just lost everything that ever mattered to me.

As time went on, I moved on to a new relationship. With this came major adjustments. I basically had only my clothes and very few personal belongings when I moved into my new boyfriend's house. He was, and still is, very accommodating. Whatever I needed to feel comfortable and at home, he provided.

But as happy as I was in this new part of my life, I still felt like something was missing, like I had nothing that was truly mine. I voiced these feelings to a friend. I shared with him how I missed my cats. A couple of hours later my new love called and told me to be ready by noon—we were going somewhere.

I had no idea where we were headed, but soon learned it was to a shelter to find a dog. Unfortunately, we didn't find one that day.

The following Saturday, a nearby pet store teamed up with shelters around the state to hold an adoption day. I was there before it even opened. As the shelters brought in dogs and cats, I looked at and held several puppies. I loved them all of course. Then I met Maggie.

The first time I held the tiny Beagle/whatever mix I fell in love. She looked at me with the saddest eyes I had ever seen, then laid her head on my shoulder and slept. I was hooked!

Maggie adjusted well. I, however, was still adjusting. One night I became very depressed. Thoughts of losing my aunt six months prior, losing my cats, wondering if I made the right decision about leaving my ex, all rushed through my head. I wondered how I was going to enjoy the holidays with a new love when I couldn't remember a holiday without my ex, who I had spent holidays with since I was fourteen years old. I got overwhelmed with emotion and felt the only solution was to end it. I had a bottle of prescription antidepressants in one hand and my Maggie on my lap.

As embarrassed as I am to admit it, I took the pills. Through my tear-filled eyes I looked down at Maggie to tell her I was sorry.

The look on her face I will never be able to explain. It's as if her eyes said, "Don't leave me, I need you just as you needed me." It was then that I ran to the bathroom to vomit up the pills. The rest of the night I sat on the couch holding Maggie and thanking her for saving me. I realized then that it was her way of saying, "You saved me from the shelter, now I'm here to save you."

Since that night I have had a love for her that I never knew possible. She never leaves my side when I am at home. She has taught me to smile and laugh when she runs around the yard like a Greyhound. She senses when I am sad and offers a paw on my leg or a "lap cuddle."

I don't know what it was I saw in her eyes that night, but I am forever grateful to her for showing me that she loved me and needed me no matter what. Together, I feel Maggie and I can get through anything.

~Melissa Barrett

Doctor Dogs

*I have found that when you are deeply troubled,
there are things you get from the silent devoted companionship of a dog
that you can get from no other source.*
~Doris Day

Dogs are wise. They know things. I don't mean things like current events, the internal workings of the space shuttle's propulsion system, or how to recite the poems of Ogden Nash (though I have seen a dog on YouTube who could say "mama").

No, dogs know important things. They know about unconditional love. Loyalty. Companionship. And they know something about healing the human heart.

My wife and I once had two Springer Spaniels. Arde (pronounced AR-Dee) was the older of the two. Liver and white, and a clown if there ever was one. Her sister, Corey, was black and white, a year younger, and the more solitary of the two. For the first three years neither was what you would call a lap dog. Arde would sit very close to my wife and Corey would lie at my feet, especially when I was at my desk, writing. But they couldn't have cared less about sitting in anyone's lap. Arde would tolerate it for a few minutes, then hop down and resume her close sitting posture. Corey would just squirm and bolt.

And all that changed overnight.

My wife and I moved from South Carolina back to our native North Carolina when her father, Richard, became ill. My wife is a nurse practitioner, and when we learned her father had a brain tumor, we sold the house, called the movers, and headed back home.

My father-in-law had always been active. He could fix anything with a motor, keep a Volkswagen running with a paper clip and two rubber bands, and had been a fireman most of his life. He loved to go out in his boat and work his fishing nets. But his body didn't cooperate. By the time the tumor was diagnosed, he tired easily and was forced to take constant breaks to complete tasks he used to complete with ease.

Prior to the final move, my wife told her mother we would be happy to move into the apartment connected to their house and help take care of her dad. But if we came, the dogs were part of the bargain. On the day we moved in, dogs in tow, the girls walked in and looked at Richard for a moment. Then, without a word (or a woof), Arde very calmly climbed in his lap and went to sleep.

My in-laws had been around our dogs before, and they were accustomed to the sitting close and stretching out at your feet routine. But none of us were ready for this.

You see, dogs know things. Important things. Life-giving things. Dogs are nature's physicians of the heart, and their medicine is powerful.

Over the next day or so my father-in-law learned about something else. He learned that a dog in your lap (even a sixty-pound "born-again lap dog") is good medicine. Every day without fail, once my father-in-law settled into his recliner for some John Wayne therapy (he had learned the therapeutic value of The Western Channel), Arde would gently climb on his lap and would stay until Richard needed to get up. Sometimes they sat there for hours. Arde receiving almost constant rubbing and Richard receiving the kind of medicine only a dog can give.

Then Corey decided to get in on the act.

One afternoon, Corey walked over to the front door and barked. Not the I'm-bored-and-need-something-to-do bark. This was the full-fledged "Come-quick-Timmy-is-in-the-well-with-a-monster" bark. Arde woke up, looked around, leaped off Richard's lap, and started barking at the door too.

Then Corey walked over, climbed onto Richard's lap, licked his hand, and went to sleep.

We were all stunned (including Arde, I think).

Then the laughing started. But that was just the beginning.

After a couple of days of the barking at the door ruse followed by Corey's stealthy climb onto Richard's lap, the tables turned. One Saturday afternoon, Arde stood up, ran to the door, and started barking like the zombie apocalypse had started. Corey jumped down, ran to the door, and joined in at the top of her lungs. At which time Arde trotted over, climbed onto her accustomed spot, and went to sleep.

A little over a year later, Richard died at home. Right where he wanted to be. But he was so frail toward the end that the dogs couldn't get on the bed with him. So they sat and watched him from the hallway. Sometimes they slept just outside the door.

On the day he died, they stood in the hallway watching the coming and going of hospice workers, EMTs, family and friends. They didn't bark. They didn't beg for treats. They just watched.

Then, after the funeral, after everyone had gone and we were alone, Arde walked in.

And climbed on my mother-in-law's lap.

You see, dogs know things.

~Thomas Smith

A Surprising Joy

I am joy in a wooly coat, come to dance into your life, to make you laugh!
~Julie Church

She was only fourteen when she took her own life. Her classmates were reeling with pain and confusion. So were we — the adults in the school. We were all trying to wrap our heads around how someone so young, so lovely, so talented could have done this.

The girls closest to her and the ones who didn't get along with her seemed to have the worst time of it. There was misplaced guilt on either end. If they were her friends, they wondered why they couldn't have stopped it. Why didn't she care enough about them not to do it? Those who hadn't liked her so much wondered if they had said or done something that had pushed her over the edge.

I was the counselor in the school and had to deal with my own pain and misgivings, because no amount of training can prepare you for the needless loss of a child. I also had to be watchful for the now emotionally vulnerable girls who seemed completely unable to pull back from their own newly found precipice of despair. There was a dark pall over the entire school. I wondered how I could ever lift it if I couldn't seem to lift myself.

I brought my Border Collie, Buzz, to school once a week as part of a reading dog program I ran in the building. The little ones loved to practice reading aloud to the dog instead of to their classmates or teachers. Buzz, "Mr. Buzz" as I had students call him while he was on the job, would listen intently with never a word or gesture of judgment. The most fearful young reader would happily try his or her hardest to read a book to my happy, willing canine partner.

As I slogged through the days following the student's death, I thought how wonderful it was for me to have Buzz at school that one day a week. Perhaps it wouldn't be a bad thing if he came along some other days to help me... so I could better help others.

My principal had no qualms since the dog was always a perfect gentleman, so Buzz was allowed to joyfully leap into the car each day, ears pricked and tail waving. He started to whine with excitement each time we drew close to the school building; his enthusiasm buoyed me a bit. I was grateful.

A few days into the new routine, my usually well trained dog—the one who waited patiently when I left the office without a complaint—bolted out my door when I opened it, racing into the hallway, ignoring my calls and standing in front of the math room where the most affected of the students were quietly working. The somber pall was like an unwelcome cloud over everything, even making the air seem heavy to breathe. Mr. Buzz looked back at me when I called to him and gave me the largest doggy grin he could and dashed into the neat, quiet classroom.

I gritted my teeth and winced, but stood straight and surprised when I heard the sounds that came to my ears, popping the pall like a bubble. There were titters, then louder giggles, then out-and-out laughter from the chronically sad students. I approached the door and found Mr. Buzz going from student to student with his tail lashing. He pushed himself into their laps.

One girl had been particularly hard for anyone to reach. She hadn't been happy and joyful before, and now she seemed determined to defy any attempts to touch her angry, pained soul. Buzz approached her, and she turned away while her classmates giggled at the surprise antics of a dog in the classroom. He crawled to her lap. I saw her lips start to twitch, but she was determined not to smile. He wriggled higher and closer still and planted a dog kiss on her chin and then it happened:

She rocked the place with her own laughter. Buzz looked like he was laughing too. He had known just what to do to help.

For the next few weeks I brought Mr. Buzz in, and groups of the students would come to my office between classes or during their recess or lunch and find joy with my unpaid therapist dog. They played tug with him, snuggled with him on the couch. Some of them took him for walks with me and tossed him tennis balls, which he gleefully caught. Once in a while I'd turn him loose on the top floor, where the junior high studied, to briefly and happily disrupt the classrooms up there.

He was so alive and so glad to be alive. He showed them how good life still was with no ulterior motive. It was something I could never have given them like he did. No human could have done it. It took both the wisdom and the openness of a good dog.

~Tanya Sousa

Sophie to the Rescue

No animal I know of can consistently be more of a friend and companion than a dog.
~Stanley Leinwoll

My husband and I know that our precious yellow Lab, Sophie, enriches our lives every day. She keeps us healthy as we walk her in rain, sleet, snow and dark of night. Just petting her luxurious fur reduces our stress. Her ears are as smooth as velvet, her eyes the color of chocolate bonbons.

She makes us laugh daily with her sleuthing antics, like taking sneakers from our closets, showing us her pirated booty and then running through the house with them. She is a master at swiping our newspapers, which she shreds with great pleasure.

We know that she loves receiving a folded paper "lunch bag" filled with tiny treats, and trotting off to her special carpet where she rips open the bag and enjoys her bounty.

But what we didn't know was that our Sophie would be a lifesaver.

We adopted her as an eight-week-old puppy from a Labrador breeder who assured us that her pups would prove intelligent, perceptive and dedicated to their families. She was the fluffiest and most enterprising puppy in the litter. She scampered up to me and began to chew my sneaker laces as if marking her territory. I picked her up and looked in her eyes; she licked my face, and I fell in love that minute.

My girlfriends surprised me with a puppy shower. This was the first such party for everyone. The restaurant was bedecked with decorations from a cartoon show about an inquisitive dog, *Blue's Clues*. Blue's plates, balloons, hats and paw prints were displayed on the table along with a huge sheet cake topped with a plastic toy dog. "It's a Girl" streamers hung from the ceiling. Many restaurant patrons came over to join in the fun. The gifts were playful and plentiful, and provided everything we needed for our puppy. What a unique experience!

We have been blessed for years with our delightful Sophie, who has chewed through several remote controls, our favorite sneakers, socks, countless bones, but never the furniture. Her scattered toys create an obstacle course throughout the house. And, she has a special place for each individual toy. She loves her quacking ducks, mooing cows, laughing koala bears, squeaking balls and assorted bones.

And that's where her lifesaving story began.

My husband wasn't feeling well. He had been having acid reflux. He had modified his diet to remedy this, but he seemed particularly uncomfortable one day. As a retired nurse, I was concerned that it was something more serious than a sour stomach as his complexion was green-tinged and he just couldn't get comfortable. But he felt that I was worrying needlessly. "I'll be fine in a bit," he said as he chewed on some antacids. I wasn't persuaded and wanted to take him to the emergency room; but he stubbornly refused to go.

Then Sophie began hunting through the house for her toys. She brought a toy and dropped it beside him and then proceeded to find another and dropped that one too. She continued until all her toys were at his side. And then she sat down next to him and waited. Now this was something that we had never seen before. We had recently read that trained Labradors were capable of detecting the scent of disease. My husband finally became convinced that there was, indeed, something extraordinary going on.

We rushed him to the hospital and, as it turned out, he was experiencing a heart attack. The main artery in his heart was blocked. His cardiologist was able to insert a stent (a small mesh tube) into this artery, which opened the blockage and prevented further heart damage.

Sophie now has her own pair of sneakers, socks and several new bones to chew as reward for motivating my husband to seek medical care in time to save his life.

~Lee Rothberg

46

Breaking the Silence

Our perfect companions never have fewer than four feet.
~Colette

We visited the special care facility on the first Wednesday night of every month. My six-year-old retired racing Greyhound, Itssy, had passed a behavior test that allowed her to visit the residents as a therapy dog. We usually visited with a group of two or three other dogs and their owners. We would travel through the building, making stops at the common areas throughout the facility, where residents would gather if they wanted to visit with the dogs. Most were wheelchair bound and eagerly anticipated the dogs.

There were some residents who did not enjoy being around other people or activity. The care workers would try to convince some residents who they believed would benefit from contact with the dogs to join us. On this particular night, they had convinced a ninety-year-old lady to join us. They mentioned that she had not spoken for a long time and they were surprised she agreed to leave her room. They pushed her wheelchair into the common area where we had gathered. The residents' chairs were in a semicircle and the dogs and owners moved from chair to chair visiting.

"Say hello!" I said to encourage Itssy to move closer to the ladies and gentlemen in the room. She moved her long snout into laps and allowed shaky hands to stroke her head and move down her sleek brindle-colored back. When she reached the quiet lady, Itssy did not require any encouragement to move closer. Even though she had been on her feet for close to an hour, she seemed to immediately perk up with excitement. She moved her head close to the lady and placed her head in her lap. The woman's eyes seemed to become more aware and Itssy looked into her tired face. Her watery blue eyes looked into Itssy's brown ones and they seemed to say something to each. The lady's hand trembled as it moved along Itssy's head, playing with the points of her ears lying flat against the sides of her head. And then the lady spoke.

"What a good dog," she murmured softly.

The care worker standing by the woman's chair looked at me, then back to the woman and Itssy in astonishment.

"Do you know," she said, "that she has not spoken a word in at least a year?"

It was difficult to take my eyes off the pair and their special moment. The woman continued to pet Itssy's head gently and speak softly to her, telling her what a good dog she was and how pretty she was. She spoke of her own dog from long ago.

"She was my dearest friend," she said as she looked off into space, a smile on her face.

The woman seemed to be taken away to a special place. All of the care workers gathered around her chair. They were so happy she had agreed to come out of her room, and wondered how this dog had inspired such an engaged reaction from a resident who had been withdrawn for so long. I smiled as I watched Itssy and her new friend, and listened to the amazed people around me. I was pleased that Itssy had made such an impact, but I was not surprised she had. I knew my dog and how special she was. She had a way of bringing joy to everyone she crossed paths with. It was all in a night's work for one amazing dog.

~Kimberley Campbell

Daisey's Sock

The great pleasure of a dog is that you may make a fool of yourself with him and not only will he not scold you, but he will make a fool of himself too.
~Samuel Butler

My twin sons had just had their wisdom teeth removed. The surgeon suggested that they sleep sitting up a bit when they returned home, so we sat them on recliners that were positioned side by side in our living room. Moans and groans filled the room. White gauze pads stuck out of their mouths.

It was a difficult day for all of us. Daisey, my Toy Poodle, tucked her tail and stared at the boys. She was terribly concerned about them, especially when they tried to talk with the gauze pads in their mouth.

Daisey left the room. I figured that she couldn't stand the boys' unhappiness. But she didn't stay gone long. In a little while she returned to the living room with a white sock in her mouth.

She lay down in front of my sons and stared at them, while holding the sock in her mouth. She decided there wasn't much she could do, but she could at least share the pain with them.

When the boys finally removed the gauze from their mouths, Daisey retired her sock as well. When they laughed at her, she jumped around, wagging her tail, happier than I had ever seen her. Daisey just knew that she had played a part in the boys' recovery.

~Nancy B. Gibbs

Musket

Dogs never lie about love.
~Jeffrey Moussaieff Masson

A hereditary disorder reduced my sight to the point where I was considered legally blind. In 2002, I went to Guide Dogs for the Blind in San Rafael, California and trained to work with a dog.

That dog was Musket, a yellow Labrador Retriever. A very sweet, friendly and beautiful dog, Musket melted the hearts of everyone he met. The bond between dog and owner can take months to develop, but the bond between Musket, my wife Jane and her parents only took seconds.

After the graduation ceremony we were in the reception area together. Dad was on the floor with our new addition. "Look at Pop-pop, Musket, come on, look at me." Mom cooed over him. "Are you Nanny's good boy?"

Very soon Musket usurped Jane in her parents' lives. Mom and Dad loved that dog. When we went to visit, Musket would run inside first while Jane and I waited outside to see how long it would take them to notice we weren't there. Six minutes was about average. Even as Dad's Alzheimer's worsened and he failed to recognize friends, he never forgot Musket.

When out on drives, Musket rode in the back seat with Dad and me. Dad's dementia resulted in tirades and random comments. But

Musket, lying by Dad, calmed him. "Musket a good boy?" He said it at least a hundred times a day.

Dad fell often, and was increasingly agitated, as his Alzheimer's worsened. Jane would pick me up at work so we could bring Musket to see him. Musket's wagging tail and kisses calmed Dad immediately. Musket was allowed to lie on the bed, which elicited smiles from his Pop-pop. And when Mom was recovering from hip surgery, Musket went to see his Nanny, keeping her happy.

In 2009, after two years of caring for her parents, Jane made the hard decision to place them in a good nursing facility, which could care for both Mom's mobility limitations and Dad's Alzheimer's. Mom could no longer care for her husband of sixty-one years.

Jane worried about how her father would react to being taken to the nursing home. But in the back seat between us sat Musket. Dad scarcely noticed where we were going. That dog made the potentially volatile and emotionally painful transition as smooth as silk.

Mom and Dad both settled in, making new friends, playing games and enjoying their well-earned retirement. Even Dad did well, meeting other WWII veterans with whom he could tell his well-worn war stories.

Just a month later Dad was rushed to the hospital with an aortic aneurism. There was no hope. Jane and her sisters went to see him, wheeling Mom in her chair. I wasn't able to be there, but Jane had a small stuffed dog that she gave to her father while he lay dying. "Daddy, this is Musket," she said, her voice trembling with sorrow. Dad held the toy and put it to his face. "My Musket. Musket gives me kisses."

Over the next few days he slipped into a coma, still holding his Musket.

Jane and I rushed to see him when we received a call late one night. He was already gone, but Jane took Musket into the room where her father lay. In his hand was that same toy. Musket stood on his hind feet and gave his Pop-pop a goodbye kiss.

At the funeral a week later, Musket was there to comfort his Nanny and family.

We visited Mom every week. She always wanted to see Musket

first. She introduced him to fellow residents and staff as "my good boy, Musket." And everybody, young and old, who met him was touched by the shining brown eyes watching protectively over his Nanny.

On the table next to her bed rested the stuffed toy dog Dad had held for the last days of his life. In it she found solace in both his and Musket's presence.

Musket was a great guide dog, a canine ambassador, setting an example of behavior and training. Yet that wasn't his greatest gift. His gift was making sick, disabled, grieving, elderly people happy. Musket changed lives with his wagging tail, smiling face and loving heart.

If I were given the choice between being blind with Musket at my side or being sighted without him, I'd gladly choose the former. We have all been blessed with Musket.

~Mark Carlson

Good Things Come in Small Packages

What really helps motivate me to walk are my dogs, who are my best pals.
They keep you honest about walking because when it's time to go, you can't
disappoint those little faces.
~Wendie Malick

As a child, I was always overweight. And I never thought I'd be able to change my life. I was addicted to food and too lazy to play sports or do any physical activities. I'd eat about ten to twelve meals a day, and didn't see a problem with it. The numbers on the scale slowly but surely rose.

Then, one June, I went for my annual checkup. The minute I stepped on that scale, I thought my life was over. I had managed to reach 184 pounds. I was only fifteen years old. I wanted to cry; I wanted to hide under a rock and never come out. I was ashamed—ashamed of what I had become because of a food obsession.

When I got home, I went online to research how to lose weight. The information I found was everything I already knew: eat healthy and in moderation, exercise daily, drink lots of water, etc. But then I spent the entire month of July doing nothing but eating like a pig.

At that time, my family was looking to adopt another dog because our Golden Retriever seemed lonely. I had always wanted a Beagle, and it was like a dream come true when my father announced we would adopt one! I promised my parents I would take excellent care of the dog. Apart from the daily grooming and feeding, I'd walk her every day. Considering I was a lazy child, this was a big commitment. But I was willing to do anything to not let my parents down and give my new puppy a chance to be healthy.

We adopted Bella at the end of July. At her first vet visit a few days later, the vet told me that I should take Bella out every day to get exercise because Beagles are known for obesity. That scared me! It would break my heart to see her get fat, and to know that I had failed in my job. I recommitted to my promise of walking Bella and our Golden Retriever, Marley, every day, no matter the weather. The only exceptions were if I was extremely busy or sick. (Those days didn't happen too often.)

I walked Bella and Marley for an hour every day, but I still kept my excessive eating habits. In September, I had another doctor's appointment. This was for my "thyroid gland" problem; I had to visit this doctor every three months. When I hopped on the scale, the doctor announced I had lost half a pound since June. It was an improvement, but not much. I wanted to give up, but then I thought about Bella and how fat she would get if I just quit. So I continued walking the dogs every day, just like I promised, even through the cold fall and winter. But I was still addicted to food.

Another three months later, the doctor announced I had lost two and a half pounds. I was shocked, in a good way. I felt like things were starting to work. I kept walking the dogs every day, and I kept overeating.

Until a Friday night in early February. It was around 8:30 p.m. and I was stuffing my face with cheese and crackers while I surfed the Web. Then, all of a sudden, I heard a voice in my head. "Why are you still eating? Do you want to be fat for the rest of your life? What is so great about eating? All it's doing is ruining you; it's making you feel bad." The voice was right—what was I doing? Stuffing my face all the time was doing me no good. I got up and dumped my snack in the garbage. From that evening on, I made another promise to myself: I would eat three healthy meals a day and drink more water.

The first few days, even the first few weeks, were really tough. I constantly felt hungry. But all through February, I continued my new eating habits and walking my dogs every day. At my next three-month appointment, I was surprised to see I had lost ten pounds! Losing weight started to become fun. All I had to do was walk my dogs every day, eat three healthy meals and drink lots of water. I slowly started adding sit-ups, squats and weight lifting to my daily walking routine.

At my June appointment, I knew the scale would show that I'd started a new, healthy life. In three months, I had managed to lose nineteen more pounds! The doctor didn't believe it; he thought the scale was broken and he kept flipping through my records. He asked me to step back on the scale—still nineteen pounds lighter. In one year, I lost thirty-six pounds and reach an ideal weight goal of 148 pounds.

I never thought I'd be able to lose weight. I truly believe that Bella saved my life. We've had dogs my whole life, and I never walked them. But the moment we got Bella, I made a promise. And that got me up and motivated. If we had never adopted Bella, I'd probably weigh over 200 pounds now.

Because of Bella, I was able to listen to that voice inside my head. Because of Bella and my weight loss, I had more energy and motivation to do things. My school grades improved so much that I was on the honor roll two years in a row. I taught myself two instruments and I'm trying learning a new language. Because of Bella, I have become a happier and healthier person. She saved my life and I couldn't be any more grateful. I guess good things really do come in small packages.

~Sarah-Elizabeth Viman

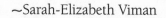

Boundless Devotion

If there is a heaven, it's certain our animals are to be there.
Their lives become so interwoven with our own, it would take more than
an archangel to detangle them.
~Pam Brown

A good set of neighbors is a lot like good health. It's something you tend to take for granted until problems arise. After our wedding, I moved into my new husband's already established abode. As a new bride, I was eager to share my gardening passion with him. Our yard was adequate in size but limited in sun. The massive branches of our trees covered a good portion of the yard. Therefore, the actual vegetable garden was regulated to the back corners of our property, where a chain-link fence bordered the property line.

One particular neighbor, Judy, also shared a passion for the great outdoors. She lived behind our house, on the other side of the fence. Rather than growing vegetables, Judy preferred to nurture flowers and decorative shrubs. She also had an interest in general landscaping. Both her front and back yards were a testament to this hobby, as they were adorned with many a figurine, bench or planter. I believe her crowning achievement was the day she had the pond installed.

My association with Judy was limited through the years. Even so, I noticed her affection for animals. At one point she had three dogs and three cats, all appearing to live in harmony. Any time Judy was outside, at least one of her furry friends would be trailing her. A black Schnauzer-Poodle, known as Elvis, was one of her most faithful companions.

At the peak of the economic recession, I was laid off from a full-time position. I eventually found a replacement job, which was on an on-call, part-time basis. Although I missed the wages and lifestyle that accompanied my earlier job, I welcomed a change. With the part-time work, I could devote more time to the house and yard. And I was able to develop deeper relationships with some of our neighbors.

It was at this time that I got to know Judy better. Her life had also seen changes... personal changes not as welcome as mine. Earlier in the year she had gone to the doctor with a pain. After examination and testing, the doctor determined that she had cancer. Her treatments left her too weak to care for her menagerie of furry friends or her gardens. That explained the overgrown shrubs that previously had been so meticulously trimmed. It also explained why one sole furry friend, Elvis, remained at her home.

Every time I saw her in the yard, Elvis was sure to follow. If Judy walked around the corner of the house, within seconds you would see Elvis running around the corner too. If I happened to drive by and they were out front, it wasn't uncommon to see Elvis curled up by her side on a bench.

Our discussions that summer covered a broad range of topics. We discussed everything from garden care to deeper subjects like cancer, prayer and the afterlife. One day she asked if she had seen me praying in my yard. I confirmed that I had been. She asked if I would pray for her. I promised we would, and my husband and I kept that promise.

The last time we talked, it was a crisp fall day and I was out raking leaves. I saw Judy walking down the street with Elvis on a leash. I stopped my raking and told her it was great to see the two of them out on a walk. I was shocked when she revealed that the doctors had only given her until Christmas. The cancer had spread.

True to that prediction, Judy left Elvis and her gardens three days before Christmas. While festive trees sparkled in neighbors' windows, her house sat dark and empty.

A couple of weeks later, the local TV news reported on a story about a faithful dog. Apparently the owner had died and the dog had been gifted to the nurse of the deceased. The first night the dog moved into his new home, he ran away. The daughter of the deceased was distraught, and she looked for the dog to no avail. She feared the worst. Against all hope she placed a Lost and Found ad in the local paper. On New Year's Eve she had a call. The dog had been found!

I looked up at the screen and saw Elvis, Judy's beloved pet! The screen had an old picture of Judy holding Elvis in her lap. The TV story was about my neighbor's faithful companion! What makes the story even more amazing was where Elvis was found after a nine-day search. He was located outside of the church where Judy's funeral service had been held days earlier. It was seven miles from our neighborhood, and it was not Judy's church. Elvis had never been there previously. But through the distance and winter weather, Elvis had somehow managed to reconnect with his human companion!

Hearing the astonished newscasters I felt a range of emotions. After my initial shock wore off I realized that Elvis was just doing what's he'd always done. Wherever Judy went, her faithful companion was sure to follow.

~Michelle A. Watkins

The Best Medicine

A dog is one of the remaining reasons why some people
can be persuaded to go for a walk.
~O.A. Battista

"Honestly, if it wasn't for Hosanna, I wouldn't let him live alone," I said.

"Is that his aide?" one of my two acquaintances asked. We were at an art opening for a mutual friend, and the conversation had drifted toward polite inquires about my aging father's health.

"No, Hosanna's his dog. She's a Husky/Lab mix," I replied. "Think of Nana Darling from Peter Pan." The acquaintance who asked the question dropped her jaw in astonishment and recoiled in horror. While the other woman nodded and said, "I know just what you mean."

"Seriously," I continued. "If I could just teach her to dial the phone, I wouldn't worry at all."

It might sound insane to many people to hear me say that I feel confident leaving my father's dog in charge of his safety. He's frail, unsteady on his feet, diabetic, and after two traumatic brain injuries, has serious memory problems. The above exchange illustrated for me the two differences in our American attitudes, not only towards dogs, but also sick or aging people. When we began the saga of my mother's and father's illnesses I was surprised at how many well-meaning friends thought Hosanna was a burden we needed to be freed from. People suggested re-homing her or boarding her long term "because dogs have germs, and you have to take them for walks and pick up after them."

My father is a dog person. Consequently for my third birthday, a Beagle puppy arrived named Copper, in honor of my father's favorite movie character: Copper from Disney's *The Fox and The Hound*. (In my childlike attempt to be original, I changed his name to Coppy.) Though Coppy and I had wonderful fun running around the yard together, tumbling and playing as only small children and puppies can, there was no doubt that Coppy was really Daddy's dog. They would sit outside together each evening and talk, Daddy sipping a cocktail, Coppy chewing on the gin-soaked ice cubes.

Eventually, it became apparent that Coppy's days were numbered. At the same time, my grandfather passed away and my grandmother, after fifty-two years of marriage, withered and followed him quickly. Losing both of his parents in eighteen months took an enormous toll on Daddy. Against all my mother's protests, I came home from college with a fluffy white puppy in tow, named Hosanna. There are two conflicting versions of this story, depending upon who is telling it. According to my parents, I had gotten this puppy for me and would be kicked out of the dorm if I didn't find a home for her, so they did me a favor and took her. Though I love Hosanna, there was never any doubt that she was intended for Daddy, and I would say whatever I had to in order to get her a home there.

Deep in depression and grief, Hosanna was the only thing that made Daddy smile. Now, lying in bed all day was no longer an option because the puppy wouldn't leave him alone to sleep. My diabetic father lost thirty-five pounds because he had to walk the puppy four times a day.

When my father took up photography, it was entirely to take pictures of Hosanna, who might be the most photographed dog on the planet by now. With Cleopatra kohl-rimmed eyes and white-colored fur, her adoring audience of one couldn't get enough of her. They would spend hours together: her posing like an Annie Leibovitz model and Daddy taking sometimes hundreds of pictures in a day.

In late 2008 Hosanna began to act differently toward my mother. Sometimes she would look at her and bark for no apparent reason. Other times she would push her head onto my mother's lap and sniff at her stomach. She became like a shadow to Mommy. We didn't understand why until March 2009 when my mother was diagnosed with Stage IV cancer that had filled most of her abdomen. When my mother didn't come home from the hospital, Hosanna grieved more visibly than anyone else. She was mad at my dad. The last time she had seen Mommy was leaving the house with him. Where had he taken Mommy? "You've got to make peace with Hosanna," I told Daddy. "This isn't going to work if she won't talk to you. You need her now more than ever."

That prophecy came true a few months later when my father had two strokes, which led to a two-and-a-half-month odyssey at the hospital. Hosanna, who had never broken out of the gate before, decided to take matters in to her own hands after the ambulance took Daddy to the hospital. She took off looking for him, checking each yard to see if she could find Daddy, and was found by a neighbor walking down the street.

Daddy has been home now for eighteen months. Hosanna knows his schedule better than I do and herds him into the rooms he should be in for meals, medicine times and sleep. They've come full circle—again, she's saving his life. The only reason he leaves the house twice a day is because she needs to be walked. If she weren't there, Daddy wouldn't get out of bed, choosing rather to waste away pining for my mother and his former life. Though I am his only child, I am thirty-two, grownup and not enough motivation for him to live; but Hosanna is. Not only is she a better caretaker than any nurse I've met, she's better medicine.

~Gwenyfar Rohler

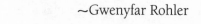

Chapter 6

The Dog Did What?

What I Learned from the Dog

Seismic Lab

Labradors [are] lousy watchdogs. They usually bark when there is a stranger about, but it is an expression of unmitigated joy at the chance to meet somebody new, not a warning.

~Norman Strung

Our dog Dylan was a lousy watchdog. He was a large Lab mix and had the potential to be intimidating. But instead of barking when strangers came to the door, he'd greet them with an eager wag of his tail.

One night, my husband Craig left Dylan in our van parked by the ice arena where Craig was playing hockey. Dylan was happy hanging out in the van (he always jumped in as soon as we opened a door, never wanting to be left behind). And Craig figured the presence of a big dog would be a better deterrent to would-be thieves than a car alarm. When Craig came out of the arena near midnight, he was surprised to see Dylan running loose around the parking lot. It took Craig a moment to register that the van was gone. Not only had Dylan not deterred the car thieves, he must have happily jumped out of the van to greet them when they forced open a door (which was just as well, because we'd rather have lost the van than Dylan).

Despite Dylan's failing as a guard dog, we soon learned that he had the ability to raise an alarm of a different kind.

From the time we first adopted Dylan from a local animal shelter, he slept in a crate in our bedroom. When Dylan wasn't yet house-trained, we locked him in the crate at night. Later, we kept the door open and

Dylan would head into the crate on his own as soon as Craig and I began preparing for bed. The crate became a place of sanctuary and security for Dylan. When anyone mentioned the word "bath," Dylan instantly hid in his crate. It was, therefore, out of character one night when Dylan refused to go into his crate. We pushed and coaxed, but he would not get inside. Instead, he slept on the floor at the foot of our bed. The next night was the same.

Coincidentally, shortly before this episode, I had been doing some research into the behaviour exhibited by animals before earthquakes. I had read that birds often stop singing moments before a quake hits and that dogs and cats have been known to avoid enclosed spaces (even to the point of running away from home) over a period of three days before an earthquake. On the third night that Dylan refused to go into his crate, I pointed out to my husband that Dylan might be displaying pre-earthquake behaviour.

"That would mean we should get an earthquake tomorrow," Craig said, half intrigued, half laughing. We both went to sleep without giving it much further thought.

The next morning around 11:00 a.m., an earthquake hit. I was in the community centre swimming pool with my daughter at the time, and we didn't feel it. But the rest of the city did. It was a small quake, with no damage reported, but it did give people a bit of a scare. As one woman interviewed on the local news said, "It was like standing on Jell-O."

That night, Dylan returned to his normal pattern of happily bedding down in his crate, and Craig and I went to bed with a new feeling of security. Dylan might be a lousy watchdog when it came to burglars and car thieves, but when the next earthquake hits, we'll be ready.

~Jacqueline Pearce

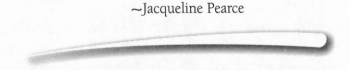

Second Chances

Go forward confidently, energetically attacking problems,
expecting favorable outcomes.
~Norman Vincent Peale

"Mom, can we get a dog for Christmas?" my daughter Piper asked.

"We already have two dogs, honey."

"But she's so cute." Piper thrust her laptop screen in my face, and the dog's oversized gremlin-like ears elicited an "awww" from me.

Piper smiled, now hopeful.

"Well, I'll certainly give her cute," I admitted. "But we can't handle another dog. Besides, getting a dog as a gift is never a good idea. It's impulsive. And most of those dogs..."

"I know, I know, end up in shelters." Piper knew the spiel from my previous dog rescue days. "But we'd never do that. Right?"

"That's right."

"I'll take care of her. I promise."

How many kids make that promise, only to ignore the dog once the novelty wears off? Wasn't that a common excuse for dumping dogs at the shelter? I raised my brows.

"Mom, I will. I promise." Piper pulled up a second photo of the red and white Corgi named Penny, and her stubby legs and soft brown eyes tugged at my heart.

I must resist, I reminded myself. I needed to identify a fault, so I scrutinized the picture. "Look." I pointed to her backside. "She doesn't have a tail."

"Mom, Pembroke Welsh Corgis don't have tails. That makes them even cuter." Piper flashed another photo of a Corgi lying frog-dog style with a full view of its thick-furred haunches. "They call their butts 'Corgi pants.' Isn't that funny?"

"Hilarious, but the answer's still no."

"The Queen of England has Corgis."

My affinity for all things British weakened my resolve. "Really?"

Piper said, "Yep."

Luckily, my sensibility immediately resurfaced. "No third dog. Period. End of discussion." I turned toward the kitchen to prepare dinner.

"Penny's a rescue."

She had to go and say the "R" word. I sighed. Piper could sense I was softening, so she brought it on home. "Mom, doesn't every dog deserve a second chance?"

As an advocate for shelter dogs, how many times had I said those same words? "Yes, they do. But it will have to be someone else who gives it to her. We have our hands full with Frodo and Dexter. It wouldn't be fair to Penny." Did I really believe that? She'd have knowledgeable and responsible dog owners, an established pack family, and a loving forever home. What was my real hangup?

Piper sulked in her chair throughout dinner. She had talked about becoming a vet or a dog trainer. Maybe Penny was just what she needed: a dog of her own.

After dinner, I went into my office to work, but I was moved by Penny's plight—her heartbreaking story unfolded on the Internet. A puppy mill survivor, she was terrified of noises, daily activity, and people. She'd require much patience and training. I recalled my days in Greyhound rescue—fostering the abused and neglected ex-racers—and the miracles that had occurred with consistency, gentleness, and love. Why had I stopped fostering anyway? Time? No. Effort? No. Burnout? Yes. I'd simply lost faith in mankind, and the sadness had overwhelmed me.

As Christmas neared, Piper no longer mentioned Penny, but she didn't have to. The little dog still needed a home for the holidays, and I knew we could provide the love and understanding she'd need to recover from her past trauma. But was I ready to jump into such an emotional commitment again? After much reflection, I decided to apply for her adoption and surprise Piper if our application was accepted. We interviewed with Linda, the founder of the adoption group, and she believed us to be a good match for Penny. Dexter and Frodo accepted her into their pack without incident during the mandatory home visit. A few days later, Penny had a new home for the holiday.

Spending the first few months in various hidey-holes throughout our house, Penny slinked into the kitchen for meals, only to retreat back into the darkness. She ducked her head and crouched whenever we reached to pet her. At times, we sat in the closet entryway, speaking her name softly and reassuringly, hoping to gain her trust. We allowed her to set the parameters of our interaction: how much and how long. The phrase "Where's Penny?" became our household mantra. While I pulled Penny out of the nooks and crannies of our home to take her outside each evening, Penny pulled me deeper into the world of Corgi rescue. Hundreds of dogs like Penny hid out of fear, and I could no longer hide from my duty to help them.

It started slowly with monetary donations, attending adoption affairs, such as meet-and-greets, and supporting Corgi fundraising events. We connected with the Corgi rescue folks, and Penny started to flourish after Piper enrolled her in obedience training and agility. As our love for Penny grew, and we witnessed her healing, I knew I had to offer more. As a professional writer, I had a skill the group could utilize. I'd help to become the voice of those who couldn't speak. I began by writing the text for the rescue's new website. The factual information wasn't sad: the application process, tips on feeding and grooming, agility opportunities, the various dogs available for adoption. I can do this, I thought.

"Would you be willing to write the dogs' bios for our annual calendar?" Linda soon asked me.

Wait. Bios would require telling the dogs' stories, their disturbing histories with the sordid facts of their abuse and neglect before they came into rescue. Facts that I didn't want to hear, stories I didn't have the strength to tell. But how could I say no? It was my chance to give back to the rescue for the love and joy that Penny had brought into our family.

Linda provided me with the heartrending details of the rescued dogs, and I wept as I read of their mistreatment: broken bones, soft tissue damage, heartworm disease, fleas, severe anxiety, and malnutrition to name a few. There was Sydney, once abandoned, frightened, obese, and suffering from severe tooth decay, who became an AKC Canine Good Citizen and now visits libraries during children's story hour. And Finley, struck by two cars while living on the streets, who now chases rabbits in his back yard and provides love to his adoptive family. Grits spent the first fourteen months of his life in a crate because his family had no time for him but, once in rescue, earned his Master Agility Champion title and the myriad accolades that followed because Linda saw promise in his athleticism and intelligence. As I spun each dog's yarn for others to read, the Corgis' mental and physical scars were swiftly counterbalanced by their successes. These dogs had been offered a second chance, and I marveled at their adaptability and fortitude.

Today, their histories of cruelty and neglect no longer make me cry. Each year, as the calendar season commences, I sit down to the gut-wrenching facts and craft stories of hope that offer people a glimpse into the dogs' strength and perseverance — the miracle of dog rescue. And, just like Penny, I've been given a second chance.

~Cathi LaMarche

Gift of the Shepherd

Mirth can be a major tool for insight, changing "ha-ha" to "aha."
~Author Unknown

As I completed one holiday chore after another, my neck and shoulders began to ache from stress. I heard music drifting out of every store at the mall. A male voice crooned "chestnuts roasting on an open fire..." The holiday spirit filled my heart, but my body needed a hot soak in the tub.

My fingertips read the Braille list that I pulled from my pocket. I visualized mountainous displays of clothes and toys to our left and right. With my guide dog Misty leading the way, the mall madness did seem a bit more manageable. Still, shoppers asked if they could pet my German Shepherd, even though her harness sign read, "Please do not pet me. I'm working." She eased me between the crowds, while I imagined their outstretched hands. Finally, my list grew shorter as the bags grew heavier.

Back home, some chores disappeared from the list while new chores were added. My husband Don and I had decorated our tree. The lights and ornaments were spaced perfectly—no "Charlie Brown" tree for us. Why were we so obsessed with our decorations? We dressed the tree as though Martha Stewart would stop by. Don and I had wrapped the presents and placed them beneath the tree. For each purchase, we had gone over budget, hoping we chose just the right gift.

The next day, ingredients lined our kitchen counter for cookie baking. My guide dog flitted at my feet. Normally, at this time of day, we would be returning from our daily walk. Then she loved being brushed. But her grooming routine needed to wait along with a walk. Once again, I felt her cold nose nuzzle my skirt, so my floured hand waved her away. She brought in her favorite toy and dropped it. I tossed the rubber ring into the next room to keep her out of the kitchen. Who wants dog hair in their cookies? Within minutes, cinnamon and vanilla perfumed our kitchen. I pulled out the first tray of cookies and turned to put them on the table. Our cookie baking reminded me of a factory. My husband, without hesitation, had the next batch going into the oven. The kitchen mess reminded me that we still didn't have any time to relax.

A bunch of stamped Christmas cards sat on the table. I still needed to Braille a message in each card sent to blind friends. Would I have the time or energy?

"After this last batch of cookies, I'm going to play with her," I told Don. Suddenly, I could not ignore a loud sound nearby. "Crunch!" Misty had swiped a cookie off the cooling tray. I used a firm tone of voice: "No." The success of our partnership depended on praise and gentle correction from me. Like a child's cry for attention, Misty's mischievous behavior announced her boredom. A few minutes later, I felt guilty for ignoring her. "Here's a biscuit, girl," I said, using the treat as a peace offering instead of praise.

Then, Misty was oddly absent from the kitchen, after being underfoot all morning. I searched the house. When I called her name, I followed the sound of her thumping tail. Her body stretched full-length beneath the Christmas tree. As I reached to pet her, my hand felt her dog biscuit. Misty had placed her treat in the manger scene next to the figurine of the Christ child. For the first time that day, I laughed.

Misty's gift to me fit perfectly, was suitable for my age, the price was just right, and I did not have to exchange it. Misty reminded me to "stop and smell the pine boughs." The blessing of the season, I learned from my furry pal, is sharing time with those we love.

~Carol Chiodo Fleischman

The Taxi Stops Here

You don't learn to walk by following rules. You learn by doing,
and by falling over.
~Richard Branson

Nikki was my third child. She was a beautiful, blond little angel. Anita was four and Michelle five, and I worried about jealousy when this new baby entered our lives. Lucky for me, the only jealousy was about who got to play with her and help care for her.

My other worry was that we had two dogs and two cats, all of which had joined our family after our daughters were well past the baby stage. The pups had grown into two majestic Collies, and the cats? Well, they were just two ordinary cats. Johnny was a small black and white cat, and Ringo was a huge gray and black striped tabby.

The old Collie I grew up with lived long enough to help raise our first two baby girls, but had passed away. I was pretty confident that my new Collies would work out well too. But I'd never had a cat around a newborn baby. I worried about one climbing into the crib or accidentally scratching her. As soon as we brought Nikki home, we saw this was not going to be a problem because the two Collies would not allow either cat to get close to the baby. One or both stayed on guard next to her 24/7. If I was nursing her, bathing her or dressing her, one of the dogs would be right there. At night, our golden sable Collie, Windsong, slept by her cradle, and later under her crib. Tiffany, our black and gold tricolor, slept on the round throw rug, blocking the doorway to the bedroom. Any cat venturing near got a growl and a quick snap.

Nikki was a bright, energetic and happy baby who seemed to learn a new capability every day, but by the time she was nine months old, she had not yet tried to take a step on her own. She crawled like a speed demon everywhere.

She did pull herself up to stand by the couch or bed. But despite our outstretched arms, she would immediately drop to her hands and knees and crawl to us. While no parent wants to compare children, at times it's hard not to. Michelle had been up and walking at nine months, Anita by ten months. I had photos of each taking their first steps. Nine months came and went. Then ten became eleven. Nikki was not walking. I took her to our pediatrician in a panic. What was wrong with my baby girl? She was almost a year old, and she not only did not walk, she refused to even try.

The doctor checked her and found absolutely nothing wrong. He assured me that all children walk at different times and that she would walk when she was ready. If she wasn't walking after she turned a year old, he would run more tests.

That evening I discussed my fears with my husband. Nikki was in the playroom with Anita and her ever-present Collie nursemaids. Michelle was sprawled on the kitchen floor with her crayons and a coloring book. My husband was trying to reassure me that the doctor was right. Nikki would walk when she was ready.

"Why should she walk when she has the taxi?" Michelle piped up, not even looking up from her coloring book.

"What do you mean, taxi?" her father asked.

Michelle explained that when they were alone playing in the playroom and Nikki wanted to get from one point to another, she just grabbed onto the two Collies and lifted her legs and the dogs simply carried her wherever she wanted to go.

"I've never seen this," I said. "I'm with her all the time."

"Mommy," Michelle said, "Nita an' me watch her too, when you're busy. She does it all the time."

"Why didn't you tell me?" I asked.

"You never asked," she said solemnly. "Bet she's doin' it right now."

My husband and I exchanged glances, then quietly went down the hall to the playroom. We went to the door, which was blocked with a security gate. I gasped in amazement. The two Collies were trotting in a circle all around the room. Nikki was between the two dogs, her little fists clutching tightly to each dog's thick ruff. She had her legs tucked up high and was giggling with delight as the two Collies took her around and around the room. Anita was playing with a doll, paying no attention to Nikki and the dogs.

I cleared my throat loudly. Nikki immediately let go of the dogs and dropped onto all fours and scuttled across the room to the door, where she sat holding her arms up to me to be picked up.

The next day was awful. We took the dogs away from Nikki and put them in the back yard. The first hours were full of Nikki throwing the first tantrums of her young life. Everyone ignored her except for tempting her to walk with favorite toys or cookies. In response to the ruckus Nikki was making, the Collies barked, whined, scratched at the back door and, as a last resort, started howling like wolves separated from their cub. Michelle and Anita went out to soothe the dogs.

After about four hours, Nikki got tired of being ignored and pulled herself up to her feet. To cheers and encouragement from her sisters, she toddled across the room to get a cookie I was holding out as a bribe. When my husband came home from work that evening, she toddled to the door to greet him. He lifted her high in the air and then hugged her.

The next day, I let Windsong and Tiffany back in, but watched them closely to make sure there were no further "taxi" incidents. They went to Nikki and kissed her all over. She showed off for them, walking all around the room. They seemed to know automatically that they were no longer needed for transportation. Windsong went back to sleeping by my bed at night, while Tiffany took on the full nanny burden. If Nikki got close to anything that might hurt her, the big black Collie was there in a flash, herding her back to safety and maybe hoping that Nikki would want a lift. But Nikki never hitched a ride again. The doggy taxi was definitely out of business.

~Joyce Laird

56

Six Pounds of Therapy

With the past, I have nothing to do; nor with the future. I live now.
~Ralph Waldo Emerson

t was the most difficult year of my life. My grown daughter had been diagnosed with a rare tumor that would require radiation and chemotherapy, followed by surgery. A beautiful, loving, smart and active young woman, she had a good job and was finally living the life she wanted. But in a flash her life had changed, and so had mine.

I'm the kind of mother who has always felt my children's pain deeply and I swore I'd always be strong for them when life threw them a curveball and they needed me to be their rock. But the seriousness of my daughter's affliction shattered my heart and sent me in a downward spiral into depression. It was unfamiliar territory and I struggled against it with everything I had. There was no way I'd let her see what was happening to me; she had enough on her plate. But the black vortex kept sucking me down.

That summer my fourteen-year-old dog and best friend, Allie, came to the end of her journey and I had to make the painful decision of letting her go. She had bladder cancer, but with medication and diapers she hung on for a year. Now she had renal failure too and her tired body was giving up the fight. Allie and I shared laughter, triumphs and tragedies and she was always by my side. She always understood me. Now I had to go on without her and I didn't know how I was going to do that. Losing her was another major blow. I was consumed with grief and spiraled downward even faster.

By September I'd reached the lowest point of my entire life. It was the first time I felt out of control and I didn't know what to do. I barely ate, couldn't sleep and spent hours a day crying. My anxiety level was through the roof and there were times I could barely breathe. I had no choice but to visit my family doctor to see if she could prescribe something that would help lift me out of this darkness.

I'd never been one to take prescription medicine, except antibiotics when I needed them. Heck, I rarely even took over-the-counter medicine! So I was nervous about taking a drug to calm my anxiety, and my stomach was in knots. I put the unopened prescription in my bag and kept trying to get a handle on things without it.

About a week later my sister suggested that I think about rescuing a little dog. She told me I was the kind of woman who needed to nurture. Taking care of a dog in need of a good home might just be the answer for me.

At first I thought the idea of bringing another dog into my life at this time would be nuts. But the more I thought about it the more I realised I really was born to nurture; it made me feel complete. Maybe I would give it a shot.

My sister found two-year-old Ziggy through a local pet network. The ad said he'd been spending most of his days alone and his owner came to the decision the little guy deserved a loving forever home with someone who had time for him.

The moment I laid eyes on little Ziggy, my heart belonged to him.

A six-pound Chihuahua mix with a small bearded face, soft brown eyes and a tiny body with a thick layer of black hair on his back and practically none on his legs and under side, he was completely adorable.

Ziggy came home with me and I quickly discovered he was the best therapy I could have asked for. He taught me to focus on one moment at a time. With every passing day, life got brighter. Before long I was sleeping like a rock, my appetite had picked up and the knot in my stomach was gone.

Ziggy has shown me how to live in the moment. He is a little clown and his antics are hilarious. He's also a great inspiration and a wonderful little snuggler when I need to hold him or he needs me close. He depends on me and I lean on him and together we make a great team.

My troubles are still there but I'm not looking at things the way I did for the past year. Now I'm able to accept the fact I can't change what's happened to my daughter and I can't fix it. All I can do is love her with all my heart and pray she's going to be okay.

Of course I still miss my precious Allie, but now I focus on the happy times we shared before she got sick. I know I did everything I could for her and gave her a happy life filled with love.

Little Ziggy is a superhero in my eyes, because I'm a giant compared to him and yet he's able to carry me with no effort at all. He keeps me smiling. And when I look into those soft brown eyes, I can see the promise of tomorrow and the happiness of today. He is love and loyalty all bundled up in a cute, energetic little body.

P.S. I never did open that prescription bottle.

~Annabel Sheila

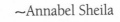

57

That Dog Can't Walk

The difference between perseverance and obstinacy is that one comes from a strong will, and the other from a strong won't.
~Henry Ward Beecher

The last thing we needed was another animal in the house. We had enough discord between the two cats and Hoss, our very naughty Dachshund. But Pumpkin was an abandoned puppy, and my daughter Alice adopted her. It was crazy to allow yet another dog into our household, but I guess I'm crazy.

"We're going to call her Pumpkin because it's almost Halloween," the kids informed me at dinner. "She even looks like a Pumpkin. Look how round she is, and her brown patches are sort of orange."

I took Pumpkin to Dr. Genet, our veterinarian, for a checkup. She greeted the vet with a happy face and wagging tail. You'd think he was her very best friend. She showed interest in everything he was saying. "She's a very young pup and healthy, but an unusual mix of breeds," the vet said. "Collie head, Basset Hound body, Dachshund feet. The tail is King Charles Spaniel." She was quite a funny looking dog.

None of it mattered. What mattered was that we had the happiest animal I ever met. She was delighted to join our menagerie, watching and imitating the other animals, eager to fit in. At first, we wondered if her vocal cords were impaired. She never barked. But after listening to our noisy cats and our other dog, she attempted to join in the racket. What came out of her sounded like a mix of meow and woof, as though she wasn't sure which language was hers.

When Hoss challenged the cats, Pumpkin pranced about behind him, imitating his dance, learning to be a dog. Pumpkin watched and learned from Hoss, but unlike Hoss, she had a dose of common sense. She'd join him in annoying the cats, but only to a point. She'd help chase them and bark at them, but never mimicked any of the more stupid moves that earned him many a scratched and bloodied snout.

As Pumpkin aged, she grew plumper and plumper and began to resemble an overinflated balloon with a head and tail. People often laughed at the sight of her. "What kind of dog is that?" they'd ask. Listing all of her breeds took too long, so my son created a shortcut. "She's a hippo spaniel," he'd say and folks would look more closely. "Interesting. I don't know the breed," they'd mumble, and walk away.

Then Pumpkin developed a problem. It showed up one evening when she couldn't move her hindquarters. My husband took her to the vet on his way to work the next morning. When I finished teaching that day, I met with Dr. Genet for his diagnosis. The news was not good. "That heavy Basset body on that elongated Dachshund spine is the problem," he said. Tests, X-rays and other imaging techniques indicated surgery.

When, after her treatment, I went to take Pumpkin home, the news was still grim. The veterinarian said they had done what they could, and there was a sixty percent chance she might recover the use of one leg. But in the meantime, to help the healing, Pumpkin needed to be confined. He brought out parts of a large cage for me to take home and assemble.

I carried Pumpkin to the car and put her in the seat next to me. She rested her chin on my lap and looked up at me with her glad-to-see-you smile. My heavy heart was lightened by her happy spirit. I stroked her head and smiled back.

The kids refused to construct the cage as I'd asked. I explained again its importance for Pumpkin's recovery. They insisted that her being free, where they could hug and hold her and let her know she was loved, was more important than the maybe recovery of some movement to one leg. I relented and Pumpkin remained uncaged.

It upset me to see her dragging her still paralyzed back parts this way and that behind the dancing Hoss, who was busy threatening the cats. My attempts to keep Pumpkin still were unsuccessful. She was so happy being back in the game. She dragged along, adding her meow-bark to the noise and grinning. I let her be.

By the end of the first week, she was pushing valiantly with her right leg, over and over again, trying to make it hold her up. It was hard to watch. Didn't she know it was hopeless?

By the second week, though, I had to wonder. Each day, she was up on her right rear leg for longer and longer stretches, with the left one now making pushing movements as well. She made progress daily.

A month passed and it was time for Pumpkin's post-op visit to the vet. My husband dropped her off on his way to the office and I went to get her after work. When they brought Pumpkin out, she dashed over to greet me. I leaned down to attach her leash.

"Don't go," the receptionist said. "The doctor needs to see you." My heart sank. I sat down, dreading more bad news. I should have kept her in the cage, I thought. The vet came out and indicated I should follow him into the examining room. Pumpkin trotted along beside me, grinning up at Dr. Genet, her tail wagging.

He had a pair of X-ray films hanging. Pointing along the first one as he spoke, Dr. Genet explained in detail the anatomy of a normal dog's spinal column. I felt like I was back in biology class.

He moved to the second frame. "Now this is the X-ray of Pumpkin's back," he said, pointing at the spinal cord. Remember what I told you about the importance of this for movement?" I nodded. "Now see where this disc has penetrated into the spinal cord here, practically severing it?" I nodded again. Dr. Genet turned his attention to Pumpkin, still prancing happily about the room, uninterested in his lecture. He pointed directly at her. "That dog cannot walk," he announced firmly.

He sounded almost angry with her. "I'm sorry," I said, "but she had cats to chase." Dr. Genet shook his head and laughed. "Motivation is powerful medicine. It's one of science's greatest mysteries. Like love." Then he leaned down and petted Pumpkin's head. "Good girl," he said. "Good girl."

~Marcia Rudoff

58

Blend Well

There is no psychiatrist in the world like a puppy licking your face.
~Ben Williams

"Let's get a dog," I said. Scott looked at the picture of a one-pound, one-ounce little white ball of fur with big black eyes looking back at him from my computer screen. The next day we were in the car "just to look."

As the woman walked out with the tiny white ball of puppy, my heart melted. I immediately reached for him. I don't remember talking about it. I just remember thinking "he's ours now." I looked at my smiling husband and knew he felt the same. I handed the puppy to Scott while I fumbled to prepare the car for our new addition.

Scott held our new baby, well, like a new baby. He stood perfectly still and upright. Fear on his face. He didn't even talk. I'm not even sure he was breathing. I grabbed the puppy back from a now relieved looking Scott and we headed home.

The ride home was filled with phone calls and announcements. "We got a puppy!"

After the flood of calls the conversation turned to logistics. What would he eat? Where would he sleep? What would we call him? Barney. We will call our newest little family member Barney. A name cleverly thought up by my mother-in-law.

Scott and I had married only three months earlier and had become a ready-made-family. He had two boys; I had one boy. We struggled to learn our roles with our new family members. Blending a family is not easy and not instant. We had different rules, different ways of life, and we needed to find common ground.

Scott and I decided to surprise the boys with the new puppy. Each boy, one by one, entered the room, smiled, and fell to the floor to get closer to our new addition.

"Who is this?"

"Did we get a dog?"

"Can we play with him?"

"He's so small."

We all fell silent as Barney took his tiny first steps over to investigate a new brother waiting across the room. As he reached his destination we all laughed and beamed with pride. I scanned the room and noticed all eyes were on Barney. The boys were laughing and calling out for him. They joked with each other and us about the tiny dog. Could Barney be the answer? Could it be this little dog could somehow bring us together?

We all watched as Barney learned his name, learned to go outside, and finally learned how much he loved treats. Eventually the little one-pounder grew to a hefty six pounds. He was still so small. But he had a giant personality. No matter what the mood of the house, Barney would change it. At any moment he would trot into a room and look at us like he was saying, "What are we doing, guys?" Everyone would smile. He had the ability to make a bad situation good or a good situation better. But most of the time he would just show up. He wouldn't expect anything. He just wanted to be a part of whatever was going on.

He didn't know he was part of a blended family. He just knew we were his family. He didn't love one more than another. He didn't see a stepbrother or stepparent. He just saw a family—his family. Barney became more than common ground for the family. For me, he became an example of how I want to live my own life.

Fill the room with unconditional love, show up, and bring treats.

~Diana Lynn

59

Wayward Setter

Thorns may hurt you, men desert you, sunlight turn to fog;
but you're never friendless ever, if you have a dog.
~Douglas Mallock

After many years of being without a dog, and at my daughter's request, I scanned the newspaper looking for one. I had raised Irish Setters for many years, so I thought that another one would fill the empty spot in our lives. I also was married at the time to a man who never seemed to take any joy in anything that I did. Surely, I thought, another Setter would bring him to his senses. In my mind, he'd be so happy that I came up with the idea, this would certainly bring the happiness back into our marriage!

I saw an ad for an English Setter from a breeder not two miles away! I knew it! This was meant to be. My daughter and I picked out an adorable puppy that was all white, except for an endearing spot of brown around one eye. Taking the wriggly pup home, we waited for my husband's approval.

Unfortunately, we were met with disapproval. Despite my best training efforts, in his eyes the puppy could do nothing right. He chewed on shoes; he jumped on furniture; he howled when left alone. Despite crate training, several long walks per day, as well as obedience training, Patrick, as we called him, was a very wayward Setter. I could handle the puppy being, well, a puppy, but what I couldn't handle was my husband's growing discontent and his conversations that began and ended with, "Get rid of THAT dog!"

My daughter was beside herself. She too had tried, but Patrick weighed fifty pounds now and he still hadn't turned into the beloved family member we had hoped. The strain on the family was ridiculous!

Then, one after another, small miracles happened. My daughter, out of the blue one day, inquired, "Mom, why don't you write a book about Patrick?"

I chuckled. "A book? Why would I write a book about Patrick? What would I say?"

She knew that I had been doing small writing jobs, but never anything big and certainly not a book. My inner fear took over. Who would want to read a book about a wayward Setter anyway? Hmm, a wayward Setter…

I sat at the computer, pulled up a blank page, and began: "Patrick was born one fine day in January, just before the coldest weather set in…." I kept writing until I had what I thought was a good, rough draft of chapter one. My daughter eagerly read it. "Yup, this is good! Now, keep going!"

Again I chuckled. Only twelve years old, she had such faith in me… and in our puppy.

Two weeks later, while gathered at a Fourth of July fireworks show, we discussed the plot of the story. Curious, my husband asked what we were talking about.

"The book that Mom is writing. It's about Patrick!" she said.

"Hmmph! Your mom can't write a book!" His lack of faith in me was so disappointing.

"She is too, and it's going to make money and then you'll see just how valuable that dog is to us!" she exclaimed.

"I doubt it. He's just a dumb dog that you just HAD to have!"

I looked at my daughter—her crestfallen face said enough. That was all the motivation that I needed. I said no more about it to him, but used every chance I had in between my jobs and caring for my kids to write. Early mornings turned into late nights, then, finally, I submitted the idea to several publishers. Within three weeks, one wrote back, asking to see my manuscript, which I sent in. The response made me cheer! It was accepted! *Patrick the Wayward Setter* would be published within nine months!

It was followed by three sequels. As I gained a following of readers, more ideas for book submissions came. Soon I was writing Western fiction, then non-fiction books. My marriage, however, took the hit. My husband, jealous of the attention, decided that I needed to make a choice: my writing or him. Our marriage had not been anything more than a piece of paper for many years. I made my choice.

In 2012, at age nine, Patrick's health took a turn for the worse. This dog, whose loyalty was proven through my book signings, where he sat patiently as readers oohed and aahed over this canine hero of stories, who saw me through a difficult divorce and the aftereffects of rebuilding my life, was now leaving me. I was heartbroken. How does one repay a dog's devotion? I stayed with him until the very end. When the injection put him to sleep for the last time, I finally broke down.

Today, I look back at how much this dog influenced my life. If not for Patrick, I would never have had the courage to write, not professionally anyway. I would not have had the chance to meet so many people who have told me what a difference my words have made in their lives. It was through this animal that I found the courage to leave a sad relationship and to love again.

~Diane Ganzer Baum

Gentle Giant

I think dogs are the most amazing creatures; they give unconditional love.
For me they are the role model for being alive.
~Gilda Radner

When we got to the shelter that day, my husband, son, and I split up in our quest to find the perfect dog. Eight months before we had lost our Bogey. We finally felt ready to open our hearts and home again, opting for an older pet.

I checked each cage, my heart constricting with emotion. Dog after hopeful dog approached, tail wagging, trusting eyes begging me to take it home.

As I approached the last cage, a massive dog stood up and wandered over. His sad, penetrating gaze captured mine and I couldn't look away. I extended my hand. He leaned forward to smell it politely, his enormous tail wagging slowly. Everything about him seemed to say, "You don't want me either, do you?"

When I read the tag hanging from his enclosure, I gasped. He'd been at the shelter for six of his eighteen months!

"This one!" I yelled out to my family, startling a young couple.

"He's gigantic," my husband declared.

"He must weigh a hundred pounds," my son added.

"One-twenty," I corrected, tapping the tag. "But I still want him." I was surprised when they both agreed.

As we led him outside, he blinked in the bright daylight, inhaling the fresh air with inquisitive, huffing snorts. We saw that his extended confinement hampered his motor skills and development. He stared blankly at the open car door, not knowing what was expected of him. We tried to coax him to jump in, but he simply stood there, uncertain and confused. We finally had to lift him into the vehicle, where he buried his mighty head into my son's lap, lying rigid with fear for the entire ride home.

The poor creature seemed even more mystified by the three steps leading to the house, needing encouragement, guidance, and soft tugs on his collar to climb them. Inside, he barely explored his new surroundings. Spotting the staircase balusters that led to the basement, he plopped down against them. A cage was all he'd known for half a year, and, recognizing bars, he gravitated to the familiar.

We named him Jack, and for the next eleven years, we were blessed to know this gentle giant. He eventually learned to take stairs, but not gracefully. He could descend easily, but going up was an entirely different matter. He would need to gather momentum from a running start clear across the yard. Occasionally, he miscalculated his speed or the distance between steps, but he persevered, repeating his process tirelessly until he succeeded. His determination was a reminder that nothing comes easy—that all goals have obstacles and require patience to achieve.

Despite his intimidating size, few people feared Jack. He emitted an aura of peaceful serenity. He'd give a warning "smile" and a low rumble that could shake the ground if he felt his "people" were at risk, but his motto seemed to be "Do no harm unless threatened."

We would watch, amazed, as he lay in the back yard surrounded by birds, some pecking at the breadcrumbs we provided, others actually daring to land on his back before flying away unharmed. Squirrels scampered by without trepidation. His only reaction was to raise his colossal head and stare at them quizzically before resuming his nap. His tolerant behavior made me rethink killing bugs, if they were merely going about their insect business.

Jack expected nothing from us. He loved unconditionally and was content with any attention or food offered. He was simply grateful to be a part of our lives, and to move freely in our home and on our property. Each time we let him out, he stopped and sniffed at the air appreciatively as if he couldn't believe that he was free.

Huge as he was in size, the biggest part of him was the heart that stored so much love, loyalty and perception. He instinctively knew when to move out of the way to avoid collision, just as he sensed the right time to lean against any of us in comfort and quiet reassurance through difficult times.

Jack was almost thirteen when his time with us began to come to an end. One morning, I found him on the kitchen floor unable to move. I'd owned enough dogs to recognize a stroke. There was little I could do except make him comfortable. Our veterinarian confirmed that.

I remained vigilant for signs of pain or discomfort, knowing Jack would tell me in that way only dogs can when it was time. For three days, I never left his side, feeding him if he wanted it, offering water as needed, and cleaning him tenderly when necessary. I would lie beside him, whispering that it was okay to leave us, yet he continued to cling to life, ever loyal, ever concerned for our sadness. On the third morning, I woke up to find him sitting up weakly, wagging his tail. Seeing I was awake, he slumped down and our eyes locked, giving me the heartbreaking message I had been waiting for.

We carefully moved him to our van for his final ride. We gave him a moment to look around his home and property for the last time before sliding the door shut. As we drove, I lifted his limp head to feel the breeze and watch the passing cars.

When we got to the vet's, we transferred him to the waiting gurney. I tried to still my shaking body and muffle my sobs, but was unable to, not then—not during the time the attendants compassionately allowed us to say goodbye.

We surrounded him and held him as he slipped away. Jack's last lesson to us was to accept death with courageous dignity. For a nanosecond before his beautiful eyes closed forever, I saw a glimpse of his former strength and spirit, almost as if he was anticipating this new journey with renewed youth. His tail swished one last time as he sagged into my arms, and I saturated his thick fur with my tears.

When we left him that day, there was no profound sign that he was okay. No rainbow split the sky, no sunbeams broke through clouds, but I wasn't surprised. Jack taught me that every day of freedom to breathe fresh air and marvel at the sights around us was a gift, one he never took for granted and embraced with heartfelt gratitude and appreciation.

~Marya Morin

Doggy-Nanny

Biology is the least of what makes someone a mother.
~Oprah Winfrey

W hen my family and I realized that our Golden Labrador, Gypsy, was going to have puppies, we were excited. After all, these would be the first puppies born on our property in well over ten years. But at the same time, a voice in my head said, "Brace yourself."

As cute as puppies are, they are a lot of work, and the circumstances were far from ideal. To begin with, Gypsy was around ten years old when a certain white German Shepherd came to visit, and she never had been known as the "sharpest tool in the shed." My parents knew from experience that Labradors had large litters of puppies. And given Gypsy's age and the risk of the birthing process, we had no doubt we would be doing more than our fair share of raising the little darlings until they were old enough to place in good homes. We needed help, but where is a nanny when you need one? Enter the doggy-nanny!

Her name was actually Freebie. She was a German Shepherd that a veterinarian had given us when our beloved Collie had passed away, hence the name. I have to admit that when our parents told us that they were acquiring a German Shepherd, I was more than a little timid. Until then the only German Shepherds I had heard of were military dogs like Rin Tin Tin or K-9s working for the police department. Freebie would make a good guard dog, the general of the yard, but would she act like a pet too?

However, Freebie turned my world around. The same dog who ripped the back pocket off an intruder's jeans was the one who came to lick my face when I fell down rollerblading in the driveway. She dealt death by whiplash to every snake that slithered into our yard and still made time to play with every pear that fell from the tree. And when it came time for Gypsy to give birth, Freebie was more ready than the humans. In fact, she was the one that let us know the puppies had arrived.

When I got up one morning, Mom said, "Melissa, don't go outside."

"Why?"

"Gypsy had her puppies last night, and Freebie brought me one of the ones that didn't make it. Melissa, she was so gentle. She carried the puppy to me in her mouth and laid it at my feet. There isn't one tooth mark on its body."

"Oh my gosh!"

"I know. She then led me to two more of them lying in the yard. Let me check on Gypsy first and make sure there are no more dead puppies outside, and then you can come see them."

Dogs will naturally separate the live puppies from the dead ones, and in large litters, these deaths are quite common. But that a dog who is not the mother would be shaken by these deaths was something we did not expect. And after she had shown Mom where each dead puppy was, Freebie set to work with the seven survivors.

For us humans, puppy duty consisted of building a good pen to protect the mother and her little ones. Freebie may not have helped with that part of the work, but she made sure that pen was an extension of her yard. The puppies were not intruders; they were her nieces and nephews, and she was going to make sure that no snakes, raccoons, opossums, coyotes, or restless neighborhood boys would give them trouble. When they whined, she was at their sides. When they scrambled over the walls of the pen, she picked them up gently by the scruff of their necks and plopped them back inside. If one made a jail break, she was hot on its trail. And when my dad let them outside the pen to play, she made sure none slipped into the street. Except for the runt, which my sister had to feed with a bottle, there was hardly any work left for us to do.

However, the best part was mealtime, even with the poor little runt! Freebie had been neglected before the veterinarian had found her, so she really loved food. When Dad went to the food container, the guard dog turned into a little puppy herself and started yipping. Mom and Dad said she was singing for her supper. Well, when it was time for her meal, Freebie figured that the puppies needed to learn to sing too. She not only started the chorus, but she went from puppy to puppy to make sure they did their part before she went to her own bowl. I have no doubt the neighbors could have set their watches by Freebie and Gypsy's little band.

It did not take long before the puppies were grown, and all but two found homes, but still every night when Dad came outside, Freebie ran to Gypsy, then to each puppy, and finally to her bowl. Freebie also taught them how to defend their yard and even how to play what I like to call "shake a snake." But one day, we learned that Freebie had come down with congestive heart failure, and in a few weeks, she quietly passed away. That was the first time in seven years that mealtime was silent, and those puppies never sang for their supper again as long as they lived.

In the Cajun culture in which I was raised, a "nanny" is not an au pair. It is the name we call our godmothers, because they are deeply involved in our lives. That is precisely what Freebie was to those puppies and to our house. Personally, if I am ever blessed with a German Shepherd of my own, I hope it too keeps away the bad snakes but still finds time to lick away my tears and sing for its supper!

~Melissa Abraham

Legacy

H₂O: two parts Heart and one part Obsession.
~Author Unknown

Our eight-week-old Shepherd-mix puppy, Annie, had all the makings of a natural swimmer: aerodynamic body, muscular legs, and glossy black fur that repelled moisture. There was just one problem: Annie wouldn't take a single step into the water.

We tried everything—coaxing, begging, hurling her favorite squeaky hamburger into the pond—but Annie stubbornly remained on land. Finally, my mom gently placed Annie in shallow water. The puppy whimpered and fled back to shore.

Mom and I sighed. Having just moved from the city, we were looking forward to watching Annie splash in our cattail-lined pond. I waded in, hoping she'd follow, but Annie stayed put, yipping anxiously as water crept past my shoulders.

"Aw, come on," I pleaded. "Just try it!"

Annie shook her head, black ears flapping. Her brown-gold eyes followed me worriedly. I swam deeper, and she started yelping again.

Then I got an idea. Holding my breath, I disappeared under the water. Fifteen silent seconds later, I surfaced to find Annie running along the shoreline, barking hysterically.

"Help me, Annie!" I called out desperately. "Come save me!"

Annie ran even faster. I started going under again and she actually sprinted a few feet into the water before retreating. An agonizing battle was taking place—fear versus love. I was the girl who came to the puppy gate whenever Annie whimpered. I was the one who played "squeaky hamburger fetch" with her. And now, apparently, I needed her help.

I dunked my head and sputtered, "Annie! ANNIE!"

Finally, Annie leaped into the water. White splashes rose on either side of her like angel wings as she charged toward me. Soon, she was swimming outright, just a small black head, harpooning across the surface.

"Come on, Annie!" I shouted. "You can do it!"

She was puffing when she reached me. My yell of triumph was followed by a howl of pain as twenty claws raked across my bare skin. My would-be rescuer had decided I was her own personal life raft. Grunting, I awkwardly helped her return to shore. Mom couldn't stop laughing.

Back on land, Annie ran in frenzied circles. Once she calmed down, I whistled and plunged back into the pond. This time, she followed willingly. Before long, we were chasing each other, filling the air with splashes, giggles and barks—the perfect music for a summer afternoon. By sunset, Annie was shoving her whole nose under as she paddled along, snorting gleefully and spraying like a dolphin.

Annie was transformed into a bona fide water dog that day. Whether it was a reward after an anxious vet visit, or delicious relief on a blistering afternoon, the pond became synonymous with joy.

Over the next several years, we adopted three more dogs—a skinny yellow stray named Pepper, an eighty-pound shelter dog named Will, and an inky black Akita mix named Cleo. Whenever we brought a new dog home, the pond was our first destination. Pepper plunged right in alongside Annie, forging the beginning of a lifelong bond. Will waded in delicately, letting the water glide over him.

And then there was Cleo.

A lonely stray who'd followed my dad home, the final member of our "pack" loved watching the others swim, but refused to enter the pond herself. If water even lapped against Cleo's toes, she'd jump back like it was molten lava. I could've resurrected the "Save me!"

technique, but by then I was old enough to know that pretending to drown was cruel — and dangerous. So, our family accepted Cleo for what she was: a land dog.

Seasons passed, and the pack bonded over long walks on tree-lined lanes, exuberant games of "dirty sock tug-of-war," and my unsuccessful attempts to use them as sled dogs. Each dog had a favorite companion. Pepper's meek nature tempered Annie's fiery, drama-queen personality, while Will's gentle soul found its match in Cleo's quiet demeanor.

Then, one night, the unthinkable happened — we lost Pepper to a terrible, sudden-onset condition known as "bloat." We were still reeling from this tragedy when more heartbreaking news arrived: Annie, who'd been struggling with a urinary tract infection, was diagnosed with inoperable bladder cancer.

Now, whenever I looked at our three dogs, a lump clogged my throat. A week ago, there had been four. Soon, there would only be two.

Despite her illness, Annie's energy never diminished. She still ran haywire around the yard, still went crashing joyfully into the water. But her ribs began to show under her shiny black coat, and her need to urinate became more frequent and painful as the cancer grew inside her bladder. Before long, she could only run a few feet before needing to go again. Even the pond lost some of its appeal — Annie had to keep climbing out to relieve herself.

One evening, as Mom and I walked the pack around the pond, we heard the plop of a bullfrog. All three dogs froze. Another step, and it happened again. Plop! This time, Annie and Will dove headlong into the pond, filling the once-quiet evening with a wet chorus of "Plop-splash! Plop-splash!"

After ten frog-frolicking minutes, Mom and I exchanged smiles. For the first time in weeks, Annie seemed pain-free, and Will was the happiest he'd been since Pepper died. Cleo, however, stood anxiously on shore, shifting from foot to foot, an invisible barrier of fear separating her from her friends. Finally, she let out a piercing bark.

Annie raised her dripping muzzle to look at Cleo. The two dogs gazed at each other, and a strange peacefulness settled over Cleo's trembling body. Annie slowly emerged from the pond and walked to Cleo. There was just a quick touch of cold noses, a brief wag of tails, before Annie waded back into the water.

This time, Cleo followed.

Step for step, the two dogs went deeper and deeper, until Cleo was immersed up to her chest. I held my breath, afraid to break the spell. Mom covered her mouth. Together, we watched our three dogs weave between the reeds, splashing and frog-hunting as if Cleo's fear had never existed at all.

Eventually, when the sun was just a fading speck, Annie, Cleo and Will reluctantly climbed out. Mom and I took them back to the house, whispering excitedly about what we'd witnessed. It was the best night Annie had had in a very long time.

It was also her last night on earth. The next day, Annie's condition deteriorated so badly that we had the vet end her suffering. I've never cried as hard as I did when I hugged her lifeless body. But even through the pain and tears, I knew Annie wasn't truly gone — she'd left behind an incredible legacy. For the rest of Cleo's life, every time she stepped boldly into the water, I could see a little Shepherd-mix puppy, diving past her fears to save me. And although Cleo and Will are gone now too, every time I walk by the pond, I can still see four dogs with pink tongues, smiling in the sunshine.

If I close my eyes, I can even hear them splashing.

~Gretchen Bassier

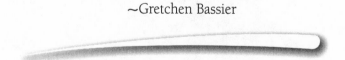

The Dog Did What?

Who's in Charge Here?

How to Find a Husband

*I once decided not to date a guy because he wasn't excited to meet my dog.
I mean, this was like not wanting to meet my mother.*
~Bonnie Schacter

I always heard that German Shepherds were obedient and protective. What I didn't know was that they could actually pick out a husband.

Soon after I chose my German Shepherd puppy, I thought I'd made a mistake. My puppy ate through the carpet, right down to the foundation, and then continued to eat the concrete and break off his canine teeth. Thus, I named him Trouble.

Trouble grew into a handsome Shepherd indeed! His black and silver coat gleamed after his baths and his ears stood at attention if he heard a noise. He seemed to understand that it was his job to protect me since I lived alone.

After a troubling divorce, I became accustomed to cuddling up with Trouble. Of course, he took up a good deal of the bed. But he never thought he was too big to plop down on the couch with me to watch a movie. We took long walks together and often shared the same food in the evenings. Steak was his favorite.

A few months after the final papers for my divorce were signed, I started dating again. I met a few gentlemen through work, and my girlfriends were always ready to fix me up with a blind date. Since Trouble had been my only companion, I felt almost giddy when it was time to open the front door to a date.

Little did I know that Trouble had his own agenda. I opened the door to greet Paul, and Trouble trotted close to my heels, almost shoving me to one side. This was a blind date, so I didn't know what to expect. As I put my hand out to shake his, Trouble leapt between us and stood stiff, growling, his eyes shooting nasty glares at Paul. "I'm so sorry," I apologized. He took a step further into the house while saying, "Oh that's okay. I love dogs." This is when Trouble grabbed hold of his pant leg and almost made Paul do a face plant on my tile floor.

This pattern repeated itself many times over the next year. I even went back to obedience basics with Trouble. I tried everything short of putting a muzzle on him. I locked him in bedrooms only to have to replace doors or at the very least repaint them.

As long as I didn't have a date, Trouble was a perfect, calm, obedient dog. I started to meet dates outside my home. I became rather attached to one gentleman in particular. Ray was a funny, charming man who dazzled me when he cocked his cowboy hat to one side. He loved to sing and had a great voice. What girl wouldn't want to have someone serenade her?

The weather turned chilly. I started a fire in the fireplace and planned a quiet romantic evening for Ray's first visit to the house. I worked on new obedience skills with Trouble—hand signals and commands—in hopes he would behave. The doorbell rang.

"Hi Ray, come on in." I put my hand out flat toward Trouble and cautioned him to sit and stay. He amazed me by sitting tall and didn't move a muscle. The evening started smoothly with the tasty meal I had prepared and cordial conversation. Trouble was perfect. He lay quietly by my side at the dinner table and walked alongside as we headed to the living room to enjoy the fireplace. Ray and I sat fairly close together on the couch.

Then Ray put his arm lightly around my shoulders. That's when we both heard the snarling growl from behind the couch. The next thing we knew, Trouble's nose was between our heads. His bright white teeth sparkled within his open mouth. He stared at Ray as his nose came under Ray's arm. Still growling, he pushed Ray's arm slowly to the side, away from my shoulder. Ray smiled. "I guess he doesn't want me to do this?" I laughed and apologized for Trouble. We resumed the evening without touching as Trouble's keen, unblinking eyes watched.

Ray visited often. Trouble continued to growl, sneer or nudge him with warnings not to touch me. Slowly, Ray's gentle ways convinced Trouble that he meant me no harm. During this courtship I continued to date other men, but every date turned into disaster when I brought him home to meet Trouble. He didn't just growl, but was always ready to clamp his pearly whites on a leg or arm. Ray seemed to be the only man he tolerated.

Trouble spent more time with Ray than with me during visits. He relished the fact that Ray threw balls for him and played rough games with him. When Ray left, Trouble sat by the door and whined. I didn't whine when Ray left but I realized I'd like to have him around more often. It occurred to me that Trouble might have found the perfect mate for me. I never imagined my dog would be the one to pick out a new husband.

Ray and I married. Trouble became Ray's best friend. They were inseparable, which made me believe all the more that Trouble had a keen sense for picking out husbands. We've been married twenty-seven years and often look back on our courtship and tell friends about how Trouble brought us together. My advice: if you are looking for a new husband, first get a German Shepherd.

~Alice Klies

Who's Number One?

Most owners are at length able to teach themselves to obey their dog.
~Robert Morley

Oreo, as you might have guessed, is a black and white dog whose markings resemble his sandwich cookie namesake. He is a Portuguese Water Dog who has graced our household for eight years now.

Oreo is primarily my wife Cheryl's dog. She bought him, she walks him (most of the time) and she showers him with unconditional love. In short, Oreo has earned a special place in our house almost akin to a second child.

For the most part, Oreo's favored status has not been a problem. After all, he's a dog and everyone loves dogs, especially one as pleasant and even-tempered as he.

Despite the constant expressions of affection directed Oreo's way, I always assumed that I still retained at least an equally favored status. After all, I've been around far longer than Oreo and I am the one who pays his food, vet and toy bills.

Well, it turns out that I may have been mistaken all these years. Recent events have led me to reconsider my current status in the Martin household. Despite my seniority and chief breadwinner status, it seems that I, rather than Oreo, may be the expendable one.

It all started last Christmas when my sister came to visit and brought along a secondhand leather chair that she thought might be helpful for my arthritic hips. We unloaded the chair from the back of her pickup truck and brought it inside to the living room.

We moved the old cloth armchair that had been sitting by the front window and put the leather chair in its place. Sure enough, it was a better fit for my aging hips. It was higher and firmer than the old chair, thereby facilitating a faster and easier entrance and exit for me.

I was just about to retire the old armchair when Cheryl spoke up and said maybe we'd better check to see if the replacement was a good fit for Oreo too. You see, the old chair has been one of Oreo's favorite resting spots for many years. He particularly likes to lie on it after lunch when the afternoon sun pours in through the front window onto his head resting atop one of the chair's wooden arms.

"I think he'll have a hard time getting up on that leather one," said Cheryl. "And he might find it hard not to fall off that slippery leather surface."

I have to admit that I was a bit surprised. Rather than accommodate my aging body, Cheryl wanted to ensure that her precious Oreo was not inconvenienced.

Since I seldom used the current living room armchair, the matter of replacing it with the secondhand leather one was not of great importance to me. So I quickly relented and Oreo retained his living room throne.

But if there had been any previous doubt, I now knew where I stood in the family hierarchy. I had a pretty good idea that I was now at least one station below the dog.

Just how far I had fallen over the years became crystal clear a few months later. Like his master, Oreo has developed osteoarthritis, albeit only in one hip and not as advanced as mine.

If Oreo goes for an extended, off-leash romp at the local dog run, he is likely to hobble about for the rest of the day. I, on the other hand, wouldn't even dream of running and bouncing about like him since that would leave me in pain for the rest of the week.

Both Oreo and I have had X-rays taken of our hips, his costing way more than mine. Both he and I take daily doses of glucosamine, which seems much more effective for him. And Oreo even has a special vet-prescribed pain medication for those occasional times when he overdoes it and stiffens up a bit. I, on the other hand, have a bottle of aspirin.

The other day, I finally realized who really was number one in our house. Cheryl had spoken to another dog owner who mentioned an experimental stem cell treatment that apparently had helped to relieve her dog's arthritic hips.

Cheryl was thrilled to find out about this new medical option for Oreo and was not deterred by its $2,000 price tag. Cheryl, it seems, is prepared to do whatever it takes to improve our dog's quality of life.

As for me, I suspect I'm on my own.

~David Martin

65

Miss Daisy and Her Pawns

In life, unlike chess, the game continues after checkmate.
~Isaac Asimov

M iss Daisy is my dog. A female Boxer. If you know anything about dog breeds, you know I am the owner of a neurotic, alpha female, gassy, I-can-jump-higher-than-your-best-Frisbee, drooling dirt dog.

And they resent, with every frantic bone in their body, when you leave them.

Like her Boxer brethren, she only likes other Boxers and thinks she's a person.

Last time she was in a kennel in Nashville she growled at everybody, and if she had been blessed with opposable thumbs, would have flung poop at them also. This place was like the Dog Ritz Carlton, with TVs and cushy beds and chairs, and she still wasn't happy.

We were planning another trip and I thought it best to try the new kennel right down the road. So a week before departure, we landed at Camp Arf Arf (the names have been changed to protect the bank account) and Miss Daisy was about to have her required pre-board exam, which they insisted on before they would "accept her."

Accept her? Geez, what sorority would she have to pledge?

I wasn't even a mile down the road after dropping her off before I got the call.

"Is this Ms. Espy, Daisy's owner?"

"Yes."

"You need to come get her right away. She has failed our pre-board exam."

"Failed? What did she do?"

"She growled and lunged at one of our attendants, and that's just unacceptable."

By the way, the attendant at Camp Arf Arf was a teenager who wouldn't stop eating her Wendy's Double Stack long enough to wait on me. She shook my hand with an unimaginable amount of grease still lingering on her palm, which was then transferred to the computer while loading my name into the database, completely misspelled.

"I'll be right back. So sorry about this," I said like a woman too familiar with kennel ejection tactics. I turned the car around and headed in the direction of defeat.

Back at the counter, I swear Daisy was smiling at me, triumphant in her bad-doggyness. As we walked passed the attendant she reportedly lunged at, Daisy jumped up and licked her face as if to say, "Sorry honey, but I had to get sprung from this joint. It was nothing personal. You're just a pawn on the chessboard of my master manipulation game. By the way, you smell like a Wendy's Stack Attack. Way to go."

The drive home was silent but deadly, if you know about Boxer gas.

I spent the next few days researching kennels that deal with female aggressors (yep, I found the name to tag onto this dog). And there it was, the Valhalla of weary dominated dog owners, the Utopia of out-of-control dog lovers... Misty Pines Dog Park.

I kid you not—Misty Pines is the real name.

They train service and hunting dogs; they have a dog park, dog pond, nature trails, kennels, doggy day care, and most of all, dog trainers on staff who know how to handle alpha-you're-not-the-boss-of-me-female dogs.

They are so good with aggressors that the local no-kill shelter sends their Pit Bulls there for rehab.

Daisy had met her match.

I took her to Misty Pines four times to acclimate her. We walked the trails. She did doggy day care... where she stood at the dog pen gate for two hours, waiting for me to come back and refusing to mingle with the other dogs. Although I think she did have a short conversation with a couple of Pugs about their shared breathing problems.

She seemed to be okay, so I officially boarded her for a week so that we could go away on that much-needed vacation.

By day three, just when I was starting to actually relax, toes in the sand, book in my hand, I got the call; Daisy was on a hunger strike.

By day four, they were feeding her canned dog food and rice cakes... her plan was working. As you can guess, we left our vacation two days early to retrieve her.

We packed up, counted the lost money on the remaining rental days, and drove back. It was a long quiet drive, the air filled with promises of "never again" and "no more dogs."

We picked her up and got the progress report: "Daisy now has diarrhea from the canned food—better not leave her alone much for the next couple of days."

So now we had to stay by her side or deal with cleaning up liquid waste on the new rugs. We (as in me) needed to feed her rice and burgers... ever so gently.

She jumped into the car victoriously wagging her entire body and put on the most sincere Boxer cute face of all—the one that says, "You can't stay mad, I am just that precious."

My husband, melted by the Boxer display of I-can't-live-without-you, patted her. The Queen had captured her King.

Later that afternoon, I prepared the special meals of rice and burger for Miss Daisy. I told her to sit and stay in the kitchen while the food cooled. She did so ever demurely, and as I walked past her to scoop the food in her dish, I could swear I heard her whisper "Checkmate."

~Carol Lee Espy

66

Small Dog, Big Attitude

Dogs got personality. Personality goes a long way.
~Quentin Tarantino

She came for a visit, a rather long visit. Her family took a posting in the Middle East and, after a little coaxing, I offered to mind Peanut for the year they would be gone. I had some rather pointed concerns as to how she would fit in, since I had a Great Pyrenees and Peanut was a longhaired Dachshund. It was truly a Mutt and Jeff story in the making.

When Peanut arrived at the house the children were all over her. She lapped it up, rolling over so her long expanse of belly could be rubbed and rubbed. Then the questions started.

"Why are her legs so short?"

"Why is her nose so long?"

"Why doesn't she trip over her ears?"

Being a writer, I offered a creative answer. "Well, you see when The Creator made the world he had an odd assortment of bits and pieces left over. He had a long tail from the monkey bin, a long snout from the aardvark drawer, a body from the hound pile and four legs from the tortoise shelf. Not being a wasteful type, he stuck them all together. What an odd-looking animal he had. The Creator sat back and shook his head, knowing that it would be too unkind to leave this creature as it was, made out of bits and pieces, none that seemed to belong to each other. After some careful reflection he remembered he had some beautiful long hairy ears and large soulful eyes. He added those and stretched the red-brown hair over the rest of the body, lengthened the tail a bit, and decided that would have to do." The children thought it was a great story and accepted this funny little furry gal without reservation. Peanut, too, accepted us and her temporary home.

What I soon learned is that The Creator had also installed attitude—big attitude. The first inkling I had that this sawed-off furry wiener dog was unaware that she had any limits was when she took one look at P2, our white mountain of a Pyrenees, and promptly made P2 aware who was boss—yep, Peanut. In that small bundle of fur dwelt the mind of a Great Dane, a large Great Dane. P2 was not the only one who came under her command—Peanut was also queen of the barnyard and my horse Missy.

Peanut was tireless, and unlike most dogs, seldom slept during the day. There were far too many things to do and she would miss none of them. Simply watching her brought me many smiles, mainly because her stature was so comical and she undertook each task with such determination. She was true to her breed and hunted the fields and meadows as she was bred to do. I would watch her lead the great white beast on many an exploration. P2 would return exhausted and plop down on the veranda for a long doze but Peanut would bounce into the house, take a long drink of water, and be ready for the next adventure.

When Peanut's family decided to extend their tour abroad, Peanut became a permanent member of our household. We have many family stories about her adventures, successful and not. She tirelessly followed the tractor as the fields were plowed and she chased rabbits and squirrels, with her ears flying behind her. She would challenge any usurper to her domain, resulting in several mishaps. She was sprayed on several occasions by visiting skunks, but the most dramatic incident was when she was ripped open by a raccoon. Her belly required fifty stitches and a lot of care.

She mastered climbing the stairs quite easily but greater heights were difficult. She gauged the distance she needed for lift-off to mount the sofa; however, when she leapt to get on the car seat she missed and twisted her back. Her hindquarters were paralyzed. I was told to put her down, but I have attitude too, so we both struggled to mend her. She let me hold her bottom up while she did her duty outside. She tolerated my regular massaging and loving care. It took two months of therapy from me, and then she healed and resumed her dominant role.

Peanut definitely had enough attitude to take on the whole world. However, she also had a temper. She had little tolerance for anything that was not to her liking and she was quick to make you aware of it. She would turn her back on you and walk away from food she didn't like. She would chase the cats off the couch, scolding them sharply should they be in her preferred spot. She refused to take her medicine when she was under the weather, and she let you know her displeasure with a low growl. This brings me to one of my favorite Peanut stories.

My mother lived next door. Shortly after mid-afternoon one day, my phone rang.

"What did you do to Peanut?"

"Why?" I asked my mother.

"She's really mad at you."

"What do you mean—she's mad?"

"She's over here complaining like crazy."

"What?"

Laughter exploded through the telephone. "You have to come over and see this. She's on my deck pacing back and forth stomping, and I mean stomping her little feet, mad as can be. If she could speak, she'd tell me that she has been badly done by and the only person she knew to tell her woes was me. Whatever did you do to her?"

Now I'm laughing. "I gave her a bath."

I'm sure Dog Heaven is now ruled by one very short, very long red-haired dog with an attitude.

~Molly O'Connor

67

Guess Who's Come to Dinner

Fortune brings in some boats that are not steered.
~William Shakespeare

We were enjoying a perfect fall afternoon, eating Sunday dinner with the nearby sliding glass door open. Suddenly my eight-year-old daughter, Amber, gazed down next to her chair to find a scruffy black and tan mutt sitting beside her. He acted like begging at the table was the most natural thing in the world... except we didn't own a dog.

As the two of them locked gazes, I knew my wife and I would need to tread carefully with this unexpected visitor. After all, with both of us avid dog lovers, Amber had received a double dose of the dog-loving gene.

Before I could say anything, Amber tossed a tidbit from her plate that was caught so quickly in midair that I wasn't sure the dog had actually moved.

"Guess who's come to dinner?" my wife asked as Amber slid off her chair, offered her hand to be sniffed before rubbing the dog's head.

"What a lucky dog you are," Amber said. "You found your way to us. Can we keep her?"

"I'm sure the dog must already have an owner," I replied. "He or she seems to be well fed. I'm sure some loving family must be looking for her." Besides, she must have learned how to beg from somewhere, I thought.

"Isn't that a collar around her neck?" I asked, trying unsuccessfully to hide my relief. I reached down to inspect more closely. Sure enough, there was also a small medallion attached to the worn collar with "Daisy" inscribed on one side and a phone number on the other.

"See, Daisy just came for a visit. We'll call her owners after dinner and let them know we have her." Which we did. Over the next several days we called and called without ever getting an answer. We learned later from our neighbors that she'd been wandering around the neighborhood for several days before she'd stumbled onto our deck and into our home and hearts.

We checked with the pound to let them know we had Daisy in case her owners notified them. Still nothing. Meanwhile Amber kept working on us to keep her. Finally into the second week I knew it was time to raise the white flag when I heard Amber call the dog to her room. "Here Lucky, time for bed."

"Lucky?" I asked my wife.

"Yea, she told me Daisy didn't fit but that Lucky was her real name."

Considering the circumstances I had to agree.

~W. Bradford Swift

Molly, The Great Communicator

Communication works for those who work at it.
~John Powell

I t's said that a Brittany will welcome a burglar, show him to the valuables and then go home with him. Molly might be the exception to the rule. She's a petite girl, the smallest in two litters totaling fifteen puppies born within a day of each other. When we saw her cowering in the corner and being pushed away from the food dishes, we snatched her up, took her home and never looked back. She was very timid at first, but soon found her feet and is one smart little girl.

We learned early on that Brits like to "talk." Molly especially liked talking during puppy class when the instructor was speaking. The instructor didn't find it amusing and gave us stern warnings about allowing such behavior. That instructor reminded me of my least favorite teacher, and since we rather enjoyed this aspect of Molly's personality, we not only allowed it, we encouraged it. Now, six years later, we have frequent conversations with her, certain she understands every word by the way she reacts.

I work from home so we have chats throughout the day, usually about treats and squirrels. When I leave the house, she almost always rides along. Molly knows the household routine well. If we don't leave on time to pick up my grandson Cody from school she lets me know.

That has worked out well, especially for Cody. She knows what day we do the grocery shopping and, understanding she can't participate, goes to her kennel when we get ready to leave. When we return she meets us at the door and carefully sniffs us over to see if we're okay, where we've been, whom we've seen, and if we have any food on us.

Every summer, just before school starts, Cody has a get-together with his friends. They have a bonfire, eat piles of pizza, watch movies and play video games. Molly knows the boys well and is always happy to see them. Last year we decided to go see a movie so, of course, Molly had to stay home.

When we returned, instead of her usual checking over, Molly started frantically "talking" and showing no apparent interest in any tidbits we might be harboring. Laughing at her crazy antics, one of the boys asked, "Is she always like this when you come home?"

"No," I said, watching Molly practically turn herself inside out. My first thought was she was overly excited because we had been gone so long.

As we made our way from the garage towards the living room she ran ahead and stopped in front of us, preventing us from entering. She took off like a shot to the front door where she crouched down frantically talking. She then took off across the room to her bed under the window that looks out to the back yard, jumped at the window and again turned to face us, crouching and continuing her frenzied conversation. She waited a moment, watching us. When we didn't get it, she repeated the routine. The louder the boys laughed, the more frantic she became.

I kneeled down. "What's the matter girl?" Loving anybody who will get on the floor with her, when Molly didn't come to me, I knew something was up. She'd been alone for over three hours and in Molly-time that was nearly an eternity. She should have been in desperate need of love, playing hard to get while we begged forgiveness for leaving her alone for so long.

It was obvious Molly wasn't going to give up, so I asked the boys to quiet down, now not only curious but a little concerned about what was on her mind. She looked at me and sighed as if to say, "Finally!" I followed as she ran to the front door again.

"Somebody came to the front door," I said. She barked, a loud sharp bark.

She made the mad dash across the room, ending in a crash landing on her bed sliding into the wall under the window. She turned, crouched and looked at me again making a variety of sounds.

With Molly close at my heels I went out the front door to investigate. There I found a notice from the electric company on the porch. It must have blown off the door. I had known they were coming, something about my meter, but they couldn't tell me exactly when. I assured them it was no problem, that I was almost always home and in the event I wasn't, they had my permission to enter the yard and do what they needed to do. I picked up the notice and Molly and I went through the house, out the back door and around the corner to the meter. At it happens, it's right below the living room window that's on the other side of the wall next to her bed. The meter had a brand new tag on it. It made perfect sense!

Back inside, Molly sat proud and tall as I explained to the boys. "She was telling us somebody was here. They came to this door," I said putting my hand on the front door. "Then," I said, walking across the living room, "they were right outside this window. She wanted us to know that somebody came inside the fence. She knows nobody belongs in the yard unless we're with them."

Molly was in heaven as all four boys dropped to the floor to lavish her with praise. She trotted around and sniffed each one to make sure they were okay, where they'd been, whom they'd seen, and if they had any food.

~Rebecca Muchow

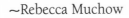

69

Don't Wash, Don't Tell

Cleanliness is next to impossible.
~Author Unknown

My friend Beth asked if I'd walk Butch, her Labradoodle, while she was out of town for a week. Husband Bob would be at work during the day, and Butch was a high-energy dog who needed a long midday walk. She'd happily pay me the going rate for dog walking.

"I'd be glad to," I said.

Several days later, I stopped by so Bob could give me a key and show me the ropes. I learned where the leash and harness were kept. Butch stood patiently as Bob showed me how to put them on correctly.

"After he comes in from a walk," Bob told me, "we wash his paws." He filled the large kitchen sink with soapy water. "He doesn't like this part, but he's good about it." Kneeling, Bob put his arms around Butch's legs, then lifted up the large dog and stood him in the sink.

That looks unsanitary, I thought as Bob washed each paw, drained the water, refilled the sink and rinsed them again. Not to mention time-consuming.

Then Bob took a baby wipe from a nearby container, lifted Butch's tail, and briskly wiped his butt. "We always do this too," he said.

Eeeew.

He lifted Butch from the sink, put him on the floor and dried his clean paws with a washcloth.

"You go through this every time he goes out?" I asked. I was beginning to understand how Beth kept her house so clean.

"Yup. He resisted at first."

"I'll bet he did."

"But now he's okay with it."

It seemed a little over the top to me, but what did I know? I didn't have a dog. I decided to ask around. Maybe every dog owner performed an in-the-sink paw wash and over-the-counter butt wipe after every walk. It could be one of those little dog-owning insider secrets that other folks don't know about. At work the next day, I queried my dog-owning co-workers.

"I wouldn't put my dog in the kitchen sink," said Eileen. "I prepare food there."

"They wipe his butt? With a baby wipe? Right over the kitchen counter?" asked Deb. "I'm sorry, but that's weird."

I was relieved to find that I was right — it WAS weird. I'd been looking forward to walking Butch. But the post-walk wash? Not so much.

When I arrived for our first walk, Butch greeted me with happy yelps and a wagging tail. It was a beautiful spring day and I enjoyed our stroll so much I forgot all about what was coming. But apparently Butch didn't. Bob had said that Butch would meekly follow me to the kitchen and submit to his post-walk wash. Instead, the moment I released him from his leash, he took one wild look at me and fled.

I found him sitting quietly on the bed in the master bedroom.

"C'mon, Butch," I said. "Time to wash up!"

He gave me a look that clearly said, "Maybe I have to put up with that routine from Bob and Beth. But you aren't getting me into that sink."

Taking his collar, I pulled gently.

"C'mon, Butchie! Let's go."

He didn't budge.

"Do I really have to pick you up and carry you down the steps and take you into the kitchen and put you in the sink?"

The look he gave me said, "Try it and die."

I fetched some wipes from the kitchen and used them to wipe his paws—and just his paws. Then I fed him a treat and rubbed his head. "If you don't tell," I said, "I won't."

It was a great week. The good weather held and we took long rambling walks all over the neighborhood. After each one, instead of going into the kitchen, Butch raced upstairs. Instead of putting him in the sink, I rubbed his head and cleaned his paws and fed him treats on his preferred spot on the bed.

"How did it go?" Beth asked upon her return.

"We had a wonderful time!" I didn't mention that Butch hadn't been anywhere near the kitchen sink. And if she or Bob noticed that any part of their dog wasn't as immaculately clean as it could have been, they didn't mention that either.

I'd really like to think they didn't check.

~Roz Warren

70

What's Good for the Goose

It is in my nature to be kind, gentle and loving... But know this:
When it comes to matters of protecting my friends, my family and my heart,
do not trifle with me.
~Harriet Morgan

For the past twenty-nine years, my wife and I have lived in Richmond Hill. Here, in this quiet suburb just north of Toronto, we raised our two wonderful children, as well as four of our six dogs.

I often like to walk in a nice little park called Rumble Pond Park, which is near our home. As one might expect, the main feature of Rumble Pond Park, is Rumble Pond. An eight-foot-wide paved pathway circumnavigates the pond, lazily ambling between trees, shrubs, rocks, and eventually crossing a quaint wood and steel bridge. A well-manicured, gently sloping embankment falls from the pathway to the pond below.

Rumble Pond is not very large but, even so, is home to a fair bit of local wildlife — frogs, fish, turtles, ducks, muskrat, several transient great blue herons, and about six breeding pairs of Canada geese. Over the past few years, within this small community of geese, an alpha pair has emerged. The male, an enormous specimen for a Canada goose, rules the park with a cruel and unwavering iron beak.

Each nesting season, once the various broods have hatched, the alpha pair kidnaps them and ends up with all the baby goslings "under their wings." The other resident geese don't seem to have much say (or "honk") about this practice of mass child abduction. But whilst caring for all the little ones, Mr. Alpha Goose becomes even more protective and aggressive.

The incident in question took place one nesting season when our dog, SchuBRT, was not quite fully mature. A week prior to the confrontation, SchuBRT and I watched, totally bemused from the opposite side of the pond, as Mr. Alpha chased a rather portly man and his two dogs (an equally portly 110-pound Labrador Retriever and a medium-sized terrier cross) halfway across the park.

SchuBRT is a lovely Black Russian Terrier, or BRT (hence, the spelling of his name). Black Russian Terrier is actually a rather ill conceived name for the breed, as these are not actually terriers, but large working dogs. The breed was created by a group of mad Soviet scientists after World War II, at the beginning of the Cold War. Their task was to create the ultimate police/military dog. After a number of years of crossing and re-crossing about seventeen different breeds, the BRT emerged as their extraordinary accomplishment.

If you've never seen a Black Russian Terrier, picture a hairy, black, bearded Schnauzer. Now imagine, under all that hair, 120 pounds of rock hard muscle, and you're envisioning our own "little guy," SchuBRT.

In reality, SchuBRT is a very sweet boy. He is highly intelligent, gentle, friendly, great with kids, and certified for therapy work. Unless necessary, he does not bark. Most of our friends have yet to hear him sound off. That is probably a good thing, as SchuBRT has retained all the protective guard dog qualities of his progenitors. When he does bark, it is serious and impressive. Beneath the kind exterior of this gentle giant is a fearless, formidable, and ferocious guardian, genetically hardwired to react to any form of aggression. But, I digress...

Back to our story, it is early summer. The local Canada geese had already hatched their new batches of goslings and, as per usual, Mr. and Mrs. Alpha have "adopted" all those fuzzy, cute little poop machines.

Taking our morning walk, SchuBRT is happily heeling off lead beside me. We casually approach the park and as we start upon the paved pathway I see, not forty yards ahead of us, the entire Rumble Pond Park Goose Gang. The alpha couple, along with all of the young ones, is busy grazing on grass whilst simultaneously depositing the fruits of this labour in countless gross green piles, strewn across the pathway and lawn, like so many squishy landmines.

The adults, upon giving us a quick gander, turn and address the young. The alphas quickly shoo their little charges down the slope and into the safety of the pond. SchuBRT, having seen geese so often, takes only a passing interest. We keep walking. And then it begins...

Once he sees his extended family is now safely pooping in the pond, Mr. Alpha, with decided deliberation, climbs back up the slope and positions himself directly ahead of us, right in the middle of the paved path. Much to my surprise, he does not lower his head in anticipation of one of his famous chases. Rather, he stands menacingly erect, stretching his entire body towards the sky. He raises his head stiffly upright, and spreads those enormous wings outwards, tensely splaying his large flight feathers like taut fingers.

Without so much as a honk, he fearlessly and threateningly waddles straight towards us, wings still outstretched, as if to prevent us from skirting around him. I think that, perhaps, I should turn around and retreat. But then my mind quickly turns towards the very intelligent guard dog beside me. I certainly don't want to send him the message that geese were something to be protected from; this would, without a doubt, set a nasty precedent for future encounters. But there is no time to ponder. I stay calm, unruffled. We keep walking forward. So does the goose.

I keep glancing down at SchuBRT to make sure he is still calm. We are now about twenty yards apart and closing. This is surreal. Here I am, playing "chicken" with a goose. Which of us would flinch first? Fifteen yards. Ten yards. And then... uh oh... a BIG flinch!

SchuBRT has had enough. He breaks ranks and charges. The goose panics. Honking like a madman (or mad goose), he quickly turns. He frantically flies towards the safety of Rumble Pond. The downward slope of the embankment helps his flight path. He is already four feet off the ground. Almost there. But unbeknownst to the goose, he has a real problem. For although SchuBRT is built like a Russian weight lifter, he actually runs like a gazelle. And just as Mr. Alpha thinks he is safely out of reach, SchuBRT leaps.

Like a deadly, hairy guided missile, SchuBRT rockets through the air. With a loud smacking thump, that massive hairy chest smashes broadside into the hapless bird. Those huge jaws close around the goose's vulnerable neck. Instant panic ensues. Oh, the humanity!

Feathers fly everywhere. The goose is screaming. The goslings are pooping in the pond. This is going to be ugly! But then suddenly, SchuBRT releases his grip, and lands with a graceful thud upon the grassy knoll. The goose, still desperately flailing its wings, continues spinning headlong out of control. Totally stripped of his former dignity, he splashes down heavily but safely into the pond below.

Without a sound, SchuBRT, tail up, tongue lolling out, and eyes filled with a mischievous spark, prances back and takes his place, heeling at my side as if nothing happened. Then smiling, hairy ear to hairy ear, he proudly looks up at me as if to say, "I could'a killed him, Dad… but I didn't!"

Seasons have since passed, but the big goose's attitude has not mellowed with age. Except that whenever SchuBRT and I approach, he turns away, throws a bitter but wounded evil eye our way and, begrudgingly, gives the two of us a respectfully wide berth to pass.

It appears that news travels fast in the goose community. Since that day, not a single one has dared to approach or threaten us, regardless of the situation. And with peace re-established, SchuBRT has kept and maintained his casual disinterest towards the geese. The truce remains intact. But now, everyone knows that there is a new Mr. Alpha at Rumble Pond Park.

~Ian Kochberg

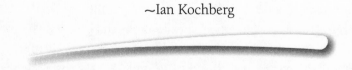

The Sentinel

Even the tiniest poodle is lionhearted, ready to do anything
to defend home, master, and mistress.
~Louis Sabin

"Here kitty, kitty," our green parakeet, Maggie, said, leaning down from her perch. "Meow." Her endless taunting frustrated our menagerie of cats. I frequently caught them eyeing her, their whiskers twitching and their tongues running hungrily across their lips.

Then it happened. I arrived home from work, surprised that my overzealous American Eskimo dog did not greet me.

"Jake," I called, but the tapping of claws across the hardwood floor didn't happen. Neither did the exuberant barked greeting I was accustomed to. Something was wrong.

I walked into the kitchen, then back out to the living room, calling for my dog again. Stepping through the door of the family room, I stopped. Maggie's cage was on the floor, seeds scattered and water spilled. Since her wings were clipped, she wasn't able to fly to safety, so she was on the floor as well. Hopping back and forth and chirping apprehensively, Maggie was being watched by five attentive cats, their tails swishing across the carpet.

There was only one thing standing between a parakeet feast and their growling tummies—Jake, the ever vigilant guard of all members of the Caye household, whether human, furry, or feathered. Jake sat facing the cats, baring a bit of teeth if one of them so much as lifted a paw, while Maggie paced behind him.

After the cats were shooed out of the room, I set the cage upright onto its stand. Maggie eagerly hopped from my finger back into her sanctuary, chattering gratefully for a moment before resuming her usual, "Here kitty, kitty. Meow. Meow."

Jake looked up at me and I patted him on the head. Then we went into the kitchen for the treat jar. If ever he earned a reward, it was the day he saved the parakeet. Good dog.

~Hana Haatainen-Caye

Puppy Love

You know you're in love when you don't want to fall asleep because reality is finally better than your dreams.

~Dr. Seuss

Although I'd dreamed of my honeymoon often, I never imagined any part of it would involve a four-month-old Dalmatian. Like most brides, I pictured an intimate get-away—even if we were just driving a few hours away, the travel would still be part of the romantic journey. On the day of the wedding, however, our puppy-sitter backed out on us. No one else was able to step in. Board our baby in a kennel? We didn't have the heart. So our honeymoon became a trip for three.

Mike and I picked up our last-minute passenger at my father's place, where he'd been waiting in the bedroom. He'd eaten my shoes.

"Not off to a good start, Schuyler," I said.

Throughout the two-hour drive from Vermont to Montreal, Schuyler whined in his crate in the back. We pulled over to take him out for a walk. Again. And again. Four-month-old puppies don't have the best control.

Then a surprise storm brought snow and ice that pelted the highway. We inched along in blizzard conditions. Gripping the wheel, Mike's knuckles turned as white as the falling flakes. When Schuyler's whines forced us to make another stop, I slogged through frigid drifts up to my knees. Finally we reached the Canadian border. We were almost there. Things were bound to improve now.

A border officer peered into our car. "May I see your immunization records?"

"Oh dear, I didn't know I'd need them. I'm sure I'm up to date,
though," I stammered. "I just had a checkup."

"Not yours. The dog's." The officer scowled.

Schuyler scratched at his crate door. Mike smiled at the officer
hopefully. "Oh, he's had his puppy shots, but we don't have the papers
with us." He laughed lightly. "We weren't planning on bringing our
dog on our honeymoon."

It didn't matter. The officer wasn't interested. "He needs a rabies
shot," the man said.

"Sir, it'll be taken care of," Mike replied. "He's scheduled for one
back home with our vet."

"Just get him a rabies shot now, or you can't take the dog across
the border."

I glanced back at our puppy. In our hurry to pack his food and
supplies, we never thought of this.

The officer gave us directions to a veterinarian about five miles
back in Vermont. There was nothing to do but turn around.

We considered giving up and going home, but the weather conditions were far from ideal, and the two-hour trip back would surely
take at least twice as long. Besides, Montreal was only a stone's throw
away, if only we could get across that border!

Happy to be out of the car, Schuyler bounded into the vet's office.
"Will the rabies shot make him feel ill?" I asked. The veterinarian assured
us it was okay. He very kindly administered the immunization, and very
kindly charged us an exorbitant fee for his services. That veterinarian
had a sweet deal being located so close to the border.

Finally, we arrived at a pet-friendly hotel in Montreal. Well, to be
clear, the hotel allowed pets, but the experience was far from friendly.
No special amenities in the room, no designated place to walk your
dog. Once again, I climbed over mountainous drifts, Schuyler and I
blazing a trail in the deep snow.

In the room, I changed into a slinky black dress to go out to
dinner. We'd managed a passing glimpse of the dining room on the

way in, and it looked inviting. Mike buttoned his new blue dress shirt. "We'll be back," he told Schuyler, scratching our pup's ears. Schuyler looked at us with sad eyes. The minute we left the room, he started crying. As we made our way down the hall, the whines turned to torturous barks.

"We can't leave him barking like that," I said. "We'll get kicked out."

Dinner that night? Room service, with an extra burger for Schuyler. And our wedding night was certainly cozy, as Schuyler squeezed his chubby little body between us and snored peacefully.

We headed back home the next morning. What was the point? And yet, as we traveled along the winter-white roads, I couldn't help smiling. At the next pit stop, Mike threw a snowball. I threw one back. Schuyler ran and jumped to catch it. The three of us romped and played together until we were nearly frozen.

We let Schuyler join us in the front seat of the parked car as we sipped takeout cups of cocoa from a nearby restaurant. He wriggled until he found just the right position, and fell asleep. Mike gave me a kiss, and we held hands.

At that moment, it was perfect—just being with the wonderful man I'd married, and our warm, spotted puppy snuggled between us on the car seat. I wouldn't have dreamed it, but yes, it was even romantic.

~Peggy Frezon

Chapter
8

The Dog Did What?

Meant to Be

That Dog

We derive immeasurable good, uncounted pleasures, enormous security, and many critical lessons about life by owning dogs.
~Roger Caras

You know that TV commercial that starts with heart-wrenching images of abused and abandoned dogs and cats while Sarah McLachlan sings "Angel," then Sarah herself appears, petting a big white dog, and asks for donations to help the animals? Well, that was my dog.

When my husband first saw Dylan in the animal shelter in Chilliwack, British Columbia (a few years before the video), we weren't even looking to get a dog. My husband was only there for an unrelated meeting with the shelter manager. But when he met Dylan through the bars of the kennel, they had an immediate connection. I was at home with our four-year-old daughter when Craig called to ask, "What would you say if I came home with a dog?" He had other meetings to go to in the area, but would stop by the shelter again before returning to Vancouver and would make the decision then.

Danielle and I waited, not knowing whether Craig would arrive home alone or with a dog. Of course, when he came through the door, Dylan was with him. We loved Dylan instantly. But he was also a handful. A Lab mix, at four and a half months old, he was already tall and gangly. And while he'd been on his best behaviour when my husband took him for a walk by the shelter, he now jumped and pulled and chewed with joyful exuberance. He also was not house-trained.

At that time, I was a stay-at-home mom and my husband worked in a building that did not allow pets, so Dylan stayed home with Danielle and me. I have fibromyalgia (similar to chronic fatigue syndrome) and found the combination of looking after a young daughter and a young dog exhausting.

But Dylan was smart, confident and good-natured. In very little time, he caught on to the house rules (happily bending a few of them if we let him) and became an indispensable part of our family. He grew up alongside our daughter. Sometimes they even had the same conflicts and rivalries that human siblings have (though usually inadvertent on Dylan's part). It was after one of the times he had knocked over a Lego set-up or chewed one of her doll's feet that Danielle remarked, "Sometimes it's hard being the sister of a dog." At other times, Danielle was happy to run around the yard with Dylan, or curl up next to him on the living room floor, her head resting on his soft, thick fur.

As much as my daughter and I loved Dylan, however, he was my husband's dog. A few years after we got Dylan, I broke my hip in a skiing mishap. By then, my husband's office had moved to a building that allowed animals. So while I was recovering, Craig took Dylan to work with him each day. Dylan soon became a fixture at the office. He had become much more laidback with age and was content to hang out most of the day on his bed near Craig's desk, reminding Craig to take a break for lunch and not work too late. Every once in a while, he got up to walk around the office, stopping to say hello and beg for a pet or a treat from everyone else who worked there. Long after my hip had recovered, Dylan continued to go to work with Craig.

Dylan was also a humane educator and meeting arbitrator. Craig took him into elementary school classes to meet with children and help teach them about animal care and safety around dogs. Dylan sat in on work meetings and negotiations, easing any tensions with his relaxed presence, and standing up to step in between people when any arguments arose (at home, he also broke up fights between our two cats).

When singer Sarah McLachlan volunteered to help the British Columbia Society for the Prevention of Cruelty to Animals (BC SPCA) with an ad to call for donations to help animals, Dylan was ready to join her in front of the camera. All Craig had to do was ask Dylan to "sit" and "stay" while the lights shone and the cameras rolled. After a few takes, the director asked, "Can you stop him from panting?"

"Sorry," said Craig. "The lights are too hot." Dylan stopped panting only long enough to lick the make-up off one side of Sarah's face. Luckily, she didn't mind.

The commercial first aired in 2006 for the BC SPCA, then was later revised for the American Society for the Prevention of Cruelty to Animals (ASPCA). Since then, it has raised over two million dollars for the BC SPCA and over thirty million dollars for the ASPCA, and has received over a million views on YouTube. It even made everyone cry on an episode of the TV series *Modern Family*.

People often asked if the big white dog in the video was available for adoption. We were happy to say that we'd adopted him, and that he was part of our family.

Dylan died of cancer at age twelve, almost three years ago now. We still miss him. It's been a while since the video with Dylan and Sarah McLachlan aired regularly, but sometimes we still see it when we're watching TV late at night. And there he is—our big wonderful dog, alive, panting, his tongue hanging out. As Sarah pets him, I remember the feel of his soft, thick fur under my own hand, and it's almost as if Dylan is sending us a message that he remembers us too.

~Jacqueline Pearce

Editor's note: Watch the British Columbia SPCA video featuring Dylan: http://youtu.be/9gspElv1yvc

74

Destiny Dog

A person who has never owned a dog has missed a wonderful part of life.
~Bob Barker

M y kids love animals. Over the years, we've collected a menagerie of lower-maintenance critters: fish, aquatic frogs, hamsters, and even briefly, a praying mantis. But those weren't enough. My kids wanted a dog.

Getting a dog posed several problems for our family. One is that three out of five of us are allergic to dogs. So any dog we adopted would have to be the hypoallergenic type.

The second hurdle was my husband. After watching our kids grieve the other critters' deaths — even the praying mantis — he didn't want more drama.

But the third and biggest obstacle was me. I had no desire to get up at night with a puppy just when my kids were finally sleeping through the night, or to worry about a dog chewing my shoes. The inevitable vet bills would surely strain our already tight budget. And I wasn't excited about dog smell in my house. But mostly, with three kids and a growing writing career, I didn't have time. I didn't need the stress of something else to take care of.

Then I started noticing dogs on the street. Kind of like when I started noticing babies shortly before I decided to become pregnant. Uh-oh. Maybe somewhere deep down, I wanted a dog too. One morning I met two gorgeous Portuguese Water Dogs outside a coffee shop.

They were sweet and, according to their owner, hypoallergenic and great with kids. Hmmm.

I mentioned this encounter to my oldest and within seconds she was researching Portuguese Water Dogs. The first fact she uncovered was that they cost around $2,000. Yikes.

I told her we couldn't possibly afford that.

But my daughter had correctly sensed the crack in my resolve. She hounded me day after day, showing me online pictures and research. But after a couple of weeks passed, I again came to my senses. I didn't have time for a dog. Especially as my youngest was headed to first grade. I would finally have the house to myself. No kids to take care of during the day! I could get work done!

I also knew that my oldest wouldn't leave me alone. So, thinking that I could pacify her, I made a list of all the criteria that would need to be met for me to agree to getting a dog. I told her that if she found a dog with everything on my list, we would adopt it. My demands were ridiculously specific and — I thought — absolutely unattainable:

- Must be a Portuguese Water Dog. Because of the dander allergy.
- Must be an adult. In fact, must be middle-aged. Old enough to be calm but not so old as to have health issues.
- Must be fully trained. No way did I have the time to train a dog.
- Must be inexpensive. We have a tight budget.
- Must be good with kids — in other words, must tolerate my five-year-old son.
- Must be black in color. I like black. Black is slimming.

I figured that no one could ever find a dog that met my specifications. I was very pleased with my own cleverness.

One week later, my daughter rescued a sick, abandoned cat on our block. A neighbor drove her to the local animal shelter to drop off the animal. While there, my daughter cruised through the adoptable dog section.

That afternoon, she came bursting through the door, babbling about a Portuguese Water Dog at the shelter. Yeah sure, I thought. But I called anyway.

"Yes, we have a Portuguese Water Dog here," the worker said. "If you're interested you'd better come now because purebreds go quickly."

My son and I drove to the shelter. We walked up to the kennel, and sure enough, the sign read Portuguese Water Dog.

Portuguese Water Dog, check.

I looked down at a mess of an animal with dark, matted fur. A long, black nose poked through the chain link and a wet tongue licked my hand.

Black in color, check. She is really cute, I thought.

I took the rug-with-a-tongue out in the yard and she chased a ball for me and my son, gently but enthusiastically.

Good with my son, check.

Then the dog jumped up on me and I nearly fell backwards from the odor. She smelled horrible, worse than any dog I'd ever encountered. As I backed away, I snapped a picture with my phone and sent it to my husband, who was out of town.

We walked the dog back to the front desk, and I flagged down a worker.

"I have some questions," I said. Surely this purebred dog wasn't up for adoption.

"Are you interested?" she asked. "If you are, you should start on the paperwork."

I didn't touch the stack of forms she slid in front of me. "Did you know she's trained?" the peppy worker continued. "She sits and walks on a leash."

Trained, check. Seriously?

"The vet thinks she's about five years old. Lots of good years left," the worker said. "That breed lives to be eleven or twelve."

Middle-aged, check. You've got to be kidding me.

I finally got a word in edgewise and asked about the cost.

"Two hundred and fifty dollars," she answered.

Inexpensive, check. (At least compared to two grand.)

The checkmarks were piling up fast. How was I going to get out of this?

Then a man walked by and pointed to the dog. "Hey," he said, "is she up for adoption?"

I instinctively pulled the furry beast close. "No!" I said. Did I say that out loud? What was wrong with me? I reached down and pushed black curls from the dog's eyes. She looked at me and my heart turned over.

I put a twenty-four-hour hold on her and went home to think it over.

As I lay in bed that night thinking, I made a deal with the universe. If my reluctant husband gave the okay, we would adopt the dog.

My phone buzzed. A text from my husband.

"Is she ours?" the message read.

The next day we drove to the shelter. When I arrived, one of the workers said, "It's a good thing you put a hold on your dog. We got over fifty calls this morning asking for her."

"Why now?" I asked. The woman explained that there had been a technical glitch, and the picture of our dog had just been posted on their website the day before. "That dog's been here over a week," the worker said. "Her picture should've been posted sooner."

It felt like destiny. Our new dog blended seamlessly into our family and is an especially good companion to me. She sits at my feet as I write, and accompanies me as I chauffeur the kids around. Instead of adding stress to my life, she calms me. We're two middle-aged ladies who suit each other.

The shelter named our dog Portia. But I changed it to Porsche, because I figure she's my midlife crisis.

I didn't want a dog, but apparently, I needed one.

~Tiffany Doerr Guerzon

75

Chicken Soup for the Soul

You Gotta Love a Tootsie

Fate loves the fearless.
~James Russell Lowell

Several years ago, I founded a Labrador Retriever rescue. With the job came many perks: kisses, handshakes and snuggle time. With it also came heartache and irritation.

I found myself in total disbelief at the number of Labs stranded and abandoned in shelters. Who would want to give up a Lab? Or any pet for that matter. It was mind-boggling, frustrating, and extremely upsetting. Those emotions were what fueled my desire to help as many of these precious animals as I could.

My rescue work often led me to a shelter in South Carolina. I lived in Georgia at the time, so making this lengthy trip was always tough, but it was worthwhile. On one particular trip, I had the pleasure of meeting one of my feistiest rescues yet.

As I pulled into the shelter, I was greeted by Brandy, the shelter manager. Brandy always tried her hardest to save as many animals as she could. She knew that my five-hour drive should not be in vain, so typically she would "save me" four or five Labs that were about to be killed.

We gave our standard greeting and then she took me to the holding tank, where she had four beautiful chocolate Labs in need of saving. They had already been spayed and neutered.

I gave Brandy a quick hug. "Thank you again for helping me help these Labs."

I noticed that Brandy had something on her mind. I was eager to get on the road, but I had time to be a friend.

"Brandy, what's up? You seem a little down."

"Lisa, I kinda need your help with something. I hate to spring this on you, but…"

I interrupted. "Go ahead. You know if I can do it I will, and if I can't I will anyway."

This made Brandy laugh and she relaxed a little.

"I have a senior Lab in the back. She tested heartworm positive and is in really bad shape. Every rescue that has come by has turned her away. Can you just look at her for me? No pressure."

No pressure? This was nothing but pressure. But I promised I would take a quick look.

We headed to the back of the shelter, which I often referred to as death row. If a shelter puts a dog all the way in the back, the chances for adoption are pretty slim.

When we approached the kennel, I looked down and just had to laugh out loud. Brandy looked at me a little strangely.

"Oh my, this Lab is adorable." I saw a chunky chocolate and rather round, older girl, with a silvery-gray muzzle. She even had gray between her paws. She looked right up at me and gave a simple bark, letting me know she didn't appreciate my chuckle. "She is built like a Tootsie Roll!"

This, of course, caused Brandy to laugh and then we both looked down to see our senior girl wagging her tail. I walked into the kennel and sat down. Looking at Brandy I said, "You know I am going to have to call her Tootsie; it would be a crime not to."

Tootsie seemed to like her new name and curled right up in my lap as if she'd known me forever. I knew beyond a shadow of a doubt that I couldn't leave her there. She needed to be in a loving home and spoiled rotten for whatever time she had left.

"I can't thank you enough." Brandy was just about in tears. "Tomorrow was her scheduled kill-date and I just didn't know what I was going to do."

We walked Ms. Tootsie to the front office and I filled out her paperwork. In the meantime the other four Labs inspected her from head to toe, and she didn't like it. Out of nowhere came a ferocious growl that made me put my pen down.

To my amazement, the other Labs crouched down in a submissive stance. This old girl had laid down the law. She was a lady, and ladies don't wish to be sniffed from head to toe. I would discover that this was one confident, savvy, and courageous dog!

I loaded up my original four Labs and realized I had nowhere for Tootsie except for the front seat. She gladly took it.

"Thanks again, Lisa," Brandy said. "You just made my day."

I smiled. "No, Brandy, you just made mine."

With that, I hopped in my 4Runner ready to go home. Glancing over at Tootsie, I smiled. This silvery, round senior sat tall and majestically, with her eyes facing forward… towards her new life.

Tootsie came through her heartworm treatments like a champ. The vet also treated her for several skin irritations and an inner ear problem. This girl had been in bad shape. She even managed to gain a few more pounds, which only added to her delightful girth.

About two months after I rescued Tootsie, a delightful couple named Sue and Bill, a little older themselves, came to spend some time with a yellow female Lab named Hannah. After about an hour, they decided that Hannah just might be the one for them.

"Honey, I'm home!" my husband announced. He had taken a quick trip to the feed store and had taken Tootsie with him as usual. As the two strolled into the den, I heard Sue let out a small gasp.

"Oh my…" Sue sat on the loveseat and motioned for Tootsie to come to her, which she gladly did.

"Is this girl in need of a home?" Bill asked. "Because I think my wife just fell in love."

The love was mutual. It was as if those two had known each other for a lifetime. Tootsie and Sue were in heaven and completely oblivious to anyone else. I knew Tootsie had just found her forever home.

Hannah went on to find her own forever home with a household full of little girls, which was just what she needed. And the last I heard about Tootsie, well let's just say that sleeping in Sue and Bill's bed, sharing their morning breakfast and vacationing at their beach house was right up her alley.

~Lisa Morris

76

Ten Pounds of Comfort

Happiness is a warm puppy.
~Charles M. Schulz

My husband wasn't thrilled about the addition of another dog—and a puppy at that—but for some reason I had to have the miniature Dachshund! At home, I placed him on the floor and watched him dart around sniffing the tile. Our other Dachshund curiously sniffed the interloper.

In the wee morning hours, I heard his slight whimpers downstairs and tiptoed down to check on our puppy. When he saw me, his cries ceased. He wagged his tail and yelped with playfulness. I took him out into the cool, still dark, yard to do his business.

That's when it hit me. This isn't right. He isn't for me! The feeling wouldn't go away. I felt compelled to give this puppy to Mom and Dad. I knew it was ridiculous, yet I wanted to present this bouncing puppy to my parents.

Long retired, my parents were aged. Dad was slow and shaky on his feet. Mom often felt trapped at home and restless. Both loved dogs, but hadn't had one in years. They won't want a puppy, I reasoned, it's way too much work. Then I mused about their reaction to this tiny bundle of love, his inviting brown eyes and gentle temperament. I knew of the research on animal therapy—animals raise spirits and help people relax.

My folks seemed depressed and lonely even though they had a busy schedule. They were involved in church and had neighborhood friends. But they were overwhelmed with weighty decisions about my elderly grandmother in the nursing home and the sale of her property. I felt sad that at this time of their life they were burdened with caring for others rather than living carefree. Their neighborhood was becoming unsafe and they needed to relocate. They repeatedly struggled with the need and the fear of moving to a retirement community. Dad blamed Mom for not wanting to move. Mom insisted that Dad was being the stubborn one. Fret, worry and numerous decisions weakened Mom's ability to think clearly. She became anxious. Her anxiety came out as hostility. Mom and Dad argued often about Grandma's care, their need to move, wills, bills, and illnesses.

I told my husband that I wanted to give the new puppy to Mom and Dad. I wanted to help my parents during this stressful time of their life.

"But they won't want a puppy," he replied.

"Yes, but I have to follow my conscience. Maybe it's some kind of divine guidance."

We kept the puppy for a few weeks to train him. He needed to be housebroken, to get on a schedule, and to learn to sit and wait at the door so he wouldn't trip Dad.

Then, on a sunny day, we drove the hour to my parents' house with the little Dachshund contentedly riding on my lap. From his mouth jutted the ever-present tongue as I stroked his soft ears. I felt a mix of anticipation and sadness at the thought of giving him away.

We pulled into their driveway and I jumped out of the car. "Here! Happy Father's Day, Happy Anniversary, Happy Birthday, and Merry Christmas," I said as I shoved the puppy into Dad's arms.

Silently he stroked the little pet. "What's this all about?"

"It's for you," I said. "I also brought you a kennel, puppy food, collar and leash. Plus he's had his immunizations and he's housebroken."

They began to examine him like a newborn. "Oh, look at that tongue," Mom said. "I forgot how little Dachshund pups are."

"He's cute," added Dad. "What should we call him?"

We talked, laughed, tried different names, and watched their puppy explore his new home. There were no ugly arguments. My husband and I drove home cheerfully chattering although I missed the little dog.

The next day, I phoned to ask about the puppy. "I think he'll be your dad's dog. He seems to favor him," Mom said, after describing their first night. Then she recounted what the dog was doing and how he was behaving. Excitedly she said, "Now he's following me around the house."

I asked, "What are you going to call him?"

"I like the name Tylo because it was my favorite aunt's name for her dog." I never knew Mom had a favorite aunt from childhood. "I take Tylo when I go for my walk," she told me. "Your dad holds him to watch TV." Warm feelings flooded over me as I heard the lightness in her voice.

Months later my husband observed, "Your folks are less stressed. It's like they have a new life to think about rather than an old, fading one. Maybe there's something to this pet therapy."

The anger, loneliness, and fretting disappeared, replaced with Tylo stories. "He's a great traveler," Mom exclaimed. They take him everywhere—even to Grandma's nursing home.

One thing bothers me. They never bought me as many as toys and treats as they do for Tylo.

~Brenda Nixon

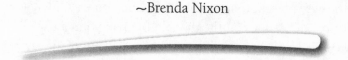

All for the Love of Patty

A dog is the only thing on earth that loves you more than he loves himself.
~Josh Billings

I knew we were in trouble. Our family's old Shepherd-Rottweiler mix, Grizz, had died. Now our middle-school-aged daughter wanted a replacement.

"Honey, we still have one dog," I said, pointing to Tundra, our Shiba Inu.

"She's yours, Mom," Patty said. "I'd miss Grizz less if I had my own dog."

That weekend my husband, Jake, showed me an ad for hybrid wolf cubs. "We won't buy one," he assured me. "We'll just go for a ride in the country to look at the pups. It'll help take Patty's mind off Grizz."

I should have known better.

When we arrived at the breeder's acreage, a large white pup with black saddle-like markings raced to greet us. He covered Patty's face with exuberant doggy kisses. It was love at first sight for both of them.

While Patty romped with the puppy my husband asked, "How big will he get?"

"He's the alpha male. He'll be around 150 pounds," the breeder replied cheerfully.

One hundred and fifty pounds?

I turned to my husband to say, "Absolutely not," but it was too late.

Patty was bouncing in her father's arms. "Pleeease, Daddy. I'll take care of him. He already loves me. I can tell."

We drove home with the pup snuggled in her lap.

"It's stormy today," our daughter said from the back seat. "Maybe I'll name him Stormy." The pup woofed in agreement, and it was settled.

When we arrived home we discovered Stormy was already as big as Tundra. The new pup playfully pounced on her. Tundra growled a "back off, I'm top dog here" warning. Stormy complied, and from that point on they were buddies.

Patty took on the task of housebreaking. For the first three nights she woke multiple times to take Stormy outside. The fourth day Patty collapsed on the sofa and exclaimed, "If taking care of a dog is this much work, I'm never having kids!"

Against my better judgment, Stormy slept in Patty's room. I'd find them snuggled together, her arm draped over his warm body, both sound asleep.

One evening I peeked in to find Patty curled in a blanket on the floor. Stormy snoozed on her bed, his furry head resting on her pillow.

"What's going on?" I asked in disbelief.

"He's so big now we can't both fit on the bed," Patty explained.

I expelled the dog with the strict instruction, "Stormy is not to sleep on your bed anymore."

The next afternoon I found them nestled together, napping comfortably on my king-sized bed.

Patty loved her new dog, and he returned her love multiplied. She taught him to stand on his hind legs and brace his forelegs against her. At first his little puppy paws reached her knees. Patty continued to employ his "up" command even when Stormy, at 160 pounds, far outweighed her, and she had to brace against a wall for support.

Stormy proved himself intelligent and curious. His exploratory missions included the kitchen garbage. I moved the trashcan to the broom closet, safely enclosed behind a wooden sliding door.

Stormy watched intently the first time I slid the door open to toss out a tantalizing pile of chicken bones. I shut the door, and Stormy immediately pushed his nose into the door's circular finger hole. He slid the door open with his muzzle, and triumphantly plunged into the trash.

When he was young, Stormy entertained himself by redecorating. He pulled pictures off the walls and knickknacks from the end tables whenever we left the house. We'd come home to claw marks in the drywall, and chewed candle stubs on the carpet.

Stormy didn't understand the correlation between his destructive behavior and our dismayed reactions. While Tundra quivered in fear in the middle of the mess, Stormy raced to meet Patty with his "I'm so glad you're home" kisses.

We began purchasing our decor at Goodwill.

The breaking point came the day Stormy greeted us at the door wearing a smashed lampshade around his neck. He'd eaten part of the lamp, including the bulb.

He couldn't squeeze into a dog crate, so we set up an outdoor kennel in our once-beautiful finished basement. Patty filled the chain-link kennel with his favorite blankets and chew toys. We congratulated ourselves on our ingenuity and left for church while Stormy settled into his plush new crate.

That afternoon Stormy greeted us at the front door, a piece of wire dangling from his raw mouth.

He'd chewed through the chain-link fence.

My husband reinforced the kennel with thick hog-wire paneling. After a few weeks of kennel training, Stormy gave up "remodeling."

When Patty left for school in a neighboring state, Stormy was inconsolable. He stopped eating and refused to play with Tundra. Stormy wandered the house looking for Patty, often staring out the window as he waited for her return.

With our daughter away, I worked overtime, sometimes coming home as late as 3 a.m. Those quiet, pre-dawn hours became my prayer time. The dogs dozed as I paced the living room, lifting my petitions to heaven.

Whenever I prayed for Patty, Stormy rose to pace with me, step by step. The moment my prayer focus shifted to someone else, Stormy lay down again.

Unnerved, I told my husband about it.

"Stormy's walking with you because you're saying Patty's name," he reasoned.

"No, Jake, he does it even when I'm praying silently," I explained.

Stumped by Stormy's uncanny knowledge, we attributed it to his love for Patty.

Years passed, and Patty laid aside her "If puppy care is this hard I'm never having kids" declaration. She gave birth to a beautiful son, Asher.

Stormy was careful and gentle around the baby. Although Stormy showed no special devotion toward little Asher, the dog kept watch over the baby. I believe he did it out of love for Patty.

When Asher started toddling, Tundra steered clear of him, leaving Stormy to suffer the indignities of a drooling child dogging his every step.

All for the love of Patty.

As Stormy aged he developed joint problems. Medications worked for a few years, but the day came when the old dog couldn't go on. Patty made the heart-wrenching decision to put him to sleep.

While Stormy lay on the table in the veterinarian's office, Patty stood at her dog's side. She stroked his fur and spoke words of love as the vet gave Stormy his final injection.

"He's gone now," the vet told Patty, and left her alone in the room to mourn.

Choking back tears, Patty whispered the words she'd repeated since their first day together, "You're a good boy, Stormy. I love you."

Her sobs cut off unexpectedly as Stormy's huge, limp body slid off the table into her arms.

The vet returned to find Patty cradling her dog's slack form.

"He was already dead," the vet said. "It must have been a muscular contraction."

My heart tells me otherwise. I believe that even as death pulled him away, Stormy heard her, and gave one final, mighty effort to snuggle closer.

All for the love of Patty.

~Jeanie Jacobson

A Better Life

*The hunger for love is much more difficult to remove
than the hunger for bread.*
~Mother Teresa

The malnourished Shih Tzu looked at the camera with sad eyes, its tail tucked between its legs. How could this sweet, helpless creature have been so mistreated? And what could I do about it? Fifteen dogs had been rescued from a woman who hoarded over fifty dogs, cats and horses. Some were so far gone it was too late for them and most were starving. Those that survived were scheduled to be destroyed. This little guy was one of them. Something about his teddy-bear-like face called to me. I knew I had to help him.

My next step was to convince my husband we should take on another pet. We already had a ten-year-old cat named Moose and a five-year-old Shih Tzu named Panda. I have a soft spot for Shih Tzus, having grown up with one as my best friend. That particular dog, Nikki, had gotten a sensitive teenager through some rough times with his unconditional love. It was my turn to pay his gift forward. I was hoping my husband would see it that way too.

After some discussion, we agreed to foster the dog to see if it would be a good fit for us. We didn't know what to expect from a dog that had been neglected and quite possibly abused. We were also unsure how our other pets would react and we needed permission from our landlords to bring another animal into the house. If we couldn't keep him, I knew he would still have the opportunity to be placed in a good home.

We met the dogs' rescuer, Judy, at the kennels and were shocked by the little Shih Tzu's condition. His coat was so short that pink skin and ribs showed through. Dried mud and what looked like dried blood was caked on some of the hairs. He had an eye-watering stench. One of his eyes had a milky white spot in the middle and he was missing all but one short front tooth, so his tongue slid partway out. His skinny little tail was tucked between his legs. This dog had seen rough times and needed some attention.

We knelt down and he approached us without hesitation. He rubbed against us like a cat and licked our hands while we petted him. He even rolled on his back so we would rub his belly. I fell in love with him then and there.

We had brought Panda with us and the two sniffed each other in greeting and seemed fine together. That was all we needed to know. Though he had no belongings, no name and we had no way of knowing his age, we brought him home with us.

Luckily, our cat Moose just ignored him as he explored his new surroundings. Loud noises caused him to jump and he flinched at sudden movements. When he lifted his leg on our couch, I was able to race him outside and praise him for finishing on the grass. He didn't seem to know any basic commands and wouldn't come when called. And when given his freedom, he would take off at full speed and we had to race to catch up to him. He had a lot to learn.

While he and Panda got to know each other in the back yard, my husband and I debated whether we had done the right thing. Here was a dog that had been traumatized and had no training. We had two pets already, limited finances and were set to move within the month.

"I'm not sure I want to take on the stress and responsibility of another dog," my husband said.

"I know," I said miserably. "I don't know that I want to either."

My husband's eyes widened in surprise.

"What is it?" I turned around to see what he was looking at. The dog was lying on the deck, his ears drooping, his sad eyes watching us.

"I think he heard us," my husband said.

I shooed the dog off the deck so we could continue our discussion, but he returned to my side immediately. I glanced at my husband, who shrugged.

"I don't really want to get rid of him, but I don't know if I'm capable of all the added work that will be necessary to train him." I kept an eye on the dog as I spoke. He dropped to the ground, put his head on his paws and stared up at us dejectedly. I was stunned. Could this dog really understand what we were saying?

"We can't get rid of him now!" my husband cried. "Look at him!"

And that's how our decision to foster a dog lasted for less than a day. We called Judy and told her we were keeping him. We got him a new collar, leash, bed, food, treats and toys. He needed three baths and a professional grooming before his coat went from tan and gray to silky black and white. And finally we gave him a name that seemed to fit him: Koala.

We were able to crate train him and teach him commands. He never went potty inside again. He still hesitated at the word "come," but we improvised by clapping and calling his name. We were always adapting, and it was always an adventure. Koala had some quirks, like swallowing my husband's earplugs, growling to get our attention, sticking his behind in the air if you scratched the right spot, doing a dance when he saw his food, panicking if someone cleared their throat, and sleeping on the floor of the closet under our clothes. The only thing that really mattered was that he had become a beloved member of our family.

Not long ago, we learned Koala had congenital kidney disease and was in the early stages of failure. It was heartbreaking because I wanted him to live a long and happy life. But my husband helped me realize that in rescuing him, loving him and taking care of him, we were giving him a great life. And no matter what, no matter how long he has left, we will never regret bringing him into our family. He shows us his love every day in the way he rubs against us, licks our hands, snorts happily when we come home or sits in our laps gazing up at us with his tongue sticking out of his mouth. And though it might have taken a few days, once that now-fluffy tail of his curled up and started wagging, it was never tucked between his legs again.

~Kristi Cocchiarella FitzGerald

79

Comet Dog

Faithful friends are gifts from heaven:
Whoever finds one has found a treasure.
~Author Unknown

I first noticed him as I drove around the boat basin in the small fishing village near where we lived. He was strutting along and was the cutest little dog I had ever seen. He had something special about him. I wondered who would have let such a beautiful creature loose.

I assumed that he must have belonged to a tourist somewhere nearby.

Later that night, I felt a restlessness I couldn't explain to my husband. "I just have to go for a drive" was the best explanation I had for leaving on one of the rare nights during fishing season when he was home.

I found myself back at the basin, parked near the restrooms and kiosk. Sure enough, the little fellow was still there. The weather had turned wet and cold, and he looked a bit bedraggled. I realized he had nowhere to go. But no amount of cajoling would get him into my car. Although he liked the attention, he stayed just out of grasp.

I went home and got food and water. No dice.

I went back home again, and explained to Tim, my husband, about the lost little dog. I thought that maybe he didn't like my car, so we headed back to the basin with our two other vehicles.

Still no success. By now the poor pooch was soaked.

Suddenly I heard a voice. It was either God or my father, and it very clearly said, "Go home and get a big bath towel, stupid. You'll need to dry him anyway." I figured God probably wouldn't call me stupid, so it must have been my dad.

We returned to the house, one mile straight uphill. I switched back to the first car, already loaded with beach towels and a very impressive heater. This time when I got out, holding open a big, fluffy towel, the puppy was mine!

Since he looked like a half-drowned red teddy bear by the time I caught him, I named him "Rainbear."

When we went to bed, he knew just where a dog should sleep. He scooted right under the covers between us.

"Too bad it's so stormy tonight," Tim said. "We could have seen Hale-Bopp while we were out."

I had forgotten the comet was passing over us in a path it took only once a century or so.

"Maybe he's the ex-dog of the Dalai Lama," I joked. "The comet picked him up and dropped him off here."

I advertised, called Petfinders, and checked the paper every day. I still could not believe that Rainbear wasn't lost from some RV. After all, he was the perfect passenger, the perfect companion, pretty much the perfect everything. Someone somewhere must have been brokenhearted.

One night we found an ad for a lost dog, similar to Rainbear, missing from Hauser, north of us just over the McCullough Bridge.

"He's probably not mine, but I'd still love to see him," said the lady who answered when I called.

Hoping he was not hers, we agreed to bring him out to her. He was not hers, but she looked him up in her big dog book for us. "The only thing that looks like him is a Tibetan Spaniel, but they are rare," she mused.

So we told her our comet story, and all had a good laugh.

Sometime later, on a warm sunny day, we were walking Bear at the boat basin. As we started down to the docks, footsteps thundered on the metal ramp behind us, increasing in speed until reaching us.

"I had to catch up with you," panted a stranger. "Do you know what you have there?" Not waiting for an answer, he said, "He is a Tibetan Spaniel! I'm a breeder. I don't often see one."

We traded stories. He told us what great dogs they are; he had turned down a chance to work in England because he didn't want to leave his.

Gradually we discovered Rainbear's roots.

When we had him checked out by a vet, we learned he had been kicked and beaten hard enough to crush vertebrae and break ribs.

Then one day when Bear and I were walking in our favorite place, a man with a tiny dog came up the ramp. Thinking the dogs would like to play, I smiled at the man, only to be upstaged by a furry streak climbing onto the top of my head, where he hung on screaming. Now, the sound of an alarmed Tibetan Spaniel has been described as "the sound of ten dragons screaming." In ancient monasteries, it was the Tibetan Spaniels' job not only to wake up the household, but also the big dogs who would chase away intruders.

"Wow," said the surprisingly calm young man. "I know him. He usually plays with my dog."

"You know him?"

"Yeah, he belonged to a guy down the street. I'm glad you have him now."

"He must be afraid you'll take him back."

I pried Rainbear off my head, and the man filled me in, Bear quivering the whole time. Rainbear had survived abuse, managed to get away, and traveled miles on busy Cape Arago Highway to find a new life.

Rainbear really believed that he had found Heaven, and we were equally sure that our little "comet dog" was Heaven sent.

~Teresa Anne Rigg

80

Run of the Mill

The reason a dog has so many friends is that he
wags his tail instead of his tongue.
~Author Unknown

Jimmy was one of those dogs who lived up to the expectations of his breed. Jimmy was a Boston Terrier—a companion dog. If Olympic medals were awarded for canine companionship, Jimmy would have earned gold.

My daughter and son-in-law bought Jimmy for me when I was newly divorced and badly in need of friendship. I had seen him in a pet store and fallen in love with his half-white puppy face and his stubby off-centered tail that made him appear to move like a car with an alignment problem. I was surprised and grateful when Tina and Chet showed up on my porch with Jimmy wrapped in a blanket. I searched for the perfect name for my new housemate and friend. I decided to name him after one of my favorites, James Herriot, the English veterinarian who penned such charming stories about his animal patients and their humans.

I had no idea Jimmy came from a puppy mill. The vet I took Jimmy to for his first well-puppy visit was happy to enlighten me. She could not find one thing right about my little pal—if it was not a clear-cut case of a clinically diagnosable problem or deficiency of some sort, then it was surely a potential problem, all caused by the puppy mill. At one point she actually asked, "How could you?" Honestly, I didn't know about puppy mills.

By now, I loved Jimmy. I certainly wasn't taking him back to the store. If getting him in the first place was socially irresponsible, how bad would taking him back be? Besides, he was a gift. I learned a lot about puppy mills and vowed to boycott their puppies in the future. I, however, could find no flaws in Jimmy. From his sandpaper tongue to his sweet puppy breath, he was my no-fault friend.

Jimmy settled into my life. He spent hours on my desk beside the keyboard. When I sang with the music playing, Jimmy howled softly in disharmonic accompaniment. When I talked to myself, he vocalized as if in response. Jimmy never barked at anything. I worked as Executive Director of a foundation that funded and operated a summer camp for children with diabetes. He spent many hours at camp with me. The children loved him. Jimmy was my perfect buddy.

When I began dating my future husband, Doug, he and Jimmy made accommodations for each other. When I started to visit Doug's home, Jimmy, my sidekick, accompanied me. Jimmy was soon comfortable there with Doug. After several months of intermittent drop-ins, Doug's cats, Jake and Tom, came out of hiding and introduced themselves to Jimmy with minimal hissing and swatting.

After a two-and-a-half-year courtship, Doug and I married. Jimmy and I moved in with Doug and the cats. Doug and Jimmy started a unique form of communication. If Doug made a grunting sound or cleared his throat, Jimmy mimicked it. I wanted to believe it was coincidence. If Doug made a long sound followed by a short one, so did Jimmy. Whatever sound pattern Doug used, Jimmy did the same. It was unreal. Still, we had never heard Jimmy bark. Even if neighborhood dogs barked, Jimmy did not.

One evening at dinner Doug said, "What good is a dog that doesn't bark?"

Well, I was somewhat offended. Obviously, Jimmy was a lot of good to me. I saw no reason to change one single hair of his black and white coat.

"I'm going to teach him to bark," Doug said.

"Okay, but you may be sorry," I warned, envisioning my timid pal becoming a boisterous four-legged pest.

Evenings, I arrived home from work to find Doug and Jimmy on the floor working on Jimmy's barking lessons. Doug woofed. He then placed his hand gently on Jimmy's throat. Doug woofed again. After a few days, Jimmy let out a soft, small yapping sound. Later, Jimmy began to yap on command.

"Now if I can get him to bark like a man," Doug said. The lessons continued.

Doug taught Jimmy well. He occasionally barked at strangers.

Jimmy lived out his years as my companion dog. Had my life depended on it, Jimmy would have barked like a man, I'm sure!

~Karen R. Hessen

Leading a Sheltered Life

The meeting of two personalities is like the contact of two chemical substances:
if there is any reaction, both are transformed.
~Carl Jung

Spots all over! Five Dalmatian puppies, all motherless, and now my responsibility at the shelter where they were dumped. RUFF was a no-kill refuge for dogs in Florida and I had just signed up to volunteer — no experience, no skills, just a love of animals and a willingness to help. The pups were little more than tiny blobs of black and white, so needy that I had no idea where to start.

"Give them a bath," someone suggested, and so I tried. Now they were wet blobs of black and white, like Oreo cookies dunked in milk. Their wriggling happy bodies were proof that I wasn't a total failure at this volunteer stuff, so I continued to show up two days a week, dragging my husband along as well.

The five spotted siblings were quite the rambunctious bunch! And each pup had its own personality. Panda was the bravest of the bunch. As soon as he saw us coming he made sure he would get singled out for attention. Gary was laid back while Gidgit was a jumping fool. Rounding out the group was Chloe, the sweetest, and JoJo, the neurotic. All five needed exercise and plenty of it. We chased; we threw balls; we pulled toys. But more was needed, so we started harnessing the troops for walks.

The shelter contained about 200 other dogs who also craved

attention. So my husband and I decided to start walking all the dogs for exercise. It was wonderful fresh air and exercise for us as well as the canines, but with 200 dogs and two volunteers you can imagine who got the most exercise. The answer was to recruit more volunteers to come every day. Thus was born the "Dogercise Crew." We enlisted the help of spry seniors, nearby business lunchers, community service participants, and the local Air Force base enlistees. In short, anyone remotely ready, willing, and somewhat able. As we paraded down the street we gathered more walkers and socialized the dogs.

One by one the Dalmatians began to find their forever homes. Gary was the first to leave. He was so cute it was hard to pass his cage without envisioning him as part of a family. Panda left next. He was not the cutest puppy but he had an adorable personality. He weaseled his way into the hearts of a young couple who took him home.

Next, wild girl Gidgit went. But she was promptly brought back, because along with being a ten on the cuteness scale, she was off the charts for rowdiness. She had what we would call "behavior issues." Chloe and JoJo shrank back from anyone at all interested in them, ending any initial interest quickly. Therefore life continued at the shelter for Chloe, Gidgit, and JoJo. We gave them as much love and attention as we could, but with 200 "clients" it wasn't nearly enough, not like a family would provide.

Gidgit, as beautiful as she was, was given another chance with another family, a family with enough patience to see her lovely, lively exuberance for what it was—joy. Gidgit had her home. JoJo was highstrung and such a crazy mess that I didn't hold out much hope for him. We took him to PetSmart to introduce him to possible adoptive families but he only keened and begged to go back home to his kennel, the only place he felt secure. We brought Chloe along too, and she hid under the closest chair. No one perceived her quiet love as an asset. Three years passed and these two precious babies were still housed at the shelter. We needed a miracle!

That miracle appeared in the form of a high-strung potential adopter. Jean was in the throes of a divorce, and just like JoJo, felt alone and insecure. We kennel helpers were not optimistic. In the past when someone looked at JoJo, he would cringe and cry and we would sadly return him to his cage. We told Jean that she would need patience in abundance. Jean came faithfully to the shelter day after day until finally she coaxed JoJo into letting her pet him. Then came another month of slowly turning JoJo into a normal dog — Jean and he adjusting to each other, taking walks, leaving the shelter for short forays, getting used to hopping in and out of cars, typical situations that other dogs enjoy, but had before seemed beyond JoJo's tolerance. The day finally came when JoJo left the shelter for good.

That left Chloe, the last of the litter, still at the shelter five years after her birth. How could we find her a place? She was too dear to spend her life in a shelter. My heart ached for her. We had seen so many puppies and dogs come and go; some we assumed could not possibly be adopted because of their age or behaviors. Chloe had no problems except for being a shrinking violet. I became more frantic for her when we were told that the shelter would need to close its doors due to lack of funds. Where would Chloe end up? I couldn't bear the thought.

About this time the adoption rules were relaxed to include people that had previously been interested in adoption but had been rejected because of age, physical handicaps or less than ideal living space for keeping a canine. An older couple stepped forward with the help of one of the shelter workers. They weren't sure they could afford a dog, and weren't sure they could handle one, but once they met Chloe all doubts disappeared. Chloe seduced them with her unconditional love. That same kennel worker who brought this couple forward promised to help the couple with any costs necessary to Chloe's wellbeing. It was a match worth waiting for. Chloe was home! A chapter of my life had a triumphant ending.

Over a thousand dogs were adopted during our six-year tenure of volunteering at RUFF. All different, and all furry friends who left paw prints on my heart. At the top of that list were the five spotted pups that began it all.

~Linda Bartlett

Hootie's Person

Animals can communicate quite well. And they do.
~Alice Walker

I sell dogs for a living, but not ones that run around or lift their legs. For twenty-plus years I've made art with dog images: paintings, drawings, and ceramic brooches. I sell my work to the public at Justin Herman Plaza across from the Ferry Building in San Francisco, where I'm known as the Dog Lady. Every day I'm open for business I talk dog.

Since my artwork marks me as a dog lover, people assume I'm a dog owner as well. "How many do you own?" I'm asked repeatedly.

My answer surprises them. "I don't own any dogs, but I've lived with two, or three, or four—and for the last three years, since Penelope died, only one."

I understand though, that by law, Hootie, my sixteen-pound, black-and-white Cairn Terrier mix, is my personal property. I'm considered his owner by the dog licensing department of San Mateo County where we live. I'm responsible for having him vaccinated against rabies every three years. I could be sued, fined, or arrested if he attacks or injures a human being or human property, such as another dog.

I'm the one you come looking for if he strolls from my front yard to yours in an occasional, unsupervised moment and poops on your lawn.

But morally and ethically, as far as I'm concerned Hootie's no piece of property. He's a living, breathing, feeling being, who knows joy, longing, anticipation, fear, and sadness. As I do. In our almost twelve years together (I adopted him from a rescue when he was three), I've observed him actively embrace pleasure, and, as actively, avoid discomfort.

I've watched him decide which of four treats laid down before him—each with different flavors and smells—was the one he wanted most. Hootie-the-toe-biter makes me laugh out loud when he backs down the hall before me, pretending to attack my toes, while I shuffle toward the kitchen and my morning cup of coffee.

The dog loves human attention. Definitely not a dog park kind of guy, Hootie's favorite recreation is walking through the streets of our town, Half Moon Bay, and allowing people to fawn over him. I've seen him speculatively eye strangers seated on park benches, wag his tail, express his willingness to be petted. Sometimes, a non-dog-person brushes by him as though he wasn't there, and he turns to me, surprised, head cocked, tail down a little, as if he's saying, "Did you see that?"

Still, he doesn't like everyone. He's clearly annoyed by people on wheels—skateboards, roller skates, bicycles—and barks them a sharp reminder that he's sixteen pounds and not to be trifled with.

Although he dislikes both youth and tallness in other dogs, he has friends. His favorite non-humans are Scrappy the Yorkie, Rollo the Cairn Terrier, and Buzz, the Sharpei/Lab—all of them laid-back dogs. (Hootie is a dignified guy and dislikes being leaped on.)

Now that he's a senior dog, I've seen bewilderment in his eyes when his upward bound onto the family bed falls short. And something resembling chagrin, as he turns to walk carefully up the bedside ramp. Lately, I've been trying to convince him to walk down the ramp as well. He's not ready to do this though. I can tell by the look he gives me just before leaping to the floor and sauntering down the hall: "I'll show you who's old."

I have no doubt that Hootie, like me, has wants, needs, preferences, longings. He's not "like a family member"—he IS a family member. And I see by the confident look in his eyes, by his proud step and tail held high, he knows this too.

"But what do you call yourself if not his owner," my customer asks. "His guardian, his caretaker, his dog/mom, his friend?"

I've considered this question over years of life with dogs. No doubt, I'm his guardian and caretaker, and dogs have a childlike quality that brings out the mom in me. And he is — except for my husband Lee — my dearest friend in the world. But none of these titles express for me the nature of what Hootie and I are to each other.

"He's my dog and I'm his person," I say, offering my best answer to the question. "Hootie's person, that's me."

~Lynn Sunday

Chapter 9

The Dog Did What?

There's No Place Like Home

The Man on the Porch

A door is what a dog is perpetually on the wrong side of.
~Ogden Nash

A beautiful, late spring afternoon was developing here in Tulsa, Oklahoma, known as "Green Country" to the locals due to the generous rainfall we receive each year. But towards evening, the skies took on an eerie grayish-green tint and it looked as if we would be drenched at any moment. The wind howled as the windows shook in response to thunder rolling in.

Our St. Bernard, Bart, hated storms so he was safe in his bed in our attached garage while our two Bichon Frises were snuggled up with my husband and me in our bedroom. Severe thunderstorm warnings kept interrupting regular scheduled network programming. Both of our Bichons began growling in tandem with each clap of thunder as the storm got closer and louder.

When you live in Northeastern Oklahoma, you become accustomed to the storms and you can sometimes see and hear the beauty in them. There can even be something strangely peaceful about the lullaby of a thunderstorm at bedtime.

We had gone to bed around eleven but I was unable to sleep, so I got up and went into the living room to read. I hadn't yet turned on a lamp, and that's when I saw the moving shadow on our back porch.

Oh my Lord! It was a man! He was almost six feet tall and pressing his horrid face against our French doors, peering directly into our pitch-dark living room, where I, in my nightgown, found myself peering right back at him!

I screamed.

The man continued staring directly at me, not even fazed by my scream.

When lightning flashed, I saw his terrifying shadowy body, not fifteen feet in front of me. I screamed again, having failed to scare him off, raise the dead, or wake a sleeping husband the first time.

My husband finally woke up and stood at the doorway to our bedroom, looked into the living room and asked me what in the world was wrong. I explained to him that clearly there was a man on the porch, looking right in at me!

"Look! He is out there! Right now! Look!"

In his recently wakened state my dear husband looked at me and dryly announced, "I don't see anyone."

There was a man on our porch looking into our house! What else did I need to report? The color of his eyes?

Dale then disappeared back into our bedroom, and I called 911.

As soon as Dale left the room, the man appeared again, pressing his face against our French doors, staring at me. This time, I actually saw the whites of his eyes as he cupped his hands around his face and leaned into the door, as if trying to push it open! Then he began banging against the door with his fists! My Lord, this man was going to come right into this house!

He was wearing dark clothes and had his stringy, red hair in a ponytail. He was soaking wet, had a beard, and his face was just ghastly. The hairs on my neck stood up as I prepared for a break-in.

I saw the rugged silhouette of his body against the darkness, as lightning dispatched shadows on the wall and thunder added even more drama to the scene unfolding before my very eyes.

Seconds seemed like hours while I waited to hear sirens, and to see the police who could catch this man and arrest him!

By now my two Bichons were barking ferociously at the man, as

I looked around for something to pick up, so I could defend them if he came in.

I prepared myself for the sound of breaking glass.

I screamed again. "Dale! He is right here! On the porch! Looking at me right now!! COME BACK IN HERE NOW! HE IS HERE, RIGHT NOW! He is about to break in!"

By the time my husband returned to the living room the man was gone again, and this was beginning to look like a bad remake of *Midnight Lace* with Doris Day while Rex Harrison delivered his creepy line into the telephone, "Mrs. Preston, I'm going to kill you Mrs. Preston."

It was at that exact moment the man looked into the living room again, and this time, I got a good enough look at him to identify him. I had seen this man before!

This time, my husband saw him too! (I'm not crazy! I'm not crazy!)

But by now the man had divulged yet another distinguishing attribute.

He barked.

Bart, our St. Bernard who had ridden out many thunderstorms in his favorite place, our garage, was so frightened by the thunder that he had jumped up and hit the garage door button, thus opening the overhead garage door.

Then Bart took himself on a little walk around the front of our house, all the way to the covered back porch where he stood on his hind legs and peered into the living room. He stood nearly six feet tall.

Bart was a dry-mouth St. Bernard with a slim face. Though he didn't have the famous St. Bernard jowls, he did have red hair and a beard. He had pressed his paws on either side of his face as he looked into the living room, no doubt trying to get me to let him inside. After all, invisible thunder monsters were out there and trying to get him.

After we determined that Bart was "the man on the porch," Dale let him inside, all 140 wet pounds of him.

I called the police back to let them know we had apprehended the "burglar," and were drying him off with a beach towel.

I scolded him saying, "Bart! You scared Mama!"

I swear to you as I live and breathe, this giant dog looked over his shoulder at me and doing his best Rex Harrison impersonation, said, "Mrs. Preston. I'm watching you Mrs. Preston."

He wagged his bushy tail ever so slightly as he sauntered to the safety of our bedroom with my husband. It was still storming hard outside and Bart knew that his frightening experience had earned him a place to sleep in our bedroom for the night.

~Robin Pressnall

84

Channeling Their Inner Gladiator

The dog, in life the firmest friend, the first to welcome, foremost to defend.
~Lord Byron

Just enough snow covered the ground that Saturday morning for the dogs to leave tracks as they trotted outside. Marcus and Maximus trailed Buffy as she led the way. I stood in the open doorway and grinned at the sight of the two large Maremma Sheepdogs following the small Beagle.

A red squirrel diverted my attention as it ran past me into the house. I spent the next half hour chasing the squirrel before I finally caught it and released it outside.

By then the dogs had disappeared. I hadn't seen the direction they took, but I wasn't worried. My home is located in a clearing in the middle of eight acres in a rural community in upstate New York.

I stood on the front deck and called the dogs' names. Marcus and Maximus were rescues, six and five years old. Although gentle in temperament, Maremmas were originally bred as guard dogs for sheep. Their timid nature caused them to be wary of strangers, but I figured they wouldn't stray too far from fifteen-year-old Buffy.

When they did not respond, I went out to look for them. Although I didn't see the dogs, their paw prints were clearly visible in the snow. Buffy still appeared to be leading the way. The tracks disappeared as they entered the wooded area surrounding my house.

It was beginning to get dark. Now I was worried. After returning home for warmer clothes, I took the car to continue my search. Still no sign of the dogs.

Back at the house, I filled their dishes and placed them on the deck, hoping hunger and the smell of food would bring them home. I continued to call their names until I grew hoarse. Then I turned on all the outside lights. Surely the lights would beckon them home.

I resumed the search early Sunday morning, this time with my nephew and his two adult sons. We split up to search the woods and fifty acres of surrounding farmland.

Were the dogs snatched? Marcus and Maximus were healthy, noble-looking purebred dogs. They would be attractive to thieves. But few strangers travelled through our rural area, so this probably wasn't something I needed to worry about.

Of more concern were the weather and the wildlife. Coyotes usually fed on small mammals in the summer and fall, but by January they were hungry enough to attack small deer… and dogs. Due to her age, Buffy would make a convenient meal.

On Monday, our search efforts extended beyond local family members. We called Animal Control and gave them our contact numbers in case they heard anything. We also called the local game warden.

Each night I left the outside lights on and clung to dwindling hope. On Wednesday, despite a snowstorm, we drove to the rescue farm where I had adopted the Maremmas. Although the farm was twenty-five miles away, they might have heard news of Marcus and Maximus.

The woman at the Maremma rescue farm suggested we speak to a local psychic. By this time I was desperate enough to consider anything that might help. The psychic said Buffy was alive and two big dogs were with her inside a red barn. I remembered an abandoned red barn a few miles from my home. It was worth a try, especially since we had no other leads.

But the snowstorm that began earlier in the day developed into a blizzard. We barely made it home safely. Poor visibility prevented us from reaching the barn until the next morning. We found no sign of the dogs. Even if they had been there, the fresh snow would have covered their tracks.

Although we continued to search daily, I imagined the worst. Freezing rain fell on top of the snow and the temperature dropped to twenty degrees. I steeled myself for the possibility that if we found anything at all, it would be Buffy's remains. Even if the Maremmas survived, an elderly Beagle didn't stand a chance in the brutal weather.

By Friday, we had covered nearly 500 acres of mostly farmland. That night, the howling of coyotes echoed through the dark, reminding me of Buffy's diminishing chances of survival. The following day we explored the last fifty acres of farmland and even returned to the barn described by the psychic.

Then we caught a break.

A woman named Lee had been hiking along a dirt road and spotted a muddy dog that appeared more dead than alive. When Lee approached, the dog lifted her head and even attempted a few steps before collapsing. Two large, white dogs watched from a nearby high ridge.

As Lee picked up the frail Beagle, she glanced back at the ridge. The two large dogs had disappeared.

Lee took the dog home and called Animal Control. They notified us. Gratefully, we picked up Buffy, a mere four miles from my house, and brought her home.

As we drove up my long driveway, I was shocked to see Maximus and Marcus sitting on the front deck of the house. True to their timid nature, they ran into the woods when my nephews exited the car.

When the guys drove away, Marcus and Maximus returned to the house. I placed Buffy in a blanket in front of the wood-burning stove. Maximus rested his head on her body and they both slept. The next morning, Maximus again walked over to her as she slept, placed his head across her body, and stayed in that position for more than an hour.

A thorough examination of all three dogs yielded strange results. Buffy was weak, dehydrated, and covered in mud, but she did not have any injuries. However, the Maremmas suffered multiple cuts and bites. A piece of Marcus's lip had been torn away, requiring several stitches.

The next day, my nephew explored the area where Buffy was found. Paw prints and hollows preserved in the snow told an amazing story. The tracks led to an impression in the snow that was about the size of Buffy. A larger impression was next to it—just the right size for Maximus. A set of dog prints circled those two hollows around and around, as if Marcus had been on guard duty.

In a wooded area nearby, bloodstains in the snow gave silent testimony to a violent confrontation.

All this happened four miles from home. Marcus and Maximus proved they were never lost when they beat us to the house and waited on the front deck as we arrived. They could have returned home any time that week, but instead they remained with a small, elderly dog who needed their protection.

Two months later, shortly after her sixteenth birthday, Buffy sat on a large pillow on the deck. Basking in the warmth of the early spring sun, she drew her final breath, surrounded by two buddies who chose to stay by her side until the end.

~David O'Neill

85

Nurse on Call

Dogs are miracles with paws.
~Attributed to Susan Ariel Rainbow Kennedy

"That puppy won't make it through the night," the vet told us flatly over the phone. That wasn't what my husband, Roy, and I wanted to hear. The little puppy had been born lifeless, still in the amniotic sac, with only a tiny muzzle visible. I ripped open the sac, and there it was—cold, not moving or breathing. Roy started puppy CPR, a technique we had only read about. Just when we had almost given her up for dead, she took a deep, lung-filling breath. She was still deathly cold, so Roy warmed her in his cupped hands while I called the vet.

"If you want to try to save her, see if you can get her to nurse, and fix a separate box with a heating pad for her tonight," the vet continued. "Don't keep her in the whelping box with the mother and other puppies—they could lie on top of her and kill her." So, before Roy left to work his night shift at the Sheriff's Department, we did what the vet recommended. The tiny puppy was so weak, she could not lift her head to nurse on her own, but she did great if I gently lifted her little head near one of her mom Lacey's nipples. Though we had grave doubts about the little pup, we would do what we could to save her.

As night fell, Lacey fed her normal three pups and I held up the tiny pup to Lacey's teats before I put her in her own little box for the night. She seemed stronger—but I tried not to get my hopes up. Before I put the runt in her box, Lacey licked her clean. I petted Lacey and all the new pups, said a little prayer for the littlest one, and went to bed.

About midnight, Lacey woke me from a sound sleep, scratching at the foot of the bed—her signal she needed to go out. Half awake, I half stumbled to the back door and let Lacey out. Since I was up, I thought I'd check on the pups. The three puppies in the whelping box were mewing sleepily—looked like Lacey had given them the midnight feeding. Then I looked in the runt's box. She was missing! Now I was fully awake. Where could that puppy be? I frantically searched in and around both puppy boxes, and behind all the furniture in the room. The puppy just was not there!

My mind raced with stories I had read about mother animals killing their young when they were not "normal." I hurried to the back door and flung it open. Sure enough, there was Lacey holding the small, limp pup in her mouth. I was so panicked; I screamed "No" at Lacey and brought her back into the house. Lacey calmly walked over to me and dropped the tiny pup on my bare foot. I was beside myself with fear until I realized she was breathing. Lacey nuzzled the pup, then my foot, then the pup again, and then my foot again. Then, she lay on her side offering to nurse the pup. Then I got it! Lacey had not wanted to go out; she wanted to feed her pup. She knew her littlest pup needed help to suckle. It was this baby's time to nurse without competition from its siblings, and Lacey was enlisting my help. I gently moved the pup to Lacey's teats and the little runt suckled. Amazing!

For three or four more days, until the little runt could lift her own head to nurse, Lacey would feed the other pups then, like clockwork, carry the runt into the bedroom and wake me to help her with the midnight meal. The little runt lived to a ripe old age of thirteen—all because Mama Lacey did something I never would have believed if I hadn't had the privilege of being part of her family.

~Janice R. Edwards

The Reluctant Host

Guests always give pleasure—if not their arrival, their departure.
~Portuguese Proverb

One January, my oldest sister and her family went on a cruise. They asked me to look after their house and take care of their pets: a goldfish, two cats, and a Toy Poodle named Scruffy.

A few months earlier, they had gone out for the day and asked me to stop by, let Scruffy out, and make sure he had food and water. Things hadn't gone well. Not only did he bark and growl at me, he also squeezed into the back corner of his cage, just out of my reach. I must have spent twenty minutes sitting in front of his cage trying to coax him out with treats, but with no luck. So I made sure he had food and water, and left a note about how I couldn't get him to come out.

I showed up at their house just before they left for their cruise, and Scruffy again just barked and growled at me. They showed me his favorite toys and held him so I could pet him, but he didn't seem pleased.

Before they left, they put him back in his cage and I turned on the TV. A couple of hours later, I figured I should try to let him out. I don't know how long I spent at the front of his cage with treats trying to get the leash on him. Eventually, it got to the point where I decided to just carry the cage outside. It had a removable bottom, so I figured I could slip it out, let him do his business, and then slip it back in. I started cleaning the dog treats and other odds and ends off the top of the cage—thinking it was going to be a very long week—when I came across an old towel.

Figuring I should give it a try, I threw the towel over him in the cage. This either calmed or confused him long enough for me to pick up the back of the cage and slide him towards the front. Then I was able to pick him up—with just a few growls—and carry him to the back door. Attached at the door was a ten-foot line. I hooked him onto it and let him run around in the snow.

During the next commercial break I went to bring him back in. He didn't like that idea. I stood at the door gently pulling on the line while he dug in between barks. Then the collar slipped over his head.

We stood looking at each other for a second or two, as if not sure what that meant. Then he turned and ran.

I took maybe three steps after him before realizing that, one, I was in my socks, and two, he already didn't like me so chasing after him probably wouldn't help.

Back inside, I put on my boots and coat. When I opened the front door, he was standing there. He barked at me and ran away again. I followed, hoping I wouldn't strangle him when I caught him.

I don't know how long I searched for him that first evening. On the one hand, I knew I needed to find him. But on the other, I knew if I chased him too much I might scare him away. With no other option, I put out food and water for him by the back door, and watched a movie on TV. Every commercial break I looked around the back yard with a flashlight, but other than tracks through the snow, I saw no sign of him.

The next morning, some of the food was gone. Whether he, some wild animal, or one of the cats—who had a habit of slipping outside—ate it, I didn't know. But I put out more food and water.

I called my mom and told her what happened, and she said to put out food and water for him and she would relay the news to my sister. Other than keeping food and water outside, and keeping an eye out for him, there wasn't much I could do.

The second or third night, a neighbor stopped by and said they thought they had seen him along the road about a mile away. So I crept along the road with my arm out my car window squeaking his favorite toy, but didn't see any sign of him.

Of course, I don't think he went that far away. Every now and then, I'd catch a glimpse of him out a window, but whenever I opened a door he would run away from me. Then one day it warmed up a bit and I saw muddy paw prints coming out from under one corner of the house. I think he was just hiding in the crawl space.

He was too quick, so grabbing him was out of the question. I decided to outsmart him. I set his cage outside and put food and some of his toys in it. I then ran a string to close the door on the cage from the back door. Once it was rigged up, I stood at the back door and waited. After half an hour, I grew bored and went to watch TV. For the next hour, I checked during every commercial break, but nothing changed. Then, on one break, half the food was gone. I kept the cage outside for a couple of more days. Every now and then the food would disappear, but I never saw him.

The night before my sister's family came back, the only animal left in the house was the goldfish. In the morning, I saw one of the cats jumping through the snow in the back yard. I opened the back door and he rushed inside. Then, about an hour before my sister and her family were due to return, I was looking out the front door and saw the other cat. He came in, and I locked the house down so they couldn't slip out again.

Finally, they pulled into the driveway. My niece stepped out and called Scruffy a couple of times. He ran around the corner of the house and went right up to her. She picked him up and carried him inside. He was a bit muddy, but apparently no worse for spending a week outside in the middle of winter. And he still barked at me. On the bright side, they haven't asked me to pet-sit since.

~Stephen L. Thompson

Grandma's Journey

Blessed is the person who has earned the love of an old dog.
~Sydney Jeanne Seward

We named her Grandma. I know it's not your typical name for a dog, but it fit her. Grandma and one of her puppies were tossed into a shelter that had a reputation for not holding onto pets long. Adoption rates were low, as they were in a secluded rural area. Grandma had never had a name—she had only been known as a number. She had survived the horrors of a puppy mill, forced to breed puppies for the owners to sell.

Now huddled in the back of a filthy cage lined with feces and urine, she shook uncontrollably and growled anytime someone tried to come near her. Her nails were curled into her paw pads, her hair had fallen out and she was infested with parasites and fleas. Severely emaciated and dehydrated, shelter workers did not understand why the small Chihuahua refused to eat.

When I heard her story, I immediately offered to rescue the two Chihuahuas in need. I did not have any foster dogs at the time, just two dogs of my own, and I was happy to offer my home to save their lives. As a foster parent for rescue pets, I drove them to safety and got them to our veterinarian right away. Among a litany of other ailments, Grandma had rotting teeth. No wonder she had refused to eat at the shelter. Shelter workers had also said that they could not touch her or vaccinate her because she growled and was angry. But the minute I reached in to take her to safety, she pressed against my chest and seemed to understand that she was now free from harm. I cradled her in my arms and promised the two dogs they would never know pain again.

I knew immediately that her name should be Grandma. At fifteen years old and having endured more than any of us could imagine, she had a spark in her eyes. She moved with pain, but I knew in time, with good nutrition and medical care, that she would be sprinting around and healthy. The veterinarian told us that all but three of Grandma's teeth needed to be pulled. We also had the girls spayed and vaccinated right away. During Grandma's spay surgery, the veterinarian discovered she had a severe case of pyometra—an internal disease which can lead to immediate death. Overbreeding in filthy conditions may have caused this. Had the surgery happened even one day later, Grandma most likely wouldn't have made it.

But she did make it and each day she grew stronger. Her hair started growing in, and her eyes continued to fill with light. She loved to sit on my lap and go for walks. She ran easily in the yard and loved to play with the other dogs. She slept beside me in bed and trotted after me throughout the house. Grandma had never been house-trained, having spent her entire life in a wire crate. But she quickly understood the concept, as she followed the lead of my two resident dogs. She fit into our family like a glove.

Watching her run after her tiny toys and wag her tail, my eyes filled with tears every time as I marveled at the miraculous recovery she had made. No one had been able to touch her at the shelter, but here in my home, her foster home, she had become a different dog. Each time I foster a pet in need I realize what a huge role environment plays in their wellbeing. In the shelter, behind bars, they are terrified. But in the loving arms of a foster home they thrive; they understand they are safe.

After several major surgeries and knowing Grandma's age, I decided to officially adopt her myself. She was attached to me and I had bonded to her. Now she accompanies me on vacations, road trips, hiking adventures—she may be a senior but that doesn't slow her down. She must be making up for lost time, because she is the most energetic of my three dogs. She is always ready to hop in the car and ride or go for a walk.

Her journey is nothing short of amazing. Now, four years later, she is a healthy, happy girl. But as astounding as her transformation has been, Grandma has taught me that senior pets have just as much, if not more, love to share with us. As happy as I know Grandma is to have been rescued and safe, I am beyond blessed to have her in my life. No matter what kind of day I have, when I come home she is always there to greet me—the smallest of my three dogs—always wagging her tail with a spark in her eyes.

~Stacey Ritz

Sisters

Bless you, my darling, and remember you are always in the heart —
oh tucked so close there is no chance of escape — of your sister.
~Katherine Mansfield

"They're sisters, and they need a home." That is what my husband said as he presented two blond Heinz 57 puppies to our family. We had just moved to the country and decided that we needed a couple of dogs to protect our home.

Blondie and Tweeter were clearly special from the beginning. Both were gentle with everyone and everything they came in contact with. They befriended our cats and their kittens and would lie down with them in the shade. They would thump their tails and entertain the playful kittens by letting them try to grab their tails.

More than anything or anyone, Blondie and Tweeter loved each other. They were inseparable. Where one went, the other followed. One day, Tweeter began to have seizures. Blondie lay next to her whining until the seizures were over. Then Blondie would comfort Tweeter by getting as close as possible to her and rest with her until Tweeter felt better. Unfortunately, Tweeter was not to recover and would eventually die. When we brought her body home from the veterinarian, we buried her where we bury all of our dear pets, by our pond, under a beautiful tree. Blondie watched everything that was done as we laid Tweeter to rest.

Many years later, Blondie had grown old. She grew weaker as the days went on. We wanted to make sure that she did not get to the point of suffering, but we wanted our oldest son to be able to return from school to say goodbye. We had gotten Blondie and Tweeter when Nathan was one year old, and now he was in college.

As Blondie rested on a mattress in the cool garage, we knew that something had to be done because she had lost the ability to walk. We decided to deal with matters after Nathan spent his time with Blondie that day.

When we came home that evening, Nathan tearfully told us a beautiful story of what had taken place with Blondie. He had gone to the garage and lain on the mattress with Blondie. He talked to her and comforted her, preparing to say goodbye. Then he went into the house to shower. As he began to go upstairs, something outside caught his eye. Blondie was walking without a problem. She seemed happy as she headed toward the pond. Then, she carefully lay down for one last time on the very spot where her sister had been buried years before. Now, they were together again, happily playing and never to be separated again.

~Ruth Ann Roy

Home Away from Home

A good dog deserves a good home.
~Proverb

My son Matt, his dog Fonzy, and I were on a mission. We had to find off-campus housing for the new school year, a task that proved to be more difficult than we ever imagined.

We studied the local newspaper in his college town. Checked out apartments, condos, and houses as close to school as possible. To our dismay, most people didn't want to rent to college students. And to make it more difficult, there was a dog involved. We decided to consult a property management company and a real estate agent. To our dismay, both offered apologies. "We're sorry, but we don't have any vacancies that allow pets of any kind. But we'll keep your application on file and let you know if something becomes available."

Our frustration grew but we continued our intense efforts—all without success. Finally, my son suggested we investigate the next town. "I won't mind getting up twenty minutes earlier to drive to my morning classes. I just want to find a place for me and Fonzy." Matt's determination spurred us on, but to no avail. It appeared Fonzy would have to return home with me until the housing situation changed.

We decided to return to the motel, have dinner, and just take it easy. We'd continue our quest the next day. But for some unknown reason,

Matt turned onto another street. "Let's just drive around. Maybe…" He never finished his thought, for right in front of us was a big red "For Rent" sign in the window of an older house bearing a handyman special add-on-wing.

It wasn't far from school and it had a small back yard. Mrs. Duffy, the friendly property owner, an elderly grandmother-type, welcomed us as if we were old friends. She explained she had never rented out space before but now needed the extra money.

"I was actually hoping for a student to come by. I need someone to mow the lawn, shovel the snow and maybe run an errand or two for me." She frowned and added, "But usually the college kids want something fancier."

Matt didn't hesitate. "This is just what I'm looking for, Mrs. Duffy. And, I have lots of experience mowing, shoveling and running errands. Just ask my mom." It appeared to be a perfect match. "There's one thing you must know," he told her before heading out to the car to get his dog. "This is my best friend, Fonzy. He's very friendly and we both need a place to live."

"I love dogs," she said. "Have one of my own. A cute little Scottish Terrier named Angus." Mrs. Duffy offered Fonzy a doggy treat.

"My home away from home," became Matt's favorite description of his new rental. As for Fonzy, he seemed to be happy wherever he lived, as long as he was with his person. When Matt would have class, he'd put Fonzy in the yard with food and water, and check on him during the day as time allowed. He always worried about his dog being home alone for a good part of the day, but resilient Fonzy never acted like anything bothered him.

One day, Matt's schedule delayed him from getting home at his usual time. When he did arrive, Fonzy was missing. He looked everywhere: under the bed, behind the sofa and in the kitchen pantry, thinking he might have forgotten to put him out; along the fence line, thinking Fonzy might have dug a hole and squeezed out; around the neighborhood, thinking he left the gate to the yard open. Heartsick, Matt finally consulted with Mrs. Duffy to see if she had seen Fonzy.

She didn't say anything—just invited him to come inside. Maybe

Fonzy was sick or injured! Matt didn't know what to think or expect. Once in the living room, to his surprise, he discovered Fonzy, curled up on a blanket, and snuggled next to Angus. Matt learned Fonzy had been visiting them every day since they moved there. "He's learned to squeeze in through the doggy door."

Embarrassed, Matt apologized for Fonzy's rudeness. "I just didn't know."

"Don't worry about it. He's become part of my family, too. This is his home away from home." She led him into the laundry room. "See, he has his own water bowl and favorite toy." Mrs. Duffy's smile assured Matt all was well. "He and Angus are like brothers."

"Well, I thank you for taking care of him, but it's time he goes home." Matt tried to coax Fonzy out of the house, but he would not budge.

Mrs. Duffy came to the rescue. "He and I have this ritual. He doesn't leave until I give him his treat."

Matt stood there, shaking his head as he watched in disbelief. Fonzy munched his biscuit, then meandered out the doggy door, without any coaxing, and straight to the back door of his house. "All I can say, Mrs. Duffy, is that having a home away from home has special meaning for Fonzy too."

~Helen Colella

Man's Best Friend

You may have a dog that won't sit up, roll over or even cook breakfast, not because she's too stupid to learn how but because she's too smart to bother.
~Rick Horowitz

My avid outdoorsman father decided our family needed a dog. He envisioned a well-trained hiking, hunting and fishing companion and set out to find a puppy who fit the bill. Sugar, a rambunctious chocolate Lab, seemed to be a perfect match. Even at a young age, she had beautiful lines, an overabundance of energy, and a sweet personality.

There were early warning signs that Sugar might not be the companion my father expected. My mother was told that Sugar could perhaps "find a better fit for an obedience class."

The first hiking outing established Sugar's innate talent and enthusiasm for finding and rolling in anything designed to make the trip home as unpleasant as possible. The second displayed her expert ability in beehive hunting and dispersing. Had my dad been a honey collector, this would have come in handy. For the average hiker, hunter and fisherman, it just meant investing in a large supply of baking soda.

My dad's hope never dimmed, however. One day, he heard the telltale signs of the bark of a dog on an animal's trail. He ran out to the back yard to see which animal had inspired Sugar to find her inner hunter. Sugar's excited bark escalated through the woods, accompanied by a large crashing noise. She had a big one! Mom was the first to see the prey emerge. She giggled. We giggled. My dad rolled his eyes. Sugar stood in the back yard, tail wagging, next to the black and white cow she had driven into our yard. Dad gave up hunting soon after.

Still, the hopes for his fisherman water dog never dimmed. The first trips up to the family's lake property, Sugar was reticent around the water.

"She's just a puppy," my mom counseled. "Maybe next summer."

The next summer Dad was ready. "This," he announced with excitement, "will be Sugar's big water year." He proudly gave Sugar a pep talk all the way down to the water. Stick in hand, he looked Sugar in the eyes, and tossed the stick twenty feet off the dock. "Go get it, girl."

Sugar stared at Dad.

"Come on, Sugar, go."

The stick floated on the surface, beckoning.

Dad got another stick.

Sugar lay down on the dock.

Dad got a treat.

Sugar left the dock.

Dad had an idea. "She's a Lab. All Labs swim. She just needs to get used to the idea." He called Sugar back down to the dock. "Watch this," he said, and then picked her up and tossed her in the water off the dock.

We all called from the shore twenty feet away. "Come on, Sugar. Come on, girl."

Her head broke the surface of the water. Sugar was not coming. Sugar was not swimming. Sugar was panicking.

Dad threw a large piece of wood for her to climb up on. Sugar ignored it. Her breaths became more and more labored as she attempted to get all four of her paws out of the water vertically. Sugar, the water Lab, was drowning.

Dad jumped in, between Sugar and the shore, to coax her in and show her the way. She spotted Dad and began swimming frantically towards him. It was working. Sugar was making her way towards the shore.

Sugar reached Dad. Instead of continuing to swim to shore, she clearly decided her rescuer had arrived. She tried to climb up on him, out of the water. The more Dad pushed her away, the more determined she was to remain on him. Now it was my dad's breaths that were becoming more and more labored. Slowly, he managed to swim the fifteen feet to shore with Sugar scratching and clinging to his back.

After that day, Dad and Sugar came to an unspoken understanding. Dad would take his children fishing and hiking and on all his outdoor adventures. Sugar would get to be the at-home cheerleader with Mom. This relationship worked wonderfully. We children avoided all things smelly, large hives of bees, and played, waded and fished with gusto in the water. Sugar stayed at home, curled in her bed, chased butterflies (and the occasional cow) and dutifully greeted the incoming adventurers with joyful barks, vigorous tail-wagging and lots of wet kisses. She was still "man's best friend."

~Julie Reece-DeMarco

An Unexpected Guest

At Christmas, all roads lead home.
~Marjorie Holmes

When my sister Catherine and I were growing up, we often helped our mother prepare for a women's group that met at our house once a month. We usually baked something special to serve to our mother's friends. Having done this for many years, we knew the ladies well and often joined them for dessert.

At one December meeting, several of the women arrived at our front door at the same time. When they entered the house, a small brown dog followed right behind them into the living room. Two of the ladies sat on the couch and the dog lay down on the carpet at their feet. Since dogs were never allowed in our house, we were shocked that someone would bring one with them. We knew our father would have a fit if he found out. After quick glances at our mother, my sister and I understood we were to remain silent and act as though having a dog in the house was a normal occurrence. Fortunately, the dog was very well behaved and never moved from its place in front of the couch.

After the meeting was over, my sister and I served dessert and visited with our mom's friends. We did our best to keep our attention on the conversation but we were distracted, knowing the cute little dog should not be in our house.

Later, when they were ready to leave, the ladies with the dog said their goodbyes and started walking toward the front door. The little dog stayed right where she was, not making a move. My mother, still not sure which of them owned it, called out, "Don't forget to take your dog." To which the two women replied in unison, "It's not my dog. I thought it was yours." We all burst out laughing.

The dog was put outside that night so she could return to her home. But to our surprise and delight, she was still there the next morning, sleeping on our front porch. She was so sweet and friendly that we begged our mom to let us keep her, and she agreed. The dog lived outdoors along with our terrier, Chris. Both our dad and the dog seemed content with the arrangement. We named her Kringle because she came to us at Christmastime. An unexpected visitor, she found her way into our home and hearts to become a faithful four-legged friend.

~RoseAnn Faulkner

Chapter
10

The Dog Did What?

Bad Dog!

92

Houdini Hound

Dogs act exactly the way we would act if we had no shame.
~Cynthia Heimel

He was an escape artist of extraordinary skill. He would have been admired for his ingenuity if he had used his talent for good instead of evil. The neighbors would probably have forgiven the occasional cat pursued through their yards or a small memento placed in their flowerbeds, but not stealing! As his caregivers, my husband Ron and I were responsible for his behavior (or should I say misbehaviors). We knew something had to be done about it.

I'm referring to our Beagle, Brandy, and events that occurred during the autumn after we returned to town. We'd spent the first summer of the little hound's life at our cottage in the country and Brandy, like Jack London's Buck in *Call of the Wild*, had tasted freedom. He'd known the exhilaration of racing across vast meadows, plunging deep into thickets, and swimming wide rivers (wide in Beagle estimations). He was not about to relinquish all of it to fences or chicken wire enclosures. Digging up flower beds, swinging from clothing hanging on the line, and playing water tag with a spouting garden hose clamped in his teeth must have seemed deadly dull pastimes.

We already had fences—basket weave along the sides and chicken wire at both ends of our property. Those had always been sufficient to keep our pets contained. But then, we'd never owned a Beagle. By the time we'd returned to town in the autumn, Brandy had grown tall and strong enough to clear the chicken wire in a single bound. Thus began his career as a canine criminal and mine as his personal prevaricator.

Unfortunately, Brandy delighted in all creature comforts, especially food. Not just any food, but takeout food, party food. And therein lay the problem. Suburbia in early fall abounds with patio parties and kitchen doors left carelessly, invitingly ajar. Fertile ground for a bored and bottomless Beagle.

By the time the leaves had turned, I'd lied my way through the Case of the Cooling Cookies, the Pizza-Party Prank, and the Brazen Barbecue Raid. Worst of all had been the Crafty Crustacean Caper. Yes, Brandy had come home one afternoon with a large, freshly cooked lobster.

Before Ron could witness the little hound's latest larceny, I seized the red-shelled creature, snapped a lead on the tricolored one, and headed for my neighbor's. Earlier that day she'd told me she was having her boss over for a lobster dinner.

When I returned the stolen property to its owner, my face as red as the shellfish in my hand, and offered the explanation that the Beagle had misappropriated it, I thought I detected an amused smirk on Brandy's face as he stood by my side.

"Dogs don't usually steal lobsters, do they?" the victim asked, haughty annoyance coloring her tone.

"No, I don't believe they do," I said lamely as the little hound sat and cocked his head appealing to one side. "But Brandy is…" I searched for a socially acceptable word… "unique."

"Really?" She took the lobster gingerly between her fingers and looked down at him. "He looks like just another Beagle to me."

Brandy's eyes narrowed. He'd understood, the wild idea fluttered across my mind. One day soon, Margaret Aims would suffer the full-blown ire of a Beagle's revenge.

Though I tried to cover up this incident and other nefarious escapades, the Houdini Hound continued to escape. Eventually tales of his misdeeds filtered back to Ron through quisling neighbors. Stronger security precautions were definitely needed, my annoyed spouse informed me. That Beagle had to be contained. Thus began what I later entitled The Great Fencing Competition.

On the day after Brandy reportedly treed Margaret Aims' cat, a delivery truck rolled into our yard and deposited several rolls of eight-foot-high green-plated chain-link fencing. Brandy, ignominiously tied to the clothesline, watched with interest.

He watched with continued interest that weekend when Ron installed steel posts around the perimeter of our property and stretched sturdy wire between them.

On Sunday evening, when Brandy was once more given the freedom of the newly secured yard, the little dog ambled around its edge, inspecting Ron's handiwork.

"That should keep him out of trouble." Ron proclaimed, a triumphant smirk curling his mouth.

Confident of the truth in his words, we went inside for supper. When I called Brandy to join us a half hour later, there was no response. And when I went out to the back yard to find him, he was nowhere to be seen. What I did see was a deep, gaping, freshly dug hole in the far corner of our lot beneath that beautiful new fence.

The next day a neighbor was overheard telling how an entire foil-wrapped, shrimp-stuffed salmon had disappeared from his barbecue the previous evening. It was purely circumstantial evidence that Brandy's snout and breath had smelled of fish when he'd returned at dusk, I tried to convince Ron.

The Great Fencing Competition continued. The next day Ron bought tent pegs and skewered the fence to the ground. Brandy jacked them out with his snout (we believe) and again (allegedly) chased Margaret Aims' cat. This time it was through her tomato bed, laden with lush, ready-to-harvest fruit. The purloined lobster incident paled in comparison.

Ron bought longer tent pegs. Brandy miraculously (because we never discovered how) removed them. Ron dug the fence into the earth. Brandy dug deeper.

Then came the day a big delivery truck backed into our yard. It roared and beeped and Brandy, once again tied to the clothesline, had the good sense to retreat onto the back step.

Two burly men alighted and began to pile cement blocks beside the house. Looking out the dining room window, I saw Brandy's eyes narrow into golden brown slits. I recognized that expression. And shuddered.

That evening Ron, puffing and sweating, piled the blocks around the edge of the yard, on the bottom of the chain link, on top of the tent pegs.

Released from the indignity of the clothesline, Brandy inspected every inch of this new barrier. Finding it impregnable, he affected a blasé attitude, wandered over to the back door and asked to be let inside.

"Got him!" Ron was triumphant as he sank into a lawn chair and I opened the door for Brandy. "That will teach him not to mess with me."

Fifteen minutes later we decided to go for a walk and went into the house to put on our sneakers.

"Got ya!" Ron couldn't resist a victory tease. He bent to tickle Brandy's belly as the little hound lay on his back, Snoopy-fashion, on the couch.

Brandy rolled over onto his stomach and watched as Ron stuck a foot into one of his sneakers. And yelled.

As Ron disgustedly withdrew his foot, the Beagle heaved a sigh and settled down for a serious nap. Using that Ron-scented shoe as a toilet hadn't taken nearly as much time and effort as distributing those cement blocks.

Thus ended the Great Fencing Competition. While some might believe Ron had succeeded in defeating the Houdini Hound, I'm convinced it was a draw. Touché!

~Gail MacMillan

93

Corn Dogs

Teamwork is essential — it allows you to blame someone else.
~Author Unknown

I looked out the window and sighed. Not again. My yard looked like a scene from *The Beverly Hillbillies* — before they moved to Beverly Hills. It was trashed. With corn stalks. Corn husks and silks. Corn cobs. Anything corn. All compliments of the Bone Mafia.

Yes, the Bone Mafia. My two dogs. They earned that name extorting dog biscuits from me. Miss Chrissie, a Border Collie mix, showed up at our farm one day and made it very clear that she was there to stay. Mr. Nellie was a Bull Terrier mix from the local humane shelter. While he is my "couch potato extraordinaire," it doesn't take much encouragement from Miss Chrissie for him to join her in wreaking havoc somewhere on the farm. Apparently, my yard was now the daily recipient of their attention.

I cleaned up corn stalks, over and over again, only to have the yard totally littered the next day. How did they do that? It took a lot of work to "fill" my yard with all of that corn stuff. I was amazed. The corn stalks even included the roots.

I knew it had to be the dogs doing this, but I could never catch them raiding the cornfield. Until one day, when I had stepped outside for a minute, and I heard rustling in the cornfield. I thought I'd better check it out. When I did, I couldn't believe my eyes. The mystery was solved as I watched the corn dogs in action.

Each dog had a firm grip with his or her mouth on the same corn stalk, on opposite sides. Chrissie tugged her way for a while. Then Nellie tugged his way for a while. Tug and pull. Tug and pull. Back and forth. They tag-teamed that corn stalk until they pulled it, roots and all, out of the ground.

Then the two of them together carried the stalk to the yard. That alone was an amazing feat to watch as they maneuvered between all the other corn stalks (the number of which was decreasing each day!) to reach the yard, neither one letting go. I wonder—did each think if he or she let go, the other one would run off with "their" corn stalk?

Once the Bone Mafia reached the yard (and some shade), Nellie lay down, positioned the ear of corn, still attached to the stalk, between his two front paws and proceeded to strip the husks off the ear, leaf by leaf, silks and all. Once the ear of corn was unhusked, he gnawed all the corn off the cob. Chrissie just lay there watching him eat. No doubt proud that the "little woman" had provided a meal for her "man."

They rested a while in the shade, leaving the stalks, husks, silks, cobs, and kernels all around the yard. It didn't take long for them to get up and stretch in anticipation of their search for another corn stalk to annihilate.

I don't remember how long I stood watching all of this transpire. I just know it was amazing to watch them. How did they figure all this out? How did they decide who tugged when? How did Nellie learn how to husk corn?

I shook my head and had a good laugh. Even though it meant my yard was a littered mess, it actually was just too funny to worry about it. Let them have fun. What are a few corn stalks missing from our field? And the Bone Mafia just looked so cute as they trotted off to fetch their next corn stalk victim. I turned and headed back to the house.

And then stopped dead in my tracks. Wait a minute. Weren't they headed the wrong way to get to our cornfield? I turned around to check on them and heard the rustling of corn stalks.

From the neighbor's cornfield.

Oh my. I shook my head as I once again turned toward the house.

This time muttering, "I know nothing." But I also have to admit — a
little smile sneaked out.

~Linda Veath Cox

Not Ready to Share

Never trust a dog to watch your food.
~Author Unknown

"Gus is coming to stay with us," I told my kids over dinner one cool, autumn night. All three of them were happy to have him. He was the perfect houseguest. Well mannered and quiet, but fun too. He loved to play in the yard with the kids, cuddle up on the couch when invited and always finished his dinner.

Gus is a Boxer/German Shepherd mix who belonged to a friend of mine, a personal trainer who also owns and runs a nonprofit organization that trains young men and women preparing to enter the military. He ran his businesses like he ran his life. One hundred percent effort. No excuses. It's also how he raised Gus—which is why he was such a great guest. This was one well-trained dog.

Each morning of his week with us, I woke to find Gus waiting patiently for me to fill his food dish. As I padded around the house, checking his water, starting the coffee maker and rousing sleepy kids for school, I was reminded of how much I enjoyed having a dog in our family. It had been two years since our Boxer, Biscuit, went to Dog Heaven and I thought I was more calm without the extra mouth to feed. But, as it turned out, I'd missed having a four-legged friend with whom I could share my thoughts. Someone who would listen completely, love unconditionally, and greet me at the end of my day.

Our week with Gus passed quickly. The day before he was to go home I was at work, thinking that maybe it was time to begin the search for our next family pet. If I could find a dog as sweet and well behaved as Gus, I thought I might be ready. My phone rang, interrupting my reverie. It was my stepmom, Mary.

"I'm out running errands," she explained. "Wondering if I can stop by your house and leave a little surprise for you guys?"

"Sure!" Mary's surprises were usually of the sweet variety. And completely irresistible. Before I hung up, I reminded her that Gus would greet her when she walked in—just so she wouldn't be surprised. "Oh, right," she remembered. "Gus! He's so sweet. Such a good dog."

"Yep, that's Gus! He won't jump on you, but he'll probably greet you at the door. Maybe give you the once over sniff and then he'll go lie down."

We hung up and I went back to work.

As I left the office later that afternoon, I called my older son to see how his school day had gone. I got the standard response of "fine," and then remembered the surprise. "Oh, hey, what'd Grandma Mary leave?" I asked before he could hang up.

"Huh?"

"Grandma Mary said she was coming by today to drop off a surprise."

"Okay, hang on," he said. Then, after a beat, "Don't see anything."

"Really? That's strange. Maybe it's in the fridge."

I pictured him turning around in our small kitchen, pulling open the door.

"Uh. There's some Cool Whip."

"Cool Whip? Oh, keep looking—I'll bet she made a pumpkin pie!"

"I don't think there's a pie…" Connor started.

"Oh, hey," I said, interrupting him, "would you let Gus out? I should be home soon."

I hung up and smiled at the thought of pumpkin pie—my absolute favorite this time of year.

Thirty minutes later, I pulled into the driveway. All was quiet inside. The younger kids weren't home yet and Connor was engrossed in homework at the kitchen table. Gus was lying on the living room rug.

"Find the pie?"

"Nope. No pie." Connor barely glanced up from his textbook.

"What? But there's Cool Whip... there has to be a pie!" I did a 360 in the kitchen, checked counter tops, peered into the oven, and then turned the corner to check the dining room when I spied Gus, still lying on the carpet. That's strange, I thought. He usually comes to the door to greet me. I walked towards him and noticed something silver poking out from under the couch. I knelt on the carpet as Gus stood up and slinked out of the room. I grabbed the silver thing and pulled out a disposable pie plate. A clean, disposable pie plate.

Realization hit me just as the phone rang, and, suspicious, I stuck my nose in the pie plate and took a sniff. Pumpkin.

"GUS!" I yelled.

I grabbed the phone before I lost the call.

"Hello?"

"Did you get your surprise?" Mary asked.

"Uh, the pumpkin pie?" I guessed. "No, but Gus sure did."

"What?" she cried. "Seriously? I put it all the way at the back of the counter!" He's normally such a good dog..."

"I guess even the most well mannered dogs can't resist your homemade pumpkin pie!" I hung up the phone and gave Gus my no-nonsense, one-eyebrow-raised look. Maybe I wasn't ready for another dog. After all, I could share my home and my life. But my pumpkin pie? Forget it.

~Beth M. Wood

Wet Diggity Dog

Anybody who doesn't know what soap tastes like never washed a dog.
~Franklin P. Jones

I am the proud owner of a fur-lined bathtub. Some people have fuzzy slippers; I have a fuzzy bathroom. It happened on a weeknight, when I opted to give the dog a bath rather than watch the season finale of *Grey's Anatomy*. Ginger, our 100-pound chocolate Lab, hated baths.

Getting her into the bathroom was the easy part. Keeping her there proved to be the workout. I coaxed her into the tub, where, initially, she stood motionless with her tail dropped and head hung low. The only things that moved were her eyebrows, alternately twitching as she stared up at me with a pitiful expression that said, "I thought you loved me."

She stood silent as I soaked her from head to tail, but the moment I popped the top on the shampoo, she attempted to scale the wall. I tried to work fast and keep up, adding shampoo and scrubbing her fur as she played Slip'N Slide on the porcelain.

I thought I was a step ahead of her, but without warning, she leapt straight up, sending me backward. My backside met the floor hard enough to rattle the mirror on the wall. One hundred pounds of furry, foamy dog stood on top of me. There we were, nose to nose, reading each other's minds. Mine said, "Ow!" Ginger's said, "I hate you." By the time I wrangled her back into the tub, I was up to my armpits in dog hair and had lost a shoe.

Halfway through the rinse cycle, her body leaned to one side and she tilted her head. I knew what was coming next and there was absolutely nothing I could do to stop it. It started at the tip of her nose. She wobbled from side to side and her ears began to flap. I dropped the sprayer to the bottom of the tub, water shot toward the ceiling and rained down on us. I lunged toward her, took a handful of wet fur in each hand and screamed, "Stop!" Her body gyrated and she flung wet dog hair, water and shampoo across the room.

Giving her tail a few quick flicks, she attempted another escape. I now had shampoo in one eye, was trying to control the sprayer with my right hand and doing my best to contain a bundle of slippery fuzz with my left. It wasn't a pretty sight. The dog-scented steam made my hair droop and my mascara run, and I smelled like a wet bath mat.

Standing ankle-deep in a marsh of wet towels, I finished the rinse cycle as clumps of gloppy dog hair slid down the shower walls and filled the drain. The sound of the water shutting off triggered another full-body shake, but this time I was ready. I tossed a towel across Ginger's back, took hold of her tail and flung my body over hers. We both hit the floor with an "oomph," and she scurried madly on the tile, trying to escape the confines of the bathroom as I attempted to towel her dry.

The minute the door opened she raced through the house like a rabid ping pong ball. With eyes wide and tongue flapping, she did laps through the kitchen, over the couch, down the hall, under the table, behind the chair and back down the hall. As much as she hated bath time, she loved the crazy, canine celebration that followed.

It took me an hour to clean my dog and twice as long to clean my bathroom. I rinsed the tub, wiped the walls, mopped the floor and did a load of laundry that consisted of eight towels and my soggy clothes.

It was the next morning that Ginger got her revenge. I stood in the shower, washing my hair, when something fell from the ceiling and landed on my shoulder. Spider! The biggest, hairiest, brown spider that I'd seen in my life. I did what any logical woman would do. Screamed at the top of my lungs and flung myself out of the tub. I ran out the bathroom door, flailing my arms and slapping at myself as if I were under some sort of naked bumblebee attack. By the time I reached the end of the hall, I realized that my assailant was actually a glob of wet, leftover dog hair.

As I turned back toward the bathroom, there sat Ginger with a dog-smile on her face, swinging her tail so hard that her whole body wagged. I had always known that dogs could love, feel guilt, express happiness and even pout. And right then and there, I learned that dogs can laugh. For Ginger, justice had been served.

~Ann Morrow

He Can't Jump

A dog desires more affection than his dinner. Well—almost!
~Charlotte Gray

" am glad we did the biopsy, Lorraine," Dr. Tom, my vet said gently. "The lump was full of cancer."

I wasn't sure how to react. I was numb. Marshall was my first yellow Lab service dog, and we had been partnered for less than a month. I was thirty and used to being on my own, still adjusting to sharing my apartment with this new creature and making him part of my life. In that short time, I had grown to love him. The devastation consumed me. I had no idea how to care for a sick animal. My cerebral palsy meant that I was the one who often needed medical procedures; I wasn't used to nursing a loved one through an illness.

I immediately called the owner of the service dog school, with whom I had worked closely when I got matched with Marshall. When he heard the situation, he said matter-of-factly, "Well, if he dies, you can get another dog." Then he hung up. My blood ran cold.

In the long days that followed, family and friends offered their advice. "You can't be too attached at this point, you just met. Why don't you just give him back and get another dog?" they said. But that wasn't an option for me. My parents didn't "get another one" when my disability was diagnosed. I had bonded with Marshall—we belonged together. I wasn't going to reject him because he had cancer. I was committed to him no matter what.

His surgery was the day before Thanksgiving. The weather was clear and cold. Marshall was prepped and anesthetized. Although I knew that he was in excellent hands, my belly did somersaults as I waited helplessly. What if something went wrong? What if his pain was out of control? What if I couldn't handle his recovery? I prayed to God fervently. Marshall had to be okay. Surgery was going to make him better, and then I was going to do everything in my power to help him get well.

Thanksgiving morning I brought him home with a big plastic cone on his head and a goofy, tired grin on his face. His abdomen had been shaved and he had a belly full of stitches. I was nervous about caring for him. Removing the tumor had been a difficult surgery for Marshall. Would his recovery be tricky as well?

The vet gave me a gentle warning: "Marshall won't be able to jump, Lorraine. He won't have much energy. And his incision site is pretty tender, so be careful."

Marshall was moving pretty slowly, but otherwise he seemed okay. We were ready to spend a quiet holiday by ourselves. Once we were home, Marshall and I snuggled for most of the day as I kept a close eye on him. He was groggy, but he seemed satisfied with the loving attention I showered on him. Late in the afternoon, while he dozed, I put the finishing touches on a small ham for my Thanksgiving dinner. As I drizzled the pineapple glaze on top, the phone rang in my bedroom. It was my sister calling to ask about Marshall. We exchanged holiday greetings for several short minutes before I returned to the kitchen.

The ham was gone.

Marshall was sitting in the corner licking his lips and looking extremely pleased with himself.

As I look back, it seems pretty hilarious, but at that moment I was panic-stricken. My dog, who was not even supposed to be able to jump, had pulled an entire ham off the counter and eaten the whole thing in less than five minutes. What if he had ripped through his stitches? What if he had done some internal damage? How was I supposed to take care of him?

I explained the situation to Dr. Tom on the phone. He was also stunned that Marshall had physically accomplished this mischief. With step-by-step instructions, he told me that I needed to make Marshall vomit. I filled a turkey baster with hydrogen peroxide and determinedly squeezed it down his throat. A little confused about the change in my demeanor, he obediently accompanied me outside and we waited.

As Marshall walked close to my wheelchair, around the grounds of my apartment complex, I talked to him. "I love you buddy. I want you to be well. We will do whatever it takes. What were you thinking?" Never before had I urged anyone to throw up, but Marshall, it turned out, exposed me to many new experiences. "C'mon buddy. Let it all out. All that salty ham isn't good for you right now."

Nothing happened.

After about half an hour, I called the vet again, and then repeated the process. Back outside, we went around and around. I petted and prodded, I threatened and encouraged. But Marshall never threw up. Not even after two more doses of hydrogen peroxide. He did burp once, though. I could tell that he thought I had unrealistic expectations.

Several hours later I called the vet for the last time that evening. Although I was quite shaken, Dr. Tom assured me that Marshall would likely be okay.

Marshall, on the other hand, seemed to wonder what all the fuss was about. This sort of stunt, I would learn, was in his nature. Jumping up on the counter to eat an entire ham was an incredible opportunity. Marshall didn't want to empty his belly, he wanted to fill it! As we drifted to sleep that night, his eyes glazed over and I could nearly hear him say, "Pass the sweet potatoes!"

Marshall and I shared nine Thanksgiving holidays thereafter. On each one, I gave Marshall a much smaller piece of ham, as a celebration of his unconquerable spirit and cast iron stomach.

He never had to jump for it again.

~Lorraine Cannistra

Everyone's a Decorator

A designer knows he has achieved perfection not when there is nothing left to add, but when there is nothing left to take away.

~Antoine de Saint-Exupéry

In high school, I considered a career in architecture and design. I loved math, science and art. Throughout childhood, while other kids had posters, unmade beds and general chaos in their rooms, mine was always magazine-photo-ready. But I lacked self-confidence. When selecting colleges, I elected to study finance and economics. It was safer.

Therefore, when I purchased my first home in my mid-twenties, I was excited at the prospect of buying furniture, selecting accessories, painting walls and hanging wallpaper. My one-bedroom condo was a first-floor unit with a covered patio and small, enclosed garden. To my upper floor neighbors' delight, I had inherited my mom's green thumb. The walled area was jammed full of bougainvillea, mandevilla, allamanda, hibiscus, begonias, bromeliads, coleus and caladiums.

With all that life growing just feet away, I felt alone. My solution involved falling in love with the sweetest eight-week-old Cairn Terrier. I named him Rascal T. Ragamuffin. Who knew that dark, chubby, sweet-smelling bundle would end up with long flowing brindled locks crowned by a shock of blond on his head? He was easy to spot in my green jungle.

From the books I had read on Cairns, my little terrier should have excavated the entire garden, along with those of my neighbors, before his first birthday. His apparent failed DNA was my win. His interest in the back yard consisted of chasing lizards and butterflies, not digging.

He did have an opinion, though, about one particular houseplant. One day, after I had dared to relocate it, I came home to a canine crime scene. The helpless victim had been dug up, dragged across the carpet, and left for dead near the sliding glass door. I assumed if he had been equipped with opposable thumbs and more height, Rascal would have tossed the offender into the garden, where he undoubtedly felt it belonged.

In a household of one dog and one fish, my little terrier was not only my primary suspect, he was my only suspect. Actually, he rolled over the minute I laid eyes on him. After performing an emergency replanting and thorough cleansing of the evidence, I came home to the same carnage the next afternoon. I decided it was in the best interest of both the victim and repeat offender to permanently relocate the plant back to its original spot. Rascal never touched it again. I speculated his uprooting spree was less a breed characteristic and more a comment on my decorating decision.

This incident seemed to have awakened Rascal's inner interior designer. At the time, my home was fully decorated except for some minor tweaks here and there. A consuming business career left little time for me to do everything I wanted. Yes, I had plans, big plans involving a tiled foyer and kitchen along with a little wallpaper sprinkled about. But they remained just that, plans. With spare time a luxury, I talked a good game but procrastinated an even better one and Rascal apparently got tired of listening.

At just over a year old, Rascal was good but still not trustworthy enough for complete run of my home all day. Upon advice from my dad, he graduated from his cage to being baby-gated in the roomy eat-in kitchen. It had two walls of cabinets in an L shape, a pass-through to the dining room, a round wood table with four wooden chairs near the outside wall, and three bifold wooden doors enclosing a pantry and separate washer/dryer closet. All sat on top of builder-grade, one-piece linoleum flooring.

Arriving home from work one day, I dropped my purse and briefcase, then rounded the corner from the foyer and headed to the kitchen. I chatted in response to Rascal's barks of happiness that I, his beloved mistress, had returned to him. At the doorway, I automatically reached for the gate latch, focusing on nothing but my happy precious boy. As I chattered, something caught my eye. I looked up and stopped in midsentence. I blinked to clear my contact lenses but the vision before me remained constant.

Everywhere, and I mean everywhere, was nothing but bare concrete. That not-so-gorgeous linoleum flooring had been reduced to pieces of varying size and scattered about like autumn leaves. Still by the gate, wagging and barking his cheerful welcome was my little Rascal. Oh, so aptly named.

My little guy, my industrious little terrier, had found the one tiny section of flooring popping out from under the baseboard. With nothing to do and nothing to lose, he gripped the linoleum and gave it a little tug. To his surprise, it gave way. With laser focus and time on his side, Rascal ripped up every bit of that nasty linoleum and put an end to my ranting and procrastinating about that floor. Rascal worked long and hard until he had pulled up every single bit of flooring that wasn't under an appliance, behind a bifold door or actually glued down.

Without a choice, doggy-proof tile was installed within a month. Unless he rented a jackhammer, I felt safe from my twelve-pound hairy demolition team. I still remember the day the tile installers came to start the job. They took one look at the floor and thanked me for helping them with the demo. I smiled as I held up Rascal and told them it was him they needed to thank. Their laughter still rings in my ears all these years later.

~Debbie Kalata

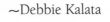

98

The Shoplifter

The odds of going to the store for a loaf of bread and coming out with only a loaf of bread are three billion to one.
~Erma Bombeck

I was the fourth generation to live on an isolated ten-acre tract of woods, fields, and lawns that had once been a working farm. Through the generations, my family watched a city spring up all around us. Gradually, neighboring families sold their properties, which were replaced with housing developments and commercial properties. On the western side of our small tract of land was a public library; on the eastern side was a funeral parlor.

When I was a senior in college, a shopping center was built directly behind us. While it was now convenient to do our grocery shopping, we also had to get accustomed to the new activity. We often heard loud noises at night from delivery trucks.

One morning, having finished my exams for the last semester, my mother and I walked the property while talking about my future plans. Meghan, our three-year-old, free-spirited Irish Setter, had disappeared into the woods. Before long Meghan reappeared, carrying a loaf of bread in her mouth. My mother had always prided herself on instilling good values in her children. It was clear by the look on her face that she had the same expectations of the dog.

"Deborah, you don't think Meghan is stealing the bread from the store do you?"

It was clear that she didn't want an answer. She looked horrified at the possibility that her dog could be a criminal and dismissed the thought. Maybe somebody had thrown it into the trash and Meghan had simply picked it up.

Mom kept a watchful eye on her to make sure that it did not happen again. For a while things seemed good. Every time Meghan would leave the property, Mom would call her back. One Saturday afternoon my mother sent me to the store to get some last-minute items. While at the checkout counter I heard the store clerk say, "Oh here comes that Irish Setter again." Sure enough it was Meghan. I watched, paralyzed, as everyone laughed. She had figured out how to work the automatic door. Nonchalantly, she headed to the bread aisle near the front of the store. She took a loaf of bread and walked out, followed by a store clerk shooing her. I was horrified. All I could think to do was to offer to pay for the bread.

When I got outside, the dog was nowhere in sight. I found her at home with the loaf of bread, and told Mom what I had just witnessed. My mother took the bread from the dog and shook her head in disbelief. She could not believe she had raised a shoplifter. She looked at me and said, "She didn't even get the right brand."

Meghan was on home confinement after that.

~Deborah Henderson Roberts

99

The Great Christmas Cookie Caper

A cat, after being scolded, goes about its business. A dog slinks off into a corner and pretends to be doing a serious self-reappraisal.
~Robert Brault, rbrault.blogspot.com

One of the most amazing gifts I've ever received came in the form of a grossly overweight six-year-old Golden Retriever named Nemo. Nemo was owned by the neighbors of my wife's hairdresser. For a variety of reasons, the dog's weight was allowed to balloon to over 170 pounds. The vet told the owners that the dog would likely die soon if something wasn't done about his weight.

I'm not normally much of a volunteer, but in spite of the fact that we were in the midst of adapting to a rambunctious six-month-old Golden Retriever puppy named Molly, I offered to do what I could to help Nemo. Something about his story touched my heart.

The original arrangement was for Nemo to alternate weeks between our house and that of his owners. We were both to do our best to get him out walking and monitor his food intake. Since I enjoy walking anyway, it wasn't hard for me to incorporate Nemo into my routine. It seemed that his owners had trouble finding the time to do their part. I was just about ready to give up on the deal when they asked if I'd adopt Nemo. I felt I shared a bond with the dog and was happy to take him full time.

Of course I had to get my wife's blessing and convince her of the benefits of having two big dogs in our house. It really didn't take much effort since she seemed to like Nemo too. Molly enjoyed having him around, and except for the occasional turf battle, the transition went smoothly. Nemo became an official member of our family.

We watched Nemo's food intake closely and walked him three or four times daily through all kinds of weather. His diet consisted of three cups of dog food per day, and his treats were mostly bits of raw fruits or vegetables. It took nearly two years to get Nemo below one hundred pounds, but he did it!

There was one major bump in the road for Nemo. When he was around eight years old, he tore his right ACL and had to undergo surgery. This injury probably resulted from being so overweight for so many years. But Nemo endured the discomfort and pushed through the arduous, boring, and likely painful rehabilitation regime. Within six months he was back to his old self.

What we found in Nemo was a gentle, wise soul who had the heart of a warrior. One day while on a walk an unfamiliar dog approached us in a very aggressive manner. In the blink of an eye Nemo positioned himself between Molly and me and the other dog so he could meet the charge head-on. He quickly ran the aggressor off. As I said, our gentle giant has the heart of a warrior.

Nemo embraced his new active life with enthusiasm, and begrudgingly put up with the reduced rations. But while Nemo lost—and kept off—over seventy pounds, he certainly didn't lose his deep affection for food! Given an opportunity, our boy has proven many times that he can and will eat just about anything. One of the more notable incidents was what we now refer to as the Great Christmas Cookie Caper.

One of my wife's holiday traditions includes baking hundreds of intricately decorated Christmas cookies for get-togethers and gifts. She would put some cookies on foil-wrapped trays and store them on our porch until needed. We never had a problem with this arrangement until one holiday season.

One night, after we had been asleep for a few hours, Nemo let me know that he needed to go outside. He barely made it out the door before his bowels exploded! This scenario repeated several more times during the course of the night. It was very unusual for Nemo to be ill and we could not figure out what was wrong. The next day I noticed that the door to the porch was slightly open.

As soon as I walked onto the porch I saw why Nemo had been sick. I remembered that I snagged a couple of cookies after lunch the previous day and I must not have secured the porch door after my cookie raid. Nemo was obviously presented with an opportunity he couldn't resist. By the looks of the demolished trays, it appeared that Nemo indulged himself with about one hundred very fancy cookies!

A quick call to the vet put us at ease when we were told that our big boy might be uncomfortable, but would be in no serious danger. As best as we could tell, our little Molly had taken no part in the Great Cookie Caper and she seemed to enjoy being the "good dog," even if just for one day.

As for my wife, I'm still trying to make it up to her.

~Jim Carey

Tropical Punch

*No animal ever invented anything so bad as drunkenness —
or so good as drink.*
~Lord Chesterton

A Westie's job description includes going to ground, which is code for chasing and capturing small animals. Being true to his breed, life with Mac meant time outdoors. Time outdoors meant pursuing butterflies, lizards and tree frogs. His "game" habitat was enclosed by stucco walls and was lush with South Florida tropical vegetation. There was even a koi pond available as an alfresco thirst-quencher until Mac fell in one too many times. Afterward, he steered clear of that watering hole. With screening secured across the wrought iron gate's bottom to prevent escapes into the greenway, my white hunter roamed the wilds before charging the kitchen door for air conditioning.

Early one spring afternoon, a day like any other day, my little terrier explored his dominion and terrorized the occupants. Afterwards, he napped, walked, played and ate — nothing special, nothing out of the ordinary. That is, until four the next morning.

Roused by the sound of hacking and heaving, I bolted out of bed, grabbed the source and made it to the bathroom in the nick of time. After cleaning dog and floor, Mac continued until the dry heaves ceased. Cradling him, I pondered whether dogs got the flu, my memory vague on the meaning of wet versus dry noses.

After showering and dressing, we were off to the vet's two miles away. I recounted the last hours as we were ushered into a room. At fifteen months, Mac had already visited several times, a few to complete his puppy shots, an overnight stay for neutering, then twice more for routine vaccines. It was a place familiar enough to elicit apprehension. My alpha dog wannabe was diagnosed early with an incurable case of white coat syndrome. Whenever a vet or technician came into view, Mac would, well, pee. Though the technical term used started with submissive, one never uses submissive and Westie in the same sentence. His notoriety was great for one so young, and the receptionist automatically provided a towel to protect the metal examination table.

After pleasantries, embarrassment and Mac's tale of woe, the doctor examined my laddie. Chatting about minor issues potentially causing his angst, he poked here, checked there, then began to run his hands over his belly. Mid-sentence, he paused.

"Ah, I feel a lump in Mac's abdomen," he said lightly.

I blinked back tears at the mention of that four-letter word. Suddenly, I was back in time, listening to another tell me about my seven-year-old Cairn.

"You mean cancer?" I choked.

"Oh my, no, don't think so. However, I need to take an X-ray to see what we're dealing with."

He suggested I leave Mac and head off to work. It would take time to set up everything. The vet would call once he knew the prognosis. Clutching Mac, wanting to stay, but knowing I had to go, I bowed to his wisdom.

That day I jumped with each ring of my phone, disappointed until I heard the vet's voice. The X-ray confirmed a blockage. It required surgery. While I was congratulated for bringing him in early, he could have been dehydrated and complicated the situation. I felt guilty for not remaining at his side. The vet's staff was prepping Mac for surgery. He'd call when it was over. I hung up, happy Mac was being cared for but upset it meant going under the knife.

The morning dragged on. Around noon, the second call came. The surgery was a success. Mac was fine and sleeping off the anesthesia. Maybe my nerves were still on edge or I was too elated all went well, but the doctor made the strangest comment. I asked him to please repeat.

"I said we removed two palm seeds from his intestinal track."

"Palm seeds?" I still thought I'd misheard.

"Yep," he laughed.

I told him there were several Christmas palms in the back yard. Yes, they occasionally dropped one-inch crimson seeds. No, I'd never seen Mac put any in his mouth. Apparently, I wasn't as observant as I should've been. Putting a screen on the gate was the least of my worries. Here I thought he was chasing the lizards and tree frogs. Instead, my puppy was sucking the jelly from the palm seeds. Ah, another Westie job, a perpetual fixation with food. Seems my laddie had accidently swallowed two seeds during his gorging.

From what the vet relayed, the jelly has a similar effect to consuming a wee bit of alcohol. My puppy had been hitting the sauce in the back yard. No wonder he had fallen into the koi pond so many times. It all began to make sense.

Unconcerned he'd become a palm seed junkie, my only thought that day was leaving to see Mac. While he was groggy and barely noticed I was there, I was grateful he was getting better. I called every morning and stopped by every evening; even my mom dropped by midday. A week later, the call came for his release.

After our reunion and his bill settlement, the receptionist asked that I wait. The doctor wanted to speak with me. A few minutes later, he walked out of an examination room, a big grin on his face and a small object in his hand. Then held out a glass container.

"Here they are, Debbie."

I was shocked at their size. They looked like two almonds.

"You might want to gold plate these guys. You know, make them into a set of dangle earrings. You've already spent enough money, might want to get some mileage out of them." That healing man snickered.

Cuddling Mac, I laughed before donning a no-nonsense face. "We'll be back to have his stiches removed but not again until his regular checkup. Everything's going back to normal. All the palm trees will have their flowers cut before ever turning to seeds. There'd be no more gorging in the back yard, no more drunken Westies." I nodded my head for emphasis.

The vet patted my shoulder and threw me a wink before turning to heal another. As if knowing this was just the beginning.

~Debbie Kalata

One Smart Yorkie

The fishing was good; it was the catching that was bad.
~A.K. Best

"Okay, I got his head out of the weeds. Now keep your rod tip up and reel like crazy—don't let him go down again." My husband Roy instructed his daughter, Shirlene, as she attempted to land a gargantuan catfish. Another good "pump and reel" from Shirlene and the fish was at the surface, "surfing" back to the shore. George Mutt, our nine-month-old fish-loving Yorkie, could no longer contain his excitement. He jumped in the lake and swam to follow the fish in. Swimming behind the fish and snapping at its tail, George Mutt became "Lake Jaws." Shirlene had to reel quickly to keep the fish ahead of the Yorkie on the hunt.

We all had gone to Lake Texana on a weekend campout with friends and had decided to catch our supper. We had tried bream at first, but they were too small to make a meal. So we changed our strategy to catfish and started catching them almost immediately. First, we caught a two-pound catfish. George Mutt waited on dry land and watched Roy reel in the fish. As soon as the fish hit shore, however, George jumped on him, mauling his tail. He liked fresh fish and really didn't care if we fried his dinner first. Roy defended his catch, unhooked him and—since one fish wouldn't feed all of us—put the fish on a stringer. He then stuck the stringer in the ground near an oak tree's roots that extended over the lake, and threw the fish into a deep hole. George

Mutt watched this process intently. Some plan was being hatched in that little doggy head—but what?

Shirlene called out—she had a second one. George, excited, ran up and down the shoreline, barking encouragement for Shirlene. She had a hard time getting it out of the lake weeds, but after a brief struggle, she landed a three-pound catfish. As it reached the shallows, George jumped in and followed it. He grabbed hold of its tail and swam in with it. "You're gonna have to let go, Mutt," Roy said as he unhooked the fish, pried off George and went over to the stringer. Again, George was mesmerized by the process.

The next time Shirlene called out, the rod was bent over double and she was having trouble staying on the shore. The fish was trying to free himself in the weeds at the bottom of the lake. Neither she nor her dad could turn that fish's head to the surface with just the rod and reel. So Roy told Shirlene to hold on as he waded out to untangle the fish. About chest-deep in the lake, he reached down and extricated the fish from the log it was caught on. Then he directed his daughter to keep its head up and reel like crazy.

With some effort, she accomplished this and the fish started "surfing" back. It was then that George Mutt jumped into the lake after that fish, chomping at the fish's tail every chance he got. This fish was a nice eight-pound catfish—almost as big as the Yorkie, who was beside himself with anticipation. He REALLY wanted THAT fish. Again, Roy pried George off the fish and strung it with the other two. When Roy put the fish back in the water this time, George continued staring at where they had gone back into the water. He was intent on doing something—but what?

I was about to call George away from the water when he put his plan in action. George picked up the stringer in his mouth and tried pulling the fish out of the water. That didn't work, so he quickly adjusted his plans. He walked to the edge of the tree root hanging over the deep hole and picked up the stringer in his mouth. He carefully placed the stringer on top of the root and backed up to the shoreline. The fish were not out of the water yet, so he laid down the stringer on the tree root, taking meticulous care to put his full body weight on the stringer. He walked back to the water, keeping his steps on top of the stringer to hold it in place. When he got to the end, he deftly picked up the next length of stringer and backed up until he got to the shoreline a second time.

George repeated this process two more times before he got the entire stringer of fish to the surface where he could see them. Then, unable to lift the thirteen pounds of fish out of the water and drag them to land, he jumped in the hole with them, trying to bite his dinner while they were still swimming.

Roy, Shirlene and I fell on the ground laughing before we could separate George from his "catch." Who would have ever thought George would "fish" for his dinner?

~Janice R. Edwards

Meet Our Contributors

Melissa Abraham resides with her husband in south Louisiana. She is a freelance translator specializing in French, Spanish, and Italian. She is the Newsletter Editor for the Writers' Guild of Acadiana and is currently working on a young adult fantasy novel. Follow her blog at www.melissaabraham.com.

Kathryn Hackett Bales lives near Elko, NV with two Pit Bulls and a Rottweiler. She is a retired bus driver and a Navy veteran. Her first novel, *Crazy Ladies on a Bus*, was published in 2013, with a sequel due in October. The proceeds from the series will go to Pit Bull rescue.

Kelsey Kate Bankert writes from a small island off the Georgia coast. She has a B.A. degree *cum laude* from Mount Holyoke College and an M.A. degree in modern European history. Her most recent book is *The Architecture of Trauma*. She is currently writing children's fiction and has happily taken up the ukulele.

Linda Bartlett, Christian, wife, mother of three, grandmother to four, teacher (forever), flight attendant (former), dog lover (big time), and now writer. Linda has traveled to all seven continents and loves to spend her free time with children, nature, books, and of course, dogs.

Gretchen Bassier holds a B.A. degree in Psychology from the University of Michigan-Dearborn. She lives in Michigan with four cats, eleven doves, and four horses—all sources of inspiration for her writing. She has written numerous short stories, one and a half novels, and hopes to start a nonprofit to benefit feral cats.

Diane Ganzer Baum has been writing professionally since 2004. *Patrick the Wayward Setter* was her first published book, followed by many more for readers of all ages, both fiction as well as nonfiction. She is married and lives in a little town on the prairie in western Minnesota, where she plans to keep writing and gardening.

Susan Blakeney is a writer of fiction for children and young adults with several novels in various stages of development. These include two historical novels and a number of works of speculative fiction, one being the story that awoke her passion for writing several years ago. E-mail her at susan@susanblakeney.com.

Cynthia Briggs embraces her love of cooking and writing through her cookbooks *Pork Chops & Applesauce* and *Sweet Apple Temptations*. She enjoys speaking to women's groups, coaching budding authors, teaching memoir writing and writing for various publications. E-mail Cynthia at info@porkshopsandapplesauce.net.

Karla Brown lives in Philadelphia with her husband and cat. She loves to garden, swim, cook, read, pursue all things chocolate, and daydream. She hopes to become a novelist, as she also writes paranormal romantic suspense, YA and middle grade.

Jill Burns lives in the mountains of West Virginia with her wonderful family. She's a retired piano teacher and performer. She enjoys writing, music, gardening, nature, and spending time with her grandchildren.

Kimberley Campbell lives in Centreville, NB, with her husband, two cats and two retired racing Greyhounds. She enjoys skating, biking and walking with her husband and hounds, as well as reading, writing and spending time with her three young nieces.

Lorraine Cannistra has a Bachelor of Science degree in English and Master of Science degree in Rehabilitation Counseling from Emporia State University. She enjoys advocating, cooking, writing and motivational speaking. Her passions are wheelchair ballroom dance and her service dog, Leah. Enjoy her blog at healthonwheels.wordpress.com.

Jim Carey lives in Sheboygan, WI with his wife Janet and their two Golden Retrievers—Molly and, the star of the story, Nemo. Jim is a practicing chiropractor and the author of the Civil War novel, *Echoes from Home*.

Mark Carlson and his wife Jane live in San Diego with his retired guide dog Musket and new guide dog Saffron. Legally blind, Mark is an aviation historian and writes for several national magazines. He is the author of *Confessions of a Guide Dog* and *Flying on Film: A Century of Aviation in the Movies*.

After spending the majority of her life with dogs, **Katharina Cirko** is convinced that the main purpose of their too-short lives is to teach humans how to love completely and selflessly. She hopes to one day write a book of stories about all the dogs who have brought such joy to her life.

Helen Colella is a freelance writer, retired teacher and grandmother of three. Her published works include educational books and materials; articles and stories for adults and children; Chicken Soup for the Soul and other anthologies; parenting magazines; *Explore & Discover National Parks*, a family activity book; consultant for blue13creative.

Linda Veath Cox lives in southern Illinois with the Bone Mafia—her two mixed breed mutts. A retired secretary from the Illinois Department of Natural Resources, she has had short stories and devotions published and is a regular contributor to Divine Detour at http://kathyharrisbooks.com/blog.

Linda Delmont lives in Orange County, CA, with her husband and a menagerie of pets: two dogs, two cats, a rabbit, and ten spoiled hens. She graduated in 2012 with an MFA degree in poetry from California State University, Long Beach and works as a substitute teacher. Her hobbies include gardening, reading, and raising monarch butterflies.

Laurie Doyle is a corporate communications executive living in Massachusetts. She received a B.A. degree in Russian from Middlebury College and an MBA degree from Simmons College. She has one daughter, Kira, who is her greatest pride and joy. In addition to her miracle dog, Charlie, Laurie has two cats, Clyde and Hannah.

Janice R. Edwards received her BAT degree, with honors, from Sam Houston State University in 1974. She taught English and journalism before working for Texaco. Now she writes freelance for *Image* magazine, showcasing Brazoria County, TX. She has published stories in *Chicken Soup for the Soul: My Dog's Life* and *Chicken Soup for the Soul: I Can't Believe My Dog Did That!*

Karen Ekstrom graduated from the University of Texas, where she majored in Chi Omega and fun. Five kids later, Karen just finished her first novel and started a blog—FlunkingFamily.com. If humor is your thing... Contact her at kcekstrom@yahoo.com.

Terri Elders lives near Colville, WA with a dog and three cats. A lifelong writer and editor, she's published stories in dozens of periodicals and anthologies, including multiple Chicken Soup for the Soul books. She co-edited *Not Your Mother's Book... On Travel* and blogs at http://atouchoftarragon.blogspot.com.

Lisa Erspamer is the president of Unleashed Media and the creator of the *A Letter to My Dog*, *A Letter to My Cat* and the upcoming *A Letter to My Mom* books. Before starting her own company, Lisa served as Chief Creative Officer for OWN and as the Co-Executive Producer of *The Oprah Winfrey Show*. Lisa lives in Los Angeles with her two pups, Lily and Grace.

Samantha Eskew received her Bachelor of Science degree from Florida State University. She is a third-year medical student and new mom to daughter, Madison. Samantha enjoys spending time with husband Ryan and their two dogs, Baron and Boden. Between a new baby and their four-legged family members, there's never a dull moment!

Carol Lee Espy is a multi-hyphenate... that's right, it goes like this: singer-songwriter-multi-Mid-Atlantic-Emmy-winner-producer-writer-TV-Radio-voice-over-artist-mom-wife-darn-good-friend. She is prone to spontaneous golf outings and stealth dawn patrols at estate sales. She employs writing and popcorn as cheap therapy.

Antonia Everts lives near Portland, OR with her family—where she teaches gymnastics. In addition to writing, she enjoys running, gardening, reading and baking. She is currently at work on a novel about the relationships between people and their dogs. E-mail her at antoniaeverts@yahoo.com.

RoseAnn Faulkner is a retired elementary school teacher. This is her third story published in Chicken Soup for the Soul books. She lives in Yuma, AZ. E-mail her at roseannfaulkner@gmail.com.

Kristi Cocchiarella FitzGerald has degrees in English and Theater and pursued graduate work in costumes until she realized she'd rather be writing. She lives in a place of spectacular beauty where she shares her life with her rugged Montana fisherman, their two Shih Tzus, Panda and Koala, and a diva cat named Moose.

Judith Fitzsimmons lives in Franklin, TN, and has been writing for personal enjoyment and professional use for over twenty years. It is with the fondest of memories that she dedicates this story to "my Ubu boy," who continues to warm her heart and spirit.

Carol Chiodo Fleischman's writing has appeared in books, newspapers, and a textbook. Her topics cover a wide range of everyday events.

A recurring theme is life as a blind person, especially the joys and challenges of using a seeing-eye dog. Pelican Publishing has scheduled a release for a children's book about her guide dog, Nadine.

Peggy Frezon writes for *Guideposts* magazine, and is author of books about the human-animal bond: *Dieting with my Dog*; *The Dieting with my Dog Guide to Weight Loss & Maintenance*; *Heart to Heart, Hand in Paw*; *Greetings at the Front Door* (2015). Fetch her free newsletter at http://peggyfrezon.blogspot.com/p/pawsitively-pets.html.

Nancy B. Gibbs is a pastor's wife, mother and grandmother. She is an author and motivational speaker. Nancy has had stories in numerous Chicken Soup for the Soul books and many other anthologies, devotional guides, newspapers and national magazines. E-mail her at nancybgibbs@aol.com or through her website at www.nancybgibbs.com.

Tiffany Doerr Guerzon is a freelance writer and the mother to three children and one dog named Porsche. Read more of her writing at www.TDGuerzon.com.

Judy Gyde is a retired nurse and a freelance writer from Toledo, OH. Her work has appeared in fifty publications and her first book, *Harvest Fields*, will soon be in print. Judy and her husband love to travel, garden, and spoil their ten grandkids. She continues to surprise her neighbors' dogs with delicious treats.

Hana Haatainen-Caye, speaker/writing instructor, has a copywriting, editing, and voice-over business. With over forty children's books published, she has won awards for her poetry, short stories, and blog (www.greengrandma.org). She is the author of the nonfiction book *Vinegar Fridays*. E-mail her at greengrandma@comcast.net.

Elizabeth SanFilippo Hall received her Bachelor of Arts degree from Augustana College and her master's from The University of Chicago. When not working part-time at The International Kitchen and freelance writing, she's a full-time mommy to a daughter born in April 2014 and Kafka the Bulldog. E-mail her at esanfilippo@lizsink.com.

Karen R. Hessen is a speaker and author of inspirational nonfiction and humor. A frequent contributor to Chicken Soup for the Soul, Karen also writes the column "Out of the Ark" for the *Seaside Signal* and *The News Guard*. Karen and Douglas live in Oregon. E-mail her at karenwrites@frontier.com.

Charlotte Hopkins is a writer from Pittsburgh. Her first book, *Everything You Wanted to Know about the Heroes in Blue*, was published in 2012. She has two children and works in childcare. She is writing a children's book series to teach preschoolers in a fun way and a life skills book for teens titled *And Then I Stepped in Gum*.

Gayle M. Irwin is a writer and speaker whose works include inspirational children's books, other Chicken Soup for the Soul compilations, magazine articles, and two devotional books for dog lovers. She conducts presentations to groups and classrooms. Learn more at www.gaylemirwin.com.

Jeanie Jacobson is on the leadership team of Wordsowers Christian Writers Group. She's currently writing a Christian fantasy series. She's active in ministries at her church, including the praise dance team. She loves spending time with family and friends, reading, hiking, and gardening. E-mail her at jeaniej@cox.net.

Pamela Jenkins lives with her husband in rural Oklahoma. Her hobbies include writing, crocheting, and growing irises on their farm.

Debbie Kalata received her BBA and MBA degrees from Florida International University. She lives in south Florida with her three-year-old Westie — Sir Brodric MacGreggor. She enjoys writing and has dabbled in essays, short stories, nonfiction, and novels. Her goal is to publish in all four categories.

Amanda Kemp earned her bachelor's degree in English and women's studies in 2002, then added to her collection in 2005 with a master's in education. After teaching for eight years, she is staying at home with her two young sons. She is an aspiring fiction writer, scribbling madly during the fleeting moments of alone time.

Alice Klies is a past contributor to *Chicken Soup for the Soul: Just Us Girls*. She is a member of Word Weavers International. She is published in *Angels On Earth*, *The Wordsmith Journal*, and four anthologies: *God Still Meets Needs*; *Grandmother, Mother and Me*; *Grandfather, Father and Me* and *Friends of Inspire Faith*.

Ian Kochberg and his wife Arlene live with their Black Russian Terrier, SchuBRT, very near to their wonderful children and beautiful grandchildren. Ian is a lifelong dog lover, as well as being a full-time artist/master printmaker. Arlene has managed the company (and Ian) for the past thirty-six years. Learn more at www.iankochberg.com.

Joyce Laird is a freelance writer living in Southern California with her menagerie of animal companions. Her features have been published in many magazines, including *Cat Fancy*, *Grit*, *Mature Living*, *I Love Cats* and *Vibrant Life*. She contributes regularly to *Woman's World* and to the Chicken Soup for the Soul anthologies.

Cathi LaMarche spends most of her day reveling in the written word as a composition teacher, college essay coach, and novelist. Her work has appeared in twenty-three anthologies. She lives in Missouri with her husband, two children, and three spoiled dogs.

Diana Lynn is a business owner and freelance writer in Washington State. This is her sixth story published by Chicken Soup for the Soul. She jokes often about how no one is safe in her world; anyone can end up in a story—even the dog. E-mail her at Diana@recoveringdysfunctional. com.

The award-winning author of thirty-two published books and a graduate of Queen's University, **Gail MacMillan** lives in New Brunswick, Canada with her husband and two dogs.

David Martin's humor and political satire have appeared in many publications, including *The New York Times*, *Chicago Tribune* and *Smithsonian* magazine. His latest humor collection *Screams & Whispers* is available on Amazon.com. David lives in Ottawa, Canada with his wife Cheryl and their daughter Sarah.

Tim Martin is a contributing writer to over a dozen Chicken Soup for the Soul books. He has two books due out in 2014: *Fast Pitch* and *Don the Dull-Shelled Turtle* (Cedar Grove Books).

Jennifer McMurrain has won numerous awards for her short stories and novels. Her novels, *Quail Crossings* and *Winter Song*, are now available on Amazon. She lives in Bartlesville, OK with her husband, daughter, two diva cats, and two goofy dogs. Learn more at www.jennifermcmurrain.com.

Melissa Meyers is a registered nurse and has a bachelor's degree in cross-cultural communications. She has worked for almost a decade in Central Asia. She loves stories of all kinds, and has recently enjoyed focusing on writing more. E-mail her at melissa.meyerswriter@gmail.com.

Marya Morin is a freelance writer. Her stories and poems have appeared in publications such as *Woman's World* and Hallmark. Marya also penned a weekly humorous column for an online newsletter, and writes custom poetry on request. She lives in the country with her husband. E-mail her at Akushla514@hotmail.com.

Lisa Morris has been an educator for the past twenty-three years and a writer for a lifetime. She recently added adjunct professor of education to her résumé. Lisa has published five educational books, two memoirs, and this is her third contribution to the Chicken Soup for the Soul series.

Ann Morrow is from Custer, SD, and is the proud pet parent to three dogs. In addition to her pet escapades, she enjoys family, writing, photography and the outdoors. Ann's humorous stories have appeared in other Chicken Soup for the Soul titles. Contact Ann through blackhillsblogger.com.

Rebecca Muchow lives in Sherwood, OR with her family and a growing collection of four-leggers. She is a self-employed medical transcriptionist and hopes to write full-time one day.

Born in England, **Irena Nieslony** received a B.A. honors degree in English and Drama from the University of London. She now lives on the island of Crete, Greece with her husband and their many rescue cats and dogs. Irena has had three murder mystery novels published, with a fourth being released in August 2014.

Speaker, author, and blogger **Brenda Nixon** lives in Ohio—home to the largest number of Amish settlements nationwide. She has two daughters, a son-in-law, and two "adopted" sons from the Swartzentruber Amish.

Molly O'Connor lives in a century-old farmhouse where she raised her children and now lives with her grandchildren. Between the children and the assortment of animals that surround her, many stories surface. Molly spends her winters in Arizona, always with her camera at the ready to capture wild flowers at their best.

David O'Neill is retired from Health & Hospitals Corporation in New York City. An avowed animal lover, David lives with his rescue dogs in upstate New York. He thanks Ava Pennington for her help in telling his story.

Joan Oen is an English teacher. Joan and her husband enjoy watching their son pal around with their beloved Sammy the Schnoodle. Check out Joan's "That's What Moms Are For" in *Chicken Soup for the Soul: The Magic of Mothers & Daughters* and "What Would I Do Without You?" in *Chicken Soup for the Soul: Devotional Stories for Wives*.

Jacqueline Pearce writes fiction for children and teens, including *Dog House Blues* and *The Truth About Rats (and Dogs)*, both written for the British Columbia Society for the Prevention of Cruelty to Animals (BC SPCA) Kids Club. She and her family still feel the absence of their dog, Dylan, who died three years ago.

Lori Phillips writes about spirituality, dreams, marriage and relationships. Visit her dreams site at the-dream-collective.com.

Robin Pressnall is Executive Director of Small Paws Rescue Inc., which has been featured on Animal Planet. She is a frequent guest on the Fox News Network's *Fox & Friends* in New York City. Robin has also appeared on *Inside Edition* with Deborah Norville and is a frequent contributor to Chicken Soup for the Soul books.

Julie Reece-DeMarco is an attorney, educator and author. She is married with four daughters and enjoys being a mom, spending time outdoors in the great Northwest and playing sports. Approximately one million copies of her books are in print.

Julie Richie received her MFA degree in creative writing in 2011 from Lesley University and a B.A. degree from Brown University in 1993. She has two boys and a dog, Lucy. Julie is working on her first novel.

Teresa Rigg is an artist, poet, and memoir writer. She is a frequent winner at county fairs and competitions for her art and poetry. An Oregon native, she is the daughter of an American serviceman and an Australian war bride who gave her words for toys. Teresa lives in Coos Bay with her adorable and adoring pet family.

Stacey Ritz is an award-winning freelance writer and Executive Director of Advocates 4 Animals, Inc. Learn more at www.Advocates4Animals. com.

Deborah Henderson Roberts grew up in Rhode Island and now makes Maryland home. She is a freelance writer currently working on a historical novel for young adults. Her story "The Middle Rock" appeared in *Chicken Soup for the Soul: Think Positive for Kids*.

Gwenyfar Rohler is proud to manage her family's independent bookstore, Old Books on Front St. in Wilmington, NC. She goes to the theatre every week as a theatre reviewer for *Encore* magazine and routinely fails to recognize the famous when they visit the bookstore.

Lee Rothberg, freelance writer and former nurse, works at the Matawan Aberdeen Public Library in New Jersey. While a medical staff writer for *The Woman's Newspaper of Princeton*, she received several awards from the National Federation of Press Women. She is compiling family stories and recipes for her three granddaughters.

Ruth Ann Roy's story about her father previously appeared in *Chicken Soup for the Soul: Angels Among Us*, released in 2013. She continues with her journey of writing as she prepares engaging books for children in lessons of good character traits.

Marcia Rudoff is the author of *We Have Stories—A Handbook for Writing Your Memoirs*. She lives and teaches writing in Bainbridge Island, WA. Favorite free-time activities involve grandkids, travel, and writing for Chicken Soup for the Soul books.

charly s. is a twelve-year member of a Barnes and Noble writers group in Norcross, GA, and published a nonfiction book in 2013 on Kindle/ Nook, completed a contemporary novel and finished a science fiction novel that has yet to find a publisher. charly enjoys writing, reading, and helping with the Red Cross as a volunteer.

John Scanlan is a 1983 graduate of the United States Naval Academy, and retired from the Marine Corps as a Lieutenant Colonel aviator. He currently resides on Hilton Head Island, SC, and is pursuing a second career as a writer. E-mail John at ping1@hargray.com.

Annabel Sheila grew up in Stephenville, a pretty little town on the west coast of Newfoundland. She now calls Moncton, New Brunswick home with the love of her life, Rick, two senior cats, and her little dog, Ziggy. E-mail her at annabelsheila@live.ca.

Thomas Smith is an award-winning writer, reporter, and TV news producer. His supernatural suspense novel, *Something Stirs*, was one of the first haunted house novels for the Christian market. He is married to his best friend, and his dog Chloe gave this story two paws up.

Cheryll Lynn Snow has been a registered nurse for over twenty-four years. She has been married for thirty years and has a wonderful son and grandson. Cheryll enjoys writing, reading, music, traveling and has been a human parent to three rescue animals—so far.

Tanya Sousa writes fiction and nonfiction about human interaction with the environment and other living things. She has published children's picture books, articles, essays, and most recently a novel, *The Starling God*.

Lynn Sunday is an artist, writer, and animal advocate living in Northern California with her husband and two senior rescue dogs. Her stories have appeared in other Chicken Soup for the Soul books, and numerous other publications. E-mail her at Sunday11@aol.com.

Dr. Swift sold his veterinary practice in the late 1980s to pursue a second career as a writer, coach and public speaker. He and his wife co-founded Life On Purpose Institute in 1996 with the vision to be a catalyst for creating a world on purpose (www.lifeonpurpose.com). E-mail him at coachbrad@lifeonpurpose.com.

Jodi Sykes is the author of *Rhyming Activities for Beginning Readers* (T.S. Denison & Co.), *I am Special — The Power is in ME!* and *The House on Pancake Hill* (Amazon.com). She is also a daily blogger of Living La Vida (Lymphoma). Jodi resides in St. Augustine, FL.

Mary Vigliante Szydlowski has published six adult novels, one novella, and three children's books under various pseudonyms. Her articles, essays, short stories, poetry, and children's stories appear in magazines, newspapers, and on the Internet. She lives in Albany, NY.

Stephen L. Thompson grew up — as he likes to say — a short drive from the middle of nowhere on his family's farm in northwestern Pennsylvania. With a B.S. degree in Physics he worked as a lab technician at a company just outside of Philadelphia for seven years. He's now returned to the peace and quiet of the country to write.

Sarah-Elizabeth Viman is a student and loves school with a passion. During her junior year of high school, she was voted student body secretary. She dreams of becoming a French teacher. Sarah-Elizabeth enjoys playing the guitar and piano, listening to music and taking her dogs for long walks every day.

Rachel Wallace-Oberle has an education in journalism and broadcasting and is working on a degree in communications. She is senior marketing writer for a software company and her work has been featured in *Reader's Digest*, *Homemakers*, *Canadian Living*, *Woman's World*, *Today's Parent*, and numerous other publications.

JoEllen Wankel received a Journalism & Mass Communication degree from Lock Haven University of Pennsylvania in 2004. She is a freelance writer and mother to two wonderful girls and one precocious boy. She has shared her life with numerous rescues, including two ferrets, Star and Gus.

Roz Warren writes for *The New York Times* and the *Funny Times*, and recently appeared on the *Today* show. Visit her website at www.rosalindwarren.com, connect with her on Facebook at www.facebook.com/writerrozwarren or follow her on Twitter at @WriterRozWarren.

Michelle Watkins received a master's degree in architecture from University of Nebraska—Lincoln while serving as a contributing editor for the architectural student publication, the Ampersand. She recently left design to work as a part-time paraprofessional and pursue interests in writing. She resides in Omaha, NE, with her husband, Gary.

Geni White is a retired RN with a B.S. and M.S. degree. Geni enjoys reading, writing, reviewing books, hiking, swimming, gardening, teaching, art, music and her husband of fifty-five years. Their three adult children live in Chicago, Maryland and Taiwan. She's been writing full-time since 2000.

Beth M. Wood is an award-winning marketer, freelance writer and mom of three. Her social media addiction pays the bills while copywriting gigs and published articles and essays feed her shopping habit. She blogs about social media at bethmwoodblog.com and digresses about life and parenting at bethmwood.blogspot.com.

Sue Owens Wright, author of the acclaimed Beanie and Cruiser Mystery series, is a multiple winner of the Maxwell, awarded annually by the Dog Writers Association of America for best writing on the subject of dogs. She is a fancier and rescuer of Basset Hounds, frequently featured in her books and essays.

Meet Our Author

Amy Newmark has been Chicken Soup for the Soul's publisher, coauthor, and editor-in-chief for the last six years, after a thirty-year career as a writer, speaker, financial analyst, and business executive in the worlds of finance and telecommunications. Amy is a Chartered Financial Analyst and a *magna cum laude* graduate of Harvard College, where she majored in Portuguese, minored in French, and traveled extensively. She and her husband have four grown children.

After a long career writing books on telecommunications, voluminous financial reports, business plans, and corporate press releases, Chicken Soup for the Soul is a breath of fresh air for Amy. She loves creating these life-changing books for Chicken Soup for the Soul's wonderful readers. She has coauthored and/or edited more than 100 Chicken Soup for the Soul books.

You can reach Amy with any questions or comments through webmaster@chickensoupforthesoul.com and you can follow her on Twitter @amynewmark or @chickensoupsoul.

About Miranda Lambert

Grammy Award-winning singer-songwriter Miranda Lambert is the reigning four-time CMA and reigning five-time ACM Female Vocalist of the Year. Her last album, *Four The Record*, made history when it debuted atop Billboard's Top Country Albums chart, making Miranda the first country artist in the forty-seven-year history of the chart to have each of her first four albums debut at # 1. All four of those albums have also been certified Platinum.

Miranda's highly-anticipated fifth album *Platinum* was released June 3rd. Her lead single "Automatic," written by Miranda, Nicolle Galyon and Natalie Hemby, is an autobiographical song that reflects on the days of pay phones, learning to drive a stick shift, driving to Dallas to buy an Easter dress, recording the country countdown on her cassette recorder and more.

In addition to her award-winning music, Miranda has designed a shoe line that is available at DSW, and other retailers across the country. She also dedicates much of her time to her MuttNation Foundation. The foundation has raised more than $1,500,000 to aid organizations and entities whose purpose is to build animal shelters for better care; increase pet adoption and encourage responsible pet guardianship; rehabilitate sick or unsocialized animals; fund spay/neuter programs; reduce/eliminate euthanasia of healthy animals. She also owns two lifestyle boutiques, general stores she named The Pink Pistol. The stores are located in her hometown of Lindale, TX and Tishomingo, OK.

About American
Humane Association

F or over 100 years, one organization has been standing guard
over America's children and America's animals, keeping them
safe and working tirelessly to improve their futures.

Born in the years after the Civil War, American Humane Association
has been behind virtually every major advance in the protection of our
most vulnerable, from creating the nation's first child labor laws to
saving the Bald Eagle, rescuing animals from war, hurricanes, tornadoes
and floods, and pioneering programs to prevent abuse, cruelty, and
neglect.

Today, American Humane Association helps ensure the welfare of
one billion farm animals, works to keep pets and children safe from
harm, protects 100,000 animal actors each year on film and television
production sets, brings life-saving and life-altering emergency services
to children, animals and communities struck by disasters, uses animal
therapy to provide healing and hope to military families and children
with cancer, and researches ways to keep more of the eight million
pets abandoned each year in loving, forever homes.

The country's first humane organization, and the only one dedicated to protecting both children and animals, American Humane
Association has been uniquely effective in working with others for the

common good: parents, teachers, scientists, farmers, ranchers, animal advocates, and anyone interested in speaking for the voiceless and effecting lasting change.

A moderate and mainstream voice in a sometimes contentious world, American Humane Association bases its programs on both science and sentiment, "heart" as well as "smart," as it strives to bring commonsense solutions to some of our most complex challenges so that together we may build more humane communities and a more humane world.

To learn more or join them in their important work, please go to www.americanhumane.org or call 866-242-1877.

Thank You

hank you dog lovers! I owe huge thanks to every one of you who shared your stories about your beloved, intuitive, heroic... and mischievous dogs. You make a strong case for running right down to the animal shelter to adopt a new friend. Your stories made us laugh a lot, nod our heads in recognition, and cry a few times.

I know that you poured your hearts and souls into the thousands of stories and poems that you submitted. Thank you. All of us at Chicken Soup for the Soul appreciate your willingness to share your lives with us. We could only publish a small percentage of the stories that were submitted, but our editorial team read every single submission — and there were thousands! Even the stories that do not appear in the book influenced us and affected the final manuscript.

First of all, I want to thank Miranda Lambert for taking the time out from her busy schedule to write her foreword for us. I loved her story about how her parents worried about how their yellow Lab would take to a new baby, and how the dog surprised them by immediately becoming Miranda's de facto nanny, sleeping under her crib and guarding her. And I want to thank our editor Jeanne Blandford, who is also the director of marketing for our pet food business. She read thousands of dog stories over many months and educated all of us about shelter dogs and the important issues that we needed to cover in this book.

Our regular editorial team did its normal fabulous job. Our VP & Assistant Publisher D'ette Corona worked with all the contributors as we edited and perfected their stories, and she and Senior Editor Barbara LoMonaco proofread the manuscript, while Managing Editor and Production Coordinator Kristiana Pastir oversaw the long journey from Word document to finished manuscript to proofs to cartons of finished books.

Lastly, I owe a very special thanks to our creative director and book producer, Brian Taylor at Pneuma Books, for his brilliant vision for our covers and interiors.

~Amy Newmark

Sharing Happiness, Inspiration, and Wellness

eal people sharing real stories, every day, all over the world. In 2007, *USA Today* named *Chicken Soup for the Soul* one of the five most memorable books in the last quarter-century. With over 100 million books sold to date in the U.S. and Canada alone, more than 200 titles in print, and translations into more than 40 languages, "chicken soup for the soul" is one of the world's best-known phrases.

Today, 21 years after we first began sharing happiness, inspiration and wellness through our books, we continue to delight our readers with new titles, but have also evolved beyond the bookstore, with wholesome and balanced pet food, delicious nutritious comfort food, and a major motion picture in development. Whatever you're doing, wherever you are, Chicken Soup for the Soul is "always there for you™." Thanks for reading!

Chicken Soup
for the Soul
Brand Pet Food ®

because Food is more than just Nutrition, it's also about Comfort, Love and Appreciation™

We offer our super premium pet food because we understand the unique relationship between people and pets. Ever since we created our first bestselling pet book, we've been reading your stories—sharing your laughter, tears and, most importantly, your love for your pets.